DISCOVERY,
CAPITALISM,
AND
DISTRIBUTIVE
JUSTICE

THE COLLECTED WORKS OF ISRAEL M. KIRZNER

Austrian Subjectivism and the Emergence of
   Entrepreneurship Theory

Competition, Economic Planning, and the
   Knowledge Problem

Competition and Entrepreneurship

Discovery, Capitalism, and Distributive Justice

The Economic Point of View

Essays on Capital and Interest

The Essence of Entrepreneurship and the Nature and
   Significance of Market Process

Ludwig von Mises: The Man and His Economics

Market Theory and the Price System

Reflections on Ethics, Freedom, Welfare Economics, Policy,
   and the Legacy of Austrian Economics

ISRAEL M. KIRZNER

Discovery, Capitalism, and Distributive Justice

Edited and with an Introduction by

PETER J. BOETTKE and FRÉDÉRIC SAUTET

LIBERTY FUND Indianapolis

This book is published by Liberty Fund, Inc., a foundation established to encourage study of the ideal of a society of free and responsible individuals.

𒂼𒄄

The cuneiform inscription that serves as our logo and as the design motif for our endpapers is the earliest-known written appearance of the word "freedom" (*amagi*), or "liberty." It is taken from a clay document written about 2300 B.C. in the Sumerian city-state of Lagash.

20 19 18 17 16 C 5 4 3 2 1

20 19 18 17 16 P 5 4 3 2 1

Library of Congress Cataloging-in-Publication Data

Names: Kirzner, Israel M., author. | Boettke, Peter J., editor. | Sautet, Frédéric E., editor.

Title: Discovery, capitalism, and distributive justice / Israel M. Kirzner; edited and with an introduction by Peter J. Boettke and Frédéric Sautet.

Description: Indianapolis: Liberty Fund, [2016] | Series: The collected works of Israel M. Kirzner | Includes bibliographical references and index.

Identifiers: LCCN 2015046058 |
  ISBN 9780865978607 (hardcover: alk. paper) |
  ISBN 9780865978614 (pbk.: alk. paper)

Subjects: LCSH: Entrepreneurship. | Capitalism. | Distributive justice.

Classification: LCC HB615 .K58 2016 | DDC 330.12/2—dc23

LC record available at http://lccn.loc.gov/2015046058

LIBERTY FUND, INC.

8335 Allison Pointe Trail, Suite 300

Indianapolis, Indiana 46250-1684

B'EZRAS HASHEM

CONTENTS

The great scientific contribution of the classical economists was the demonstration that within a system of private property rights and freedom of contract, individuals pursuing their self interest produce a peaceful and productive social order. The "invisible hand" proposition identified with Adam Smith set the stage for all subsequent developments of economic science. The great classical liberal political economists of the nineteenth century, such as J. B. Say and Frédéric Bastiat in France and David Ricardo and James Mill in England, refined Smith's argument and claimed that the private property order with free and open trade resulted in the simultaneous achievement of individual autonomy, prosperity, and peace. The empirical record in the eighteenth and nineteenth centuries seemed to support this claim, as the relatively free economies of Europe, especially the United Kingdom, and of the new world, especially the United States, grew prosperous and the expansion of the rights of man was achieved.

But somehow, the late nineteenth century saw an increasing dissatisfaction with the capitalist order among intellectuals. The socialist critique of capitalism resonated with the youth and the literary class. James Buchanan argues that this was due to the fact that the classical liberal political economists had failed on the intuitive test of the justice of the distribution of resources, even though they had demonstrated the compatibility of individual autonomy with generalized prosperity.

The development of the marginal productivity theory of wages provided a rigorous answer to the question of the discrepancy of income in a capitalist system. The results, however, followed only under the highly restrictive assumptions of perfectly competitive equilibrium. The theory did not adequately address the moral intuitions of the social critics of capitalism. Furthermore, the "technical" defense of capitalist distribution did not adequately explain, let alone justify, the source of pure or speculative profit. This is where Israel Kirzner enters the discussion and seeks to contribute a better understanding of the nature of the capitalist economic process and the role of pure profit in the functioning of the system. To understand Kirzner's contribution, one must go back to classical economics.

John Stuart Mill is taken to have argued that production and distribution could be treated separately.[1] A fair division of the social product could be determined without any concern for adverse incentives on the process of production or the efficient allocation of scarce resources. But thinkers who are more market-oriented, using the latest development of marginalist economics, emphasized that production and distribution could not be so neatly separated. The way the social pie was divided would have an impact on the size of the social pie produced. Incentives indeed matter. Thinkers who are more socialist oriented, on the other hand, thought the tools of marginal analysis could be marshaled to serve the ends of socialism more effectively. In other words, neoclassical economics could serve the distributional goals of socialism. This was a central idea behind Fabian socialism and the founding of the London School of Economics.

In spite of the major dispute in the 1920s and 1930s over the economic analysis of socialism, the sides never really engaged each other in a common language, and both walked away declaring themselves victors. Unfortunately, at the height of this debate the major modern world economies sank deeply into an economic crisis. The Great Depression had the consequence of not only ushering in a great growth in the size and responsibility of governments in the United States and United Kingdom, but it destroyed the "faith" in the efficacy of the capitalist order for more than a generation of intellectuals throughout the world. Capitalist distribution had been seen as unjust; now capitalism was seen as inefficient altogether, and it didn't work as the classical theory had suggested. After the Great Depression, it became commonplace to argue that capitalism didn't work and the distribution that resulted from it was unjustified on moral grounds. The "invisible hand" was revealed to be palsied, and the very "visible hand" of the government was required to fix, in addition to the injustice of the capitalist system, the inability of the market economy to self correct. In the 1940s and 1950s the dominant voices in economics declared loudly that unfettered capitalism suffered microeconomic inefficiencies and macroeconomic instability, and resulted in gross social injustice.

---

1. There is some controversy over whether J. S. Mill was actually committed to this separation, but subsequent discussions proceeded as if he was, and thus argued that questions of distribution should be treated separately from the laws of production.

The counterargument of the 1960s and 1970s associated not only with the Chicago School but also with the various strands of a resurgent classical liberal political economy in Law and Economics, Property Rights Economics, Public Choice, New Economic History, Market Process, and New Institutionalism focused their analytical and empirical attention on demonstrating that the claims of market failure theory were flawed. In other words, upon close examination, the market economy was indeed a self-regulating system that generated social cooperation and wealth creation. In short, the market worked and the "invisible hand" thesis proved to be more robust to deviations from ideal conditions than former theory had led us to believe.

But the economists of that generation largely left the questions of justice and the moral assessment of capitalism alone. The economist *qua* economist, it was argued, had nothing to say on such questions. The position held is not intellectually unjustified. Economics is after all a "positive" science in that it seeks to understand what is and not necessarily what should be. But it is important to stress that economics is not rendered completely silent by such a position. Indeed, economic theory may not be able to tell you whether profits are deserved or not, but it can specify the consequences of your answer to those questions of just desert. And that knowledge is essential for the task of moral and social philosophy. Perhaps nothing is as dangerous as an economist who knows only economics except a moral philosopher who knows no economics at all.

Robert Nozick's *Anarchy, State, and Utopia* put the fundamental question of justice in distribution at the center of discussion in modern political theory. Nozick basically defended the style of reasoning associated with "invisible hand" explanations that raises doubts about aggregate and end-state ideals of just distributions. He laid out the case for individual rights and fairness in the processes of exchange and production, and thus the resulting distribution. Nozick legitimated the classical argument that the market economy works and the resulting distribution is morally just. The critical debate between John Rawls (the two principles of justice: [1] maximum equal liberty, and [2] maximize the minimum position of anyone in society) and Nozick (rights as trumps and process versus end-state ethics) became the centerpiece of every discussion in modern political theory. It is not an exaggeration to say that Nozick impressed with his wit and analytical skill but did not persuade, and Rawls came to define modern political liberalism.

This was a debate of political theory that touched on political economy, but many of the core economic issues, such as pure profit, remained unexamined. Marginal productivity theory of distribution could hardly be used in understanding the role that speculation and pure profit play in a market economy, let alone in justifying the pursuit and grasping of those pure entrepreneurial profits. Israel Kirzner's *Discovery, Capitalism, and Distributive Justice* sought to make those unexamined economic issues more widely understood in the hope that the positive science of economics could contribute greatly to our understanding of the justice in capitalist distribution.

Kirzner argues that standard criticisms of the justice of capitalist income distribution are not correct because they fail to see capitalism as a "discovery procedure" in which the way the social pie is created and distributed is never fully known prior to its distribution. He argues that the capitalist system consists of innumerable acts of entrepreneurial discovery by all market participants. These acts must be sharply distinguished from acts of deliberate search and deliberate production. On the basis of these insights, Kirzner argues for what he calls a "finders-keepers" rule as a commonsense ethical rule that has moral weight. In a fundamental sense, Kirzner argues that the society that does not accept the finders-keepers rule will be unable to enjoy the fruits of capitalism in terms of technological innovation and wealth creation that we are too often led to take for granted. Economists' theory of the market generally ignores or underappreciates entrepreneurial discovery and the institutional conditions and moral prerequisites that make possible a vibrant entrepreneurial society.

Discovery, Capitalism, and Distributive Justice is Kirzner's work that comes the closest to normative political economy, but reading the book in such a way would do the work a disservice. Kirzner goes to great lengths to avoid being a normative economist. He is, instead, limited to laying out the implications of the positive analysis of entrepreneurial market process for arguments concerning the role of pure profit and the capitalist distribution of resources.[2]

2. For more discussion of the main themes of the book, see Charles Baird's, Richard Ebeling's, and David Gordon's reviews of the book. See also two articles that discuss Kirzner's book: David Schmidtz's "Finders, keepers?" and Martin Rickett's "Kirzner's theory of entrepreneurship: A critique."

The arguments contained in *Discovery, Capitalism, and Distributive Justice* are particularly timely given the turmoil of the global financial crisis that started in 2008. Those events are this generation's "Great Depression," and the old Keynesian arguments about capitalist instability, market failure, and ill-gotten market gains have been resurrected with a vengeance. The story of the financial crisis, just as the story of the Great Depression of the 1930s, is not a simple one. But the larger debate over the capitalist system needs to be reengaged in light of the arguments that logically follow from an economic analysis that sees entrepreneurship as the driving force.

This volume comprises two sections. The first section contains Kirzner's book *Discovery, Capitalism, and Distributive Justice*. Section 2 offers three important articles by Israel Kirzner on the subject of economic justice. The first one dates back to 1973 and was written at the time *Competition and Entrepreneurship* was published. The second paper was written in 1978 and presents an assessment of Robert Nozick's entitlement theory of justice, including an insightful discussion of the Lockean proviso. Kirzner saw very early on the importance of the entrepreneurial framework for the subject of economic justice, and one can find in those two papers the themes that Kirzner will develop further in his 1989 book. After his book came out, Kirzner was concerned that his ideas on justice were neglected, which led to the publication of the third paper in 1992. That paper offers refined insights into the issue of discovery and economic justice. Section 2 also includes a critique of Kirzner's theory by Theodore Burczak published in 2002 and Kirzner's reply.

ACKNOWLEDGMENTS

We would first like to thank wholeheartedly Israel Kirzner for his unparalleled contribution to economic science. Kirzner's research program has deeply enriched the discipline and has shed light on some of economics' most difficult puzzles. Economists owe him an immense intellectual debt.

The publication of the Collected Works of Israel M. Kirzner would not be a reality without the participation of Liberty Fund, Inc. We are extremely grateful to Liberty Fund, and especially Emilio Pacheco, for making this project possible. To republish Kirzner's unique oeuvre has been on our minds since our time spent at New York University in the 1990s—where one of us was a professor (Peter) and the other a post-doctoral student

(Frédéric). We are thrilled at the idea that current and future generations of economists and other scholars will have easy access to Kirzner's works.

Finally, we wish to thank Emily Washington for her invaluable help in the publication of this volume.

Peter J. Boettke and Frédéric Sautet

REFERENCES

Baird, Charles. (1990) "Book review: *Discovery, Capitalism, and Distributive Justice* by Israel Kirzner." *The Freeman*, 40 (8).

Buchanan, James. (1991) "The potential and the limits of socially organized humankind." In James Buchanan, *The Economics and the Ethics of Constitutional Order*. Ann Arbor: University of Michigan Press.

Ebeling, Richard. (1990) "*Discovery, Capitalism, and Distributive Justice* by Israel M. Kirzner." *Freedom Daily*. The Future of Freedom Foundation.

Gordon, David. (1991) "*Discovery, Capitalism, and Distributive Justice* by Israel M. Kirzner." *Review of Austrian Economics*, 5 (1): 117–22.

Nozick, Robert. (1977) *State, Anarchy, and Utopia*. New York: Basic Books.

Rawls, John. (1999) *A Theory of Justice*. Rev. ed. Cambridge, Mass.: Belknap Press.

Rickett, Martin. (1992) "Kirzner's theory of entrepreneurship: A critique." In Bruce J. Caldwell and Stephen Boehm (eds.), *Austrian Economics: Tensions and New Directions*. Boston and Dordrecht: Kluwer Academic Publishers, 1992, 67–84. Republished in this collection in the volume entitled *The Essence of Entrepreneurship and the Nature and Significance of Market Process*.

Schmidtz, David. (1998) "Finders, keepers?" *Advances in Austrian Economics*, 5:277–89.

DISCOVERY,
CAPITALISM,
AND
DISTRIBUTIVE
JUSTICE

For a number of years my work has emphasized the importance of the entrepreneurial role in market processes. The bulk of this work has focused on understanding the way in which market processes depend on entrepreneurial alertness and discovery for any systematic equilibrative properties they display. In this work in positive economics, insights concerning entrepreneurial discovery were able to illuminate the Austrian tradition in economics, as developed in recent decades by Mises and Hayek. This tradition, while overlapping on key elements of economic understanding with the dominant, neoclassical tradition, differs from it in significant respects. Grasping the entrepreneurial role turned out to be crucial for an appreciation of how the Austrian theory transcended the scope of mainstream equilibrium formulations. While at work on these matters, it was difficult to avoid noticing how profoundly important the entrepreneurial role is, not only for positive economics, but also for the philosophical and ethical evaluation of market processes. This little book develops some simple but important ideas along these lines. It argues that criticisms of the justice of capitalist income distribution suffer severely as a result of failure to see capitalism as (to employ Hayek's felicitous phrase) a "discovery procedure."

It turns out that when equilibrium economics treats economic gains as being *either* the fully expected results of deliberate plans, *or* the fortuitous expression of pure luck, it is excluding consideration of a third, morally significant possibility, namely, that gain may emerge as a result of the alert grasping of a hitherto unnoticed opportunity. Such gain, I maintain, must be seen as *discovered* gain—a category with a moral character entirely of its own. This book pursues this idea at some length, and reaches, as a result, some radically novel conclusions concerning capitalist distributive justice.

Many of the matters discussed in the book have been debated around the colloquium table of the Austrian Economics Program at New York University. Portions of the book were also presented at seminars at the Center for the Study of Market Processes, George Mason

University, and under the auspices of the Social Philosophy and Policy Center, Bowling Green State University. Appreciation is gratefully expressed to participants in these seminars, especially to Mario Rizzo, Lawrence H. White, Jack High, James Buchanan, Karen Vaughn, Robert Tollison, Don Boudreaux, Richard Epstein, Alec Nove, John Roemer, Loren Lomasky, and John Gray. Financial support from Sarah Scaife Foundation and Moorman Fund is gratefully acknowledged. Theorists of distributive justice may differ on the degree of credit to which these friends and supporters are respectively entitled. All of them will agree, I believe, that only the undersigned deserves censure for remaining errors.

Israel M. Kirzner

1. INTRODUCTION

This book aims to clarify an aspect of the morality of the capitalist system—the idea of *justice* as it relates to the market economy. Probably no other moral dimension of capitalism has sparked such bitter controversies and aroused such fierce emotions. Critics of capitalism have denounced this system as one of exploitation; they have condemned it as generating a pattern of income distribution that is unjustified and unfair. Sometimes these denunciations have focused on the economic *inequality* that is inseparable from capitalism. But it is the charge of *injustice* that almost invariably supplies the moral fuel for these and similar criticisms.

What I will be dealing with is, therefore, certainly not the full gamut of ethical and moral concerns arising from capitalism. The morality of the capitalist system depends not only on its justice or injustice, but also upon the extent to which it promotes or obscures human freedom, the extent to which it can succeed in efficiently serving the needs and promoting the goals of its members, the extent to which it promotes the emergence of noble or ignoble qualities among its members, and on and on. As I shall be emphasizing, clarity in regard to the idea of justice in capitalism requires that we be careful to treat this idea separately from all other moral aspects of capitalism. Lack of compassion is not the same as the perpetration of injustice; moral criticisms of capitalism that claim that it promotes heartlessness and selfishness have not—even were these criticisms to be accepted—thereby established that capitalism is an inherently unjust system. Conversely, the defense of capitalism against the charge of injustice does not by itself invest the system with overall moral worthiness.

Yet, while I freely acknowledge that my topic is relatively modest in the scope of its ethical concerns, we must not underestimate its importance. It is because capitalism is seen as at least permitting rank injustice that many of its defenders feel compelled to couch their defenses in apologetic terms: it is true, they concede, that exploitation and injustice are rampant under capitalism, but, after all, the system promotes prosperity and/or individual liberty, and so on. It is because capitalism is seen by millions as being built on injustice as one of its essential and defining characteristics, that the system is despised and even hated in much of the world. It is largely because of this violent antipathy to capitalism on the grounds of its alleged injustice that no modern country has permitted unrestricted capitalism to flourish within its borders. To claim, as this book will claim, that virtually all of these criticisms of capitalism as being unjust, are themselves deeply flawed and are even, perhaps, in principle invalid, is to make a counter-intuitive and iconoclastic claim concerning a vitally important issue. Whether my claim is itself persuasive will be for the reader to decide; but the intrinsic importance of the issue as being at the very forefront of moral and ethical debate regarding capitalism, should not be a matter of dispute.

DISAGREEMENT WITH THE LITERATURE

My thesis is to charge that existing discussions of economic justice under capitalism have—whether they attack or defend capitalism—seriously misperceived the issue. Considering the substantial volume of work which has been devoted, during the recent decade, to economic justice, and considering the unquestioned competence and eminence of many of the philosophers and economists who have addressed this theme, the charge will properly be met by skeptically raised eyebrows. It will be necessary, in subsequent chapters, to identify with great care the lapse in vision I wish to attribute to the existing literature, and to seek to persuade the reader that this lapse is indeed crucial for a proper evaluation of the justice or injustice of the capitalist system. In this introductory chapter I can only outline the basic insights that I wish to introduce into the discussion, to sketch their significance, and briefly show how existing discussions have consistently failed to incorporate these insights.

I should emphasize at the outset that my disagreement with the existing literature is not, at the core, a disagreement on ethics. In fact very little in what I shall be arguing anywhere in this book depends on proposing any novelties in the moral evaluation of economic phenomena. My contention will be that the ethical assessments of capitalism have failed primarily because these assessments have misperceived the nature and the mode of operation of the capitalist system. My disagreement with the existing literature will, then, turn out to be not a disagreement in ethics but a disagreement in economics—but an economics disagreement with direct implications for the ethical assessment of capitalism. Some further remarks on this aspect of the problem may be of help.

ON THE INTERFACE BETWEEN ETHICS AND ECONOMICS

To judge adequately any aspect of social reality from the ethical perspective calls, of course, for a valid framework of ethical criteria to serve as the evaluative yardstick. But such judgment also requires, perhaps even more importantly, a valid positive understanding of the particular slice of social reality being ethically appraised. The same is true, after all, for all kinds of moral appraisal: that which is being appraised must, first of all, be properly identified and understood. To condemn the bad manners of someone creating an unruly disturbance in a concert hall during the course of a sublime artistic performance, requires that one should correctly identify the nature of the disturbance. One's moral condemnation might be softened if the noisemaker turns out to have noticed an unsecured ceiling girder dangling precariously over a portion of the audience. Two observers who are equally outraged by rude interruptions of orchestral performances will react differently if one of them does and the other does not, understand what has motivated the horrified girder-discoverer.

To judge the morality of a particular economic transaction requires that we fully understand the motives and the likely consequences of that transaction. To judge the justice of a market system requires that we fully understand the workings of that system. Two judges who share the same set of ethical values may judge the morality of the market system quite differently from each other, if one does and the other does not, understand how markets work.

These are rather obvious observations, but are often overlooked. It is frequently assumed that in order to defend the market system against its ethical detractors, it is necessary that the defender should disagree with his adversaries more or less profoundly on ethical standards. Of course such disagreements on standards *may* be responsible for quarrels about the morality of the market. But very frequently this is not the case. The quarrels over the morality of markets merely reflect different views concerning economic reality.

So sound "positive" economic reasoning is important, in the most simple and direct way, for arriving at sound ethical judgment concerning economic reality. It will be my contention that a fairly subtle flaw in the standard economic understanding of the function and operation of markets is in fact responsible for much that is inappropriate in contemporary discussions of economic justice under capitalism.

ON THE DEFINITION OF CAPITALISM

I have been using the term "market system" synonymously with "capitalism." This means I am defining capitalism, for my purposes, as a "pure" system, one in which all economic activity proceeds through laissez-faire markets. I do not, in other words, wish to comment directly on real-world modern day capitalism, in which a large, often enormous, volume of government regulation modifies the operation of otherwise free markets. For present purposes it is important to disentangle the market elements in modern capitalism from those other elements in it which circumscribe and constrain the market elements. My concern is with the justice of the market system; with the justice of real-world capitalism only insofar as relates to its market elements.

More specifically, I conceive of pure capitalism, for purposes of appraising its justice or injustice, as a system of *decentralized decision making*. Such a system, as we shall see, presumes a legal framework defining individual private property rights. Given this framework each individual is free to decide for himself what to do with each item that he owns. The individual may use it for consumption, may use it in productive processes, or may sell it to anyone able and willing to buy it from him at an agreed price. No one finds that his power to determine the use to be made of an item of property that he rightfully owns, has been arbitrarily interrupted by the decision of someone—legislator, central economic planner, criminal, or whomever—other than himself. No one finds that his ability to sell his property to a willing buyer has been obstructed by laws declaring the agreed price to be illegally too low or too high, or by laws declaring his sale to be harmful to the physical well-being or the morals of the purchaser. Notice that the postulation, in capitalism, of a system of individual rights is merely an alternative way of identifying capitalism as a system of decentralized decision making. To be able to make a decision with regard to the disposition of a unit of resource or product *is* to have rights over the entity the disposition of which is being considered. Decentralized, individual decision making *is* nothing but a system of inviolate individual rights. Centralized decision making, involving one or other form of central planning, implies, at the very least, significant limitations on the extent to which individuals may exercise economic decision rights. The system I wish to examine is the pure, decentralized decision-making system. Such a system is described as a market system because, typically, decentralized decision-making systems tend to generate active and complex markets and systems of markets, and these markets are defined as exempt from outside regulation. Questions concerning economic justice under pure capitalism relate, therefore, to the operation of and outcomes generated by unregulated markets, for land, for labor, for capital goods—as well as for financial capital, and for intermediate and final consumer products of all kinds. But, at least conceptually, we must distinguish sharply between two different kinds of questions that may be asked concerning the justice of a system based strictly on individual rights. Only one of these two kinds of questions is our direct concern in this book.

One kind of question—the kind we are *not* directly concerned with—has to do with the justice of the specific pattern upon which individual rights are initially assigned, *before* the market process gets under way. Conceptually this question is prior to that of the justice of the market. This first question asks whether the property which individuals bring to market is justly theirs, that is, whether the legal system assigning such property rights to them is a just one.

The second kind of question begins only after the first has been satisfactorily answered. Given a just system of individual rights-assignment, the second kind of question then addresses the extent to which the *operation* and *outcomes* of the system—any just system—of individual rights conform to canons of justice. Admittedly in practice the property rights an individual enjoys in a given market economy are themselves the outcomes of earlier market economy processes, but conceptually we can distinguish between the assignment of existing rights at the moment when we begin our examination, and the subsequent market processes through which rights are exchanged and exercised.

It matters a great deal that I declare myself in this book, not to be directly addressing the first kind of question. The idea of capitalism, of a market economy, of a system of decentralized decision making, does not presuppose and is not dependent upon any one system of property law. One can imagine a wide range of alternative systems of private property, each one of which would satisfy the institutional prerequisites for capitalism. Clearly any given criteria of justice are unlikely to pronounce all these alternative systems of property law to be equally just—yet all could serve in a capitalist system. Full acceptance of the justice of one legal system specifying private property rights is entirely consistent with moral revulsion against a second legal system specifying a different mode of acquiring property rights. The institution of human slavery, for example, is consistent with a narrowly defined system of private property, but moral approbation of capitalism in the abstract does not at all imply the moral acceptance of slavery.

By confining myself to the second kind of question referred to earlier, I avoid having to choose between alternative systems of property law. I concern myself with principles of justice that can relate to any and all systems of private property—without committing myself to the justice of any one of them. This means that I will be supposing, for the rest of this book, that individual participants in capitalism are, somehow, justly in possession of their property—at least, they are before the market process that we are examining gets under way. I am concerned only whether the justice of this initial state of affairs is enhanced or jeopardized by the subsequent operation of the free market economy. My concern to avoid addressing the question of the justice of systems of property law is not merely because that question is a difficult one, and, moreover, one which is different from the question I do wish to address. My avoidance of that difficult and different question is due, in addition, to the insight that the justice of capitalism as an abstract system of social organization is, in logic, entirely independent of that question. We may indeed wish to declare a capitalist system that permits slavery to be unjust; but the injustice of that system has nothing to do with the capitalist character of that system—a character which in no way depends on the institution of slavery. If we are to address the issue of the justice of capitalism, we had better steer clear of other questions which have little directly to do with the justice of capitalism as a system. The way to achieve this must be to assume, for the sake of our discussion, that *some* ethically acceptable private property system is in place.

To be sure, it may be objected that by thus narrowing the scope of our study we avoid considering not merely the justice or injustice of particular systems of private property, but also the question of whether *any* private appropriation of the gifts of nature can be justified. Surely, it can be objected, while the capitalist character of a social system does not depend on the particular system of property law governing it, that capitalist character does very much depend on the institution of private property as such. So that a full discussion of the justice of capitalism as an abstract system should surely not avoid the question of whether the very idea of private property can be reconciled with the idea of justice. There is much merit in this objection. I offer two exculpatory observations in regard to my not addressing the justice of the idea of private property. My first observation is that the issue of the justice of the private property idea is one to which the fresh argument offered in this book is almost entirely irrelevant. So that, where a full treatment of the justice of capitalism would have to pay its respect to the formidable literature on private property, my more modest essay need not do so. My second observation is that, insofar as the fresh argument offered here does have limited relevance for the justice of private appropriation, we shall indeed take note of it.

ON THE IDEA OF DISTRIBUTIVE JUSTICE

The justice of capitalism has usually been discussed in terms of the idea of *distributive* justice. That is, the market system, in the course of allocating the resources of society among competing branches of production, at the same time determines the incomes that the individual members of society receive. It is through the market process that wage incomes, interest incomes, rental incomes, and pure profit receipts are determined and assigned. The market system is seen in this discussion as not only producing a social "pie," but at the same time slicing up that pie and assigning the respective slices to the specific individuals who participate in the market process. The market is seen as "distributing" social output among its participants. And the justice or injustice of the market is identified with the justice or injustice of the pattern of income distribution. The question of social justice under capitalism is seen as the question of its distributive justice. It will be a central thesis of this book that in reality the entire notion of distribution is a flawed one, and the identification of the question of justice as being one of distributive justice is, consequently, equally flawed and quite misleading.

My challenge to the notion of "distribution" in a capitalist system is, to be sure, by no means the first such challenge to have been made, but my reasons for rejecting this notion seem not to have been advanced in the earlier challenges. Earlier critiques of the idea of capitalist income distribution centered on the absence, in capitalism, of any central entity responsible for slicing and distributing the pie. Incomes, it was pointed out, are determined impersonally, as a result of the interaction of innumerable market participants. There never is an entire pie which is subsequently sliced up and distributed. "There is in the operation of a market economy nothing which could properly be called distribution. Goods are not first produced and then distributed, as would be the case in a socialist state."[1] Individual incomes are earned *simultaneously* with the process through which the size and composition of the supposed "pie" are determined. In fact the size and composition of the pie are as much dependent upon the pattern of income "distribution" as the latter depends on the size and composition of the pie. Hayek, in particular, has argued that all this renders the very question of social justice under capitalism rather nonsensical. If no one agency distributes incomes it cannot, Hayek maintains, ever be said that the pattern of income distribution is either just or unjust. In "a system in which each is allowed to use his knowledge for his own purposes the concept of 'social justice' is necessarily empty and meaningless, because in it nobody's will can determine the relative incomes of the different people, or prevent that they be partly dependent on accident. 'Social Justice' can be given a meaning only in a directed or 'command economy' . . . in which the individuals are ordered what to do . . . ."[2]

I can readily acknowledge the force of these earlier challenges; yet it seems to me that important additional insights must be introduced in order to fully appreciate the flaws in the standard treatments of social justice under capitalism. Even if, with Mises, we recognize the metaphor involved in the term "income distribution" in capitalist societies, we might yet wish to consider the justice of incomes received under capitalism *as if* the social pie were being sliced up by some central authority. And while we may concur with Hayek in denying strict meaning to the concept of social justice as applied to the results of a spontaneous process, a critic of capitalism might nonetheless coherently declare the system to be intolerable if these results turn out to form a pattern which under a directed or "command" economy would have been pronounced unjust. Hayek himself recognizes that a "feeling of injustice about the distribution of material goods in a society of free men" while in no way providing a basis for any valid complaint against any individual or any cooperating group of people, may yet imply a measure of generalized blame insofar as "we tolerate a system in which each is allowed to choose

1. L. Mises, *Human Action* (New Haven: Yale University Press, 1949), p. 255.

2. F. A. Hayek, *Law, Legislation and Liberty: The Mirage of Social Justice*, vol. II (Chicago: University of Chicago Press, 1976), p. 69.

his occupation and therefore nobody can have the power and the duty to see that the results correspond to our wishes."[3]

My dissatisfaction in this book with the standard notion of income distribution is rooted, not in the decentralization out of which the pie is spontaneously created and "distributed," but in the circumstance that what is distributed is never in fact fully known, prior to its distribution. The spontaneous process through which the social pie is created and "distributed" is *a process of discovery*. Incomes are received in the course of the production process in which the pie is discovered; or, to put it differently, the pie is produced in the course of the process in which incomes are discovered.

In order to establish my thesis I will have to show (a) that the capitalist market process is indeed a discovery process, and (b) that the discovery character of the capitalist process thoroughly undermines the relevancy of standard discussions of distributive justice under capitalism.

THE MARKET AS DISCOVERY PROCEDURE[4]

Among economists who recognize that a price system is capable of fulfilling the allocative functions of an economy without central direction, there are two sharply divergent ways of seeing the capitalist market. The first, the dominant, view widely presented in most textbooks of microeconomics, sees the competitive market economy as one more or less pervaded by perfect knowledge. That is, market activity is seen as made up of innumerable independently made buying and selling decisions, each of which, in effect, more or less correctly anticipates and takes account of, all the other decisions being made in the market. Even though it is not claimed that each decision maker is in fact omniscient, it is held that each decision maker *is* aware of all market prices and thus in effect correctly taking into account all relevant decisions (since market prices are held to reflect those decisions). What an individual chooses, in this view of things, is the best out of an array of clearly perceived alternatives. These alternatives are, so to speak, offered by the market. Given the prices of all available goods, each decision maker can translate his available budget

---

3. Ibid.

4. The phrase "discovery procedure" is Hayek's. See F. A. Hayek, "Competition as a discovery procedure," in *New Studies in Philosophy, Politics, Economics and the History of Ideas* (Chicago: University of Chicago Press, 1978).

into an array of alternative market baskets. These baskets are, as it were, laid out in front of each decision maker, available for his choosing. These alternatives are *known* to be "there." They are not *discovered* to be there; they are implicit in the known budget constraints and known arrays of market prices. From these alternative market baskets available to him, each decision maker selects the one he most prefers. This selection constitutes the set of purchases and sales that he then makes in the market. The achievement of the competitive market, in this view of it, is that the individual items bought and sold in these myriads of market decisions turn out, as a result of the commonly known equilibrium prices, to fit exactly. Every attempted purchase is successful; every attempted sale is successful. All items for which a possibility of sale exists at a price that will make both buyer and seller better off (in their own prospective judgment) are in fact so sold. In this picture of the market there are no surprises, no pure profits, and no pure losses. There is nothing that is not, in effect, fully known at all times; there is no scope for discovery.[5] This picture contrasts sharply with the second view of the market economy.

This second way of seeing the capitalist market emphasizes, contrary to the first view, the deep fog of ignorance that surrounds each and every decision made in the market. The achievement of the market is not seen, in this second view, as consisting in its ability to generate precisely that set of equilibrium prices that will inspire myriads of dovetailing decisions, each of them made with complete knowledge of all prices. Rather, the market's achievement is seen in its ability to generate discovery. In other words, starting at each instant of time with a background of given mutual ignorance among market participants, the market process spontaneously offers the incentives and opportunities that inspire market participants continually to push back that fog of mutual ignorance. It is this fog of mutual ignorance that is to blame for the market's failure to achieve complete dovetailing of decisions; it is because the market process is continually generating the insights which operate towards dispelling this fog, that markets achieve the degree of dovetailing among decisions that they do. The first, dominant, view of the market emphasizes how, without central direction of individual decisions, these

5. This very brief capsule description of the mainstream view is, unavoidably, an oversimplification in several respects. Necessary qualifications will be added in later discussion as they become relevant.

decisions have somehow all been made so as to fit each other. The second view emphasizes how, without central direction, errors now being made come to be revealed and corrected through the incentives of the market. For the first view, "central direction" is seen as representing, in essence, the body of centralized knowledge sufficient to permit direct calculation of patterns of dovetailing activities. For the second view "central direction" suggests no such complete body of knowledge.

Because the first view of the market emphasizes the completeness of knowledge possessed by market participants it is reasonable, in this view, to treat aggregate output as something *definite*. The size and composition of this aggregate pie are not discovered; they are, in this view, already entirely implicit in the given resource endowments, preference rankings, and relevant technological possibilities that are the data for the system at any specific date. The emergence of this aggregate output is seen as inevitable, given these data. This is the case because the outcome of each buying, selling, and production decision is, as noted above, completely determined by these data. These outcomes are, for each decision maker, merely those bundles (of inputs or outputs) ranked highest among the respective ranges of alternatives spelled out by the known prices and known budget constraints.

But on the second view of the market this is not so at all. To be sure the aggregate outcome comprises the outcomes of all of the individual decisions made in the market. But these decisions are, in that second view, by no means the inevitable outcomes of the actual situations in which individuals respectively find themselves (when faced with given prices and budget constraints). What an individual decides to do is the outcome, not necessarily of his given preferences and of the arrays of market baskets marked out by prices and budget constraints—but of what the individual *believes* to be the set of available opportunities. Because of the ignorance that pervades the market the perceived set of opportunities may sharply differ from the opportunities implicit in market prices. More to the point, the opportunities the market participant sees must be attributed to his alertness at noticing what he might easily otherwise have missed. Ignorant though he may be, he nonetheless knows a great deal about his surroundings—knowledge derived from his *noticing* items of information that might redound to his benefit. The opportunities he sees, he has discovered. Just as he is still ignorant of so much that might have been useful and profitable to him, he *might* have been ignorant also concerning the opportunities he does see. What he has noticed and discovered about his surroundings and about the opportunities they afford, has been glimpsed as a result of the incentives offered by the market. The aggregate result that emerges from these discoveries by countless market participants can in no way be described as having been already implicit in the data of the market. This aggregate result—the aggregate pie that emerges from the independent productive activities of so many alert, but yet ignorant, decision makers—can only be described as having been discovered by those who make up the market.

It is true that the relative stability over time of market outcomes tends to mask this discovery-character of aggregate output. Each week the citizens of a city are fed, clothed, and housed not very differently, it seems, from the manner in which they were fed, clothed, and housed during the preceding week. So that to the superficial observer the weekly supply of the food, clothing, and housing services that make all this possible seems to flow routinely from the relevant resources—almost as if the economy resembled a machine generating its output or a tree yielding its fruit. But the view of the market we are now describing recognizes the superficiality of seeing the economy as a smoothly operating machine or a luxuriant tree. There is nothing automatic or predetermined about the productive efforts put forth in the market economy. Output does not flow automatically from inputs; rather, the owners of resources discover the productive potential that resides in their resources and move purposefully to implement their discoveries. It can be fairly stated that producers indeed *create* their product. Their creation is, as it were, *ex nihilo*. The car that emerges from the assembly line was not implicit in the steel and labor power from which it is fashioned. Access to steel and to labor power does not ensure—even under favorable price conditions—the emergence of the car. The decision to produce the car is a determination that the necessary resources are indeed within one's grasp, and that their deployment to fashion the car is indeed likely to be profitable. This "determination"— in the face of radical uncertainty—is ultimately responsible for the emergence of the car. This determination is not implicit in steel and labor power; nor is it in any sense implicit in the personality of the entrepreneur himself. This determination, the entrepreneurial decision to produce, is a genuine discovery; the act that implements this discovery is an act of creation. The output that the entrepreneur produces as a result of these creative acts is thus *discovered* output. The aggregate output of a nation—output of which each component has been discovered—must itself be treated not as a pie that is simply there, but rather as a pie that has been found, a discovered aggregate pie. I shall argue in this book that the circumstance that national output has been discovered drastically alters the way in which we should judge the manner of its "distribution." In particular, the discovered character of the social pie renders thoroughly irrelevant much of the standard literature on the justice of capitalist distribution.

JUSTICE AND PIE-SLICES

A pie is presented to a group of individuals. They must somehow share it between themselves. An observer may pronounce ethical judgment on the justice or injustice of the formula on the basis of which the pie is sliced and shared out. It may be held that it is unjust for the pie to be shared out unequally. Or, on the other hand, it may be held unjust for the pie to be shared out equally when some of the claimants are held to be hungrier than others, or when some of the claimants are in some sense held to be more meritorious or worthy than others. Or some other theory of justice may be advanced. Whatever the theory of justice that is being applied, the ethical observer's starting point is the simple existence of a given pie that has already been presented to the group. A good deal of the literature on economic justice has approached the question of capitalist distributive justice by treating aggregate national output in exactly this way, as a given pie that has been presented to society and must somehow be shared out among the various claimants or claimant groups.

Much of the literature is, of course, far less simplistic than this. Most writers now recognize that after all the social output is not a given pie; social output is a pie that has been produced by the joint productive contributions of the relevant resources. But, I shall argue, this insight, fundamental as it is, has not by itself very much altered matters for the literature of justice. This literature, even if it recognizes that the social pie is a pie baked out of arrays of resources, has nonetheless still treated the pie, in effect, as a given pie. More precisely, what is perceived as having been "presented" to society is not actually the pie itself, but the arrays of resources from which the pie emerges. Justice in sharing out the future output may, in one way or another, indeed depend on the efforts contributed by the respective resource owners. But once the ability to contribute these efforts has itself ultimately been, in the aggregate, seen as "presented" to society,

it has proven difficult to escape from the "given pie" perspective on capitalist distributive justice. Given pie ingredients may be seen as not drastically
different, justice-wise, from a given fully baked pie. In fact, many of the
classic controversies and dilemmas in regard to distributive justice, stem
from ethical intuitions vainly seeking to address the given-baked-pie case
and the given-pie-ingredient case simultaneously with a single set of criteria. Some of these dilemmas may, of course, easily be avoided by recognizing that applying a specific set of criteria to the given-pie-ingredient case
will generally yield quite different final prescriptions than would emerge
from an application of the very same set of criteria to the given-baked-pie. But
the point I wish to make is that both kinds of application share the same
initial premise in common. This premise is that that which is being shared
out is already in existence and known to be "here," prior to and independently of the criteria for distributive justice to be adopted. The argument of
this book denies this premise.

My position will be that neither the ingredients for pie-yet-to-be-baked
nor (*a fortiori*) the final consumable pie itself, are ever in fact "given" to
society to be shared out. Both the final pie and its ingredients must always
be discovered, imagined, created. And the forces that shape the process
of discovery are themselves powerfully affected by the criteria for distributive justice held to be relevant. These circumstances, I claim, raise fundamental challenges for standard treatments of economic justice.

Notice that my objection to standard treatments is not quite captured
in the argument that the size of the pie to be shared out is itself a function of the adopted criteria for distributive justice. This latter argument,
valid as it certainly is, has of course *not* been overlooked in the standard
literature. But recognition of this argument does not at all necessarily
presuppose any insight into my "discovery" perspective. This argument,
in standard treatments, simply calls for recognition that what is in fact
given to society is not the final pie but only its ingredients. The argument
then simply points out that the size of the pie that will be baked from
these given ingredients may depend on the way in which the pie is to be
shared out—and that this dependency may hold ethical significance. We
have already seen that this recognition, while a definite advance over simplistic theories of economic justice, which seem to assume that drastic
alterations in the pattern of distribution will leave the size of the distributed pie unchanged, need not at all involve any "discovery" insights. Even
if the size of the final pie may depend on the way it is to be distributed,

the volume of the originally given ingredients is surely invariant to alternative patterns of distributive justice.

My argument, on the other hand, is that there is nothing at all that is already given (and thus not dependent on the adopted criteria for distributive justice). Not only the final pie is not given, but also its ingredients are not given. Moreover, even if some criteria for justice were clearly to fix just title to each unit of discovered productive resource, this would not end the matter. This is because there is yet a further element of discovery that is needed to translate pie ingredients into the fully baked pie. And this discovery element introduces new questions for economic justice that transcend the simple determination of just ownership in the pie ingredients.

What is needed, therefore, in a theory of economic justice, is an approach that recognizes that at each stage in capitalist economic activity what is won has been, in some degree, found. Whether we deal with the justice of resource ownership or the source of just title in produced output, we are dealing with the ethics of assigning that which has been discovered. There is every reason to believe that, in the judgment of many ethical observers, it matters a great deal that we are concerned with the assignment of discovered, created, products, rather than with economic goods that are seen, essentially, as having been known to be here from the beginning of time.

THE RELEVANCY OF A FINDERS-KEEPERS ETHIC

It will be my contention that, for many observers, the circumstance that economic activity involves discovery does indeed alter matters a great deal. These observers, I believe, are likely now to invoke a simple ethical principle that would, in the absence of our discovery-perspective on capitalism, have had little scope within the market economy. This is the principle of finders, keepers. I will *not* take it as my goal to argue in favor of a finders-keepers ethic; but will argue that this ethic is consistent with what appear to be widely shared moral intuitions. I will, then, consider it important to establish that, *if* a finders-keepers ethic is subscribed to, then it should, out of consistency, be applied to any assessment of capitalist assignment of incomes.

A finders-keepers ethic means, for our purposes, something a little different from a simple first-claimant ethic. One who finds a beautiful, previously unowned seashell and takes possession of it is entitled to that seashell, we interpret the finders-keepers ethic to mean, not because he was the first to register a claim to it, but because he found it. Not only was the seashell unowned and unclaimed before he found it, but it was in fact undiscovered as well. In other words the seashell had, insofar as human awareness goes, no *existence* prior to its discovery. By finding it, the sea-shell's discovery has, in a sense, *created* it. Those subscribing to a finders-keepers ethic apparently attribute the very existence of the discovered item to its discoverer to a degree that confers natural ownership upon him.

A finders-keepers ethic offers a superficial parallel to the ethic on the basis of which John Locke developed his labor-mixing theory of private property. What a man's labor has brought into existence (out of unowned materials) is naturally his, Locke argued. The finders-keepers ethic maintains that what a man's discovery has brought to light is naturally his. Yet the two intuitions are not the same. To be convinced that the discoverer-creator of an item *ex nihilo* is its natural owner is one thing. To be convinced that mixing one's labor with unowned materials renders one the natural owner of the resulting artifact, is another.[6] But while these ethical intuitions are distinct, they are not necessarily contradictory. (Nor need the finders-keepers ethic preclude yet other ethical principles in which private property rights may be held to be rooted.) After all, one ethical intuition may apply to discovered items, while other ethical intuitions may be held to apply to items produced without discovery.

The last point is important both for elucidating the relevancy of the finders-keepers ethic for assignments of incomes under capitalism, and for recognizing the possibility of a certain convergence between this and the Lockean (or some other) ethics.

To accept the validity of ethical principles of just ownership that apply to items produced without discovery, need not at all compromise the universal relevance of a finders-keepers ethic—if it can be shown that all production must involve an element of discovery. On the other hand, subscribing to a finders-keepers ethic need not mean that this is the only

---

6. The reader may wonder if the discussion in the text is not inconsistent with the statement earlier in this chapter concerning not wishing to deal directly with the issue of the justice of private property institutions in general. I am *not* in fact primarily concerned with this question—except insofar as it holds implications for the justice of the market process. It is because there *are* important implications of this kind, that *some* attention will certainly have to be paid to these issues.

intuition that can be relevant to capitalist economic justice—if it can be shown that central aspects of capitalist production do not depend on discovery at all. In criticizing the existing literature on economic justice I am not, therefore, arguing that this literature offers fallacious reasoning or totally irrelevant ethical intuitions. I argue, instead, that this literature has been decisively flawed by its failure to recognize the centrality of discovery in the capitalist process, and the profound implications for distributive justice that follow from this centrality. I am now in a position to sum up the thesis of this book.

DISCOVERY AND THE JUSTICE OF CAPITALISM

The market process is one that is generated, at each and every moment, by entrepreneurial decisions. These decisions are not to be understood as merely selecting the highest out of an array of given and ranked alternatives. Entrepreneurial decisions embrace, most importantly, the perception and evaluation of the alternatives identified as relevant, in an environment of ineradicable uncertainty. Such perception and evaluation involves, especially, the perception and evaluation of opportunities seen to be waiting in the near or distant future. To see and evaluate such opportunities by peering into the future through the inescapable fog of ignorance, is, in a very real sense, to discover and to create them.

The incomes that are won in the market are thus won, in significant degree, through discovery. Such incomes are different from incomes imagined to consist solely of the revenue received from selling productive services in an equilibrium market for such resource services. Revenue received from selling in an equilibrium market has not been discovered. Such revenue received, say, from the sale of labor, is merely the highest ranked among two already fully perceived alternatives: the leisure to be enjoyed by not working, and the wage income to be received as a result of working. To choose to work and thus to receive income is to select one out of two alternatives *previously* discovered to be available. Because incomes under capitalism are never in fact received under equilibrium conditions they necessarily display aspects of discovered gain. In order to appraise the justice of capitalist income distribution, therefore, it is necessary to take explicit account of the justice of ownership of discovered value. There are plausible grounds for believing that, for many observers, the principles of justice likely to be held relevant to discoveries differ significantly from those likely to be held relevant to non-discovery contexts.

In particular, one type of income under capitalism has consistently incurred the moral castigations of critics of capitalism: the winning of pure economic profit. I shall show that, especially in regard to pure profit, the discovery aspects of capitalism generate a much higher degree of acceptability than might be forthcoming from perspectives from which discovery perspectives are excluded. To the extent that capitalist processes are driven by pure-profit-motivated entrepreneurial activity, we must enrich our conceptions of justice to take adequate account of such activity. To the extent that capitalist incomes, even in disequilibrium, do display characteristics that do not depend on pure entrepreneurship, we may continue to apply conceptions of justice that do not take discovery into account.

2. THE MEANING OF DISCOVERY

The notion of discovery is so central to the thesis of this book, and the nuances of this notion are so subtle and elusive, that it will be useful to devote a brief chapter to a discussion and clarification of its meaning. It will be my contention that incomes under capitalism—especially pure economic profit—are *discovered* incomes. It will be my contention that the aggregate national output of a capitalist economy—the pie that is supposedly "distributed"—is a discovered pie. I shall be contrasting these characterizations of incomes and aggregate output with the perceptions of them that appear to underlie the standard literature on economic justice under capitalism. I shall be associating the concept of discovery with that of creativity and alertness; I shall be identifying the context in which discovery is made as a context of radical uncertainty. All these contrasts and associations require discussion. I begin with some paradigmatic cases of discovery and its absence.

LUMBER AND LADDERS

Imagine that Jones, by accident, finds himself trapped in a deep hole, at the bottom of which happens to be, fortunately enough, a good deal of loose lumber, old nails, and some discarded tools, including a hammer. Wishing to escape from his predicament Jones sets about constructing a crude ladder with the materials and tools he finds to be at his disposal. We would probably all agree that Jones *discovered* the lumber and the tools that enabled him to construct his ladder. (He certainly did not *produce* them.) On the other hand, we would, at least at first glance, probably not wish to say that Jones discovered the ladder. We would rather say that Jones has produced the ladder with discovered materials and tools. Let us analyze the two kinds of human activity, the discovery of the materials and tools, on the one hand, and the production of the ladder, on the other.

What distinguishes the discovery stage from the production stage in the process culminating in the completed ladder? Several related features of these two stages suggest themselves as important in formulating the distinction.

i. The discovery of the lumber, nails, and hammer was unpremeditated. Jones did not deliberately search, let us suppose, for these materials and tools; he simply noticed them and realized their potential usefulness in making an escape from the hole. On the other hand, the construction of the ladder was completely deliberate. Once the materials and tools were clearly at his disposal, once he had made up his mind that the best available means of escape was by making a ladder, Jones's decision and its implementation were both typically planful. He had a clear-cut goal (the achievement of a ladder needed to fulfill the yet further goal of escape); the means to achieve this goal were at hand; he proceeded deliberately to deploy the means to attain his goal.

2. Because the construction of the ladder was deliberately planned, we can assume that the process of ladder production conformed to the standard paradigms of economic decision making. Because we may assume that Jones would prefer to escape sooner rather than later, that Jones would prefer to build his ladder with less fatigue to himself rather than with more, that he prefers to climb ladders that are safe rather than ladders that might perhaps collapse under his weight, that he prefers to take nourishment rather than to remain hungry, we can be sure that his method of ladder construction has taken into account all of these goals and constraints. His method of ladder construction will have been chosen so as to balance his urge to escape at the earliest, with his distaste for fatigue and for working on an empty stomach, and with his desire to avoid making a dangerously flimsy ladder. The discovery of the materials and tools, on the other hand, involved no such exercise in constrained maximization; Jones simply noticed them and recognized their potential value to him. Only then was he able to engage in calculation and in balancing possibly conflicting objectives.

3. In the construction of the ladder we do not see, at first glance, any of that element of chance or good fortune that surrounded Jones's discovery of the lumber, nails, and hammer. Once the means to attain his goal had been discovered, the construction of the ladder appears to have been completely under Jones's control from start to finish. The discovery of the materials and tools has—barring unforeseen and unanticipated accident—placed the ladder definitively within his grasp. On the other hand, precisely because his discovery of the lumber was undeliberate, we are inclined to ascribe it to good luck, divine intervention, and so forth—to favorable elements beyond Jones's human control. Absent these fortunate elements that somehow appear to have led Jones to notice the lumber, he might still be at the bottom of the hole.

4. On the other hand, although the discovery of the lumber was unpremeditated and appears largely a matter of good fortune for which

Jones can take little credit, that discovery must yet be attributed in part to Jones's alertness and resourcefulness. Had Jones dozed, he would have made no discoveries. Discovery requires human alertness and resourcefulness—qualities which do not seem to have played any obvious role in the building of the ladder. Once the materials and tools were known to be at hand, once their qualities had been ascertained, the decisions on what kind of ladder to build, what work schedule to follow, and so on, were made "mechanically," in textbook fashion. Given the objectives and the constraints (embodied in the available materials and tools), the production decisions did not call for human alertness; they could have been turned over, in principle, to a computer for their solution. The discovery of the ladder-materials, however, could hardly, even in principle, have been made by any conceivable machine—since we begin from the premise that Jones had no inkling that any lumber was to be found at the bottom of the hole. He could not have programmed any scanning device to search for lumber, since he had not even the remotest idea that any such search was likely to be successful; in fact he had no thought of building a ladder at all. Only *after* he noticed the lumber did he realize that he had within his reach the means of building an escape ladder. His discovery of the lumber cannot, therefore, be divorced from his human qualities of alertness and resourcefulness. Had he been less alert to his surroundings and their possibilities, he might never have noticed the lumber. Even if we describe Jones as having literally accidentally stumbled on the lumber, we must yet credit him with the alertness of noticing the potential usefulness of what he stumbled upon.

5. Clearly both lumber discovery and ladder construction involve prior *knowledge*. For Jones to be able to build a ladder, we must assume him to know how to hammer in nails in old lumber. For Jones to notice the potential usefulness of the lumber, we must assume him to have known about such things as ladders and their possible uses in climbing out of deep holes. But the two kinds of knowledge are quite different. The knowledge of how to build a ladder was in the nature of a resource at Jones's disposal. While he may not have given the matter much thought, he would, if he were questioned, agree that just as he was aware of his command over the lumber, nails, and hammer, he was also conscious of his ability to fashion a ladder out of them. In building a ladder he is, in a very real sense, *using* the knowledge he knows he possesses, exactly as he is using the lumber and the nails and the services of the hammer. If

in fact he did *not* initially know how to convert lumber, nails, and hammer into a ladder, we can imagine him deliberately learning how to do so through diligent practice at hammering in nails. But the prior knowledge that permitted Jones to make his discovery was not deliberately used in order to make his discovery. After all, I have described his discovery as having been unpremeditated. We may imagine psychologists analyzing the alertness with which I have credited Jones (and to which we have in part attributed his discovery of the lumber) as being constituted in certain items of knowledge that Jones may have "tacitly" commanded. But the point is that Jones did not deliberately deploy his alertness (or any items of tacit knowledge into which we may decompose that alertness) in order to find lumber. He simply noticed the lumber.

DISCOVERERS AND PRODUCERS

Our example has taught us some important differences that separate the alert discovery of valuable things from the deliberate production of valuable things. These differences are important precisely because, as we have seen, both the process of discovery and the process of deliberate production are essentially *human* processes. These differences may perhaps be summed up as follows. In processes of deliberate production, output is simply extracted from inputs. The product is seen as *already* inherent in the relevant mix of input services; once all of the relevant and necessary input services have been assembled, the intended product can be said to have been obtained entirely from these inputs. Naturally the list of inputs must be complete; it must include all necessary knowledge and technical skills. The decision to produce is then seen as simply the decision to pull the switch that permits the inputs to become effortlessly metamorphosed into outputs. The presence of the inputs *ensures* the emergence of the product. The product is completely attributable to the inputs. Command over inputs constitutes complete command over output. Given the decision to produce, the emergence of the product is *inevitable*. In contrast, the valuable things that one commands as a result of a discovery cannot be attributed to *any inputs whatsoever*. Nothing in the past rendered the occurrence of the discovery inevitable. The discovery was, I have repeatedly emphasized, undeliberate: no inputs were deployed to achieve it. To be sure we have attributed the discovery to human alertness, but such attribution is a different kind of attribution than that relevant to the squeezing of outputs from inputs. In the latter case, outputs are traced back to inputs in the context of a deliberately undertaken procedure. In the discovery case, alertness was never deliberately deployed to achieve discovery; all one can say is that, because Jones was alert, he noticed the lumber. One can never say that alertness "ensured" discovery—in the sense that possession of alertness rendered its possessor sure that he would successfully discover that which he later discovers. This is so (1) because the alert agent has as yet no inkling that the item-to-be-discovered is indeed available for discovery and (2) because, as we have seen, alertness is not enough; discovery involves also those elements of sheer good fortune that were noticed in the preceding section. One may describe a great tree as having, in some sense, been implicit in the seed from which it grew and developed; the growth process was simply the "unfolding" of that seed. One may, as we have seen, describe output as having already "existed" in embryonic form, in the bundle of inputs from which it finally emerged; the process of production may be seen as merely extracting that output pearl from the input oyster. We can fully account for the emergence of the tree, or the output, by reference to the prior existence of seed and inputs. Each stage of production is fully explainable by reference to the past. But one is quite unable to attribute the *discovery* of anything wholly to the prior existence of anything else. The process of discovery is not at all a process of conversion; each discovery is a genuine novelty. In a sense, no discovery can be explained in terms of the past. The past history, no matter how complete, is unable to ensure or wholly account for, an act of discovery. In this sense we may describe discoverers as having been responsible for, as having originated, "created," something entirely new, *ex nihilo*.

DISCOVERY AND SEARCH

I now turn to take note of the sharp distinction that we must draw between discovery, which is central to the theme of this book, and the quite different activity of *search*. Our preceding discussion will be most helpful here. One may, as a result of searching, "find" something valuable that one sought. But the verb "to find" in this context, is not at all the same as the verb "to discover." The distinction is of great importance.

Let us imagine I wish to look up Smith's telephone number. I have before me the telephone directory in which that number is listed; I know the full and correct spelling of Smith's name and address; my eyesight and education are such that I can read. My search for his telephone number is no act of discovery at all; it is a simple act of production. The resources necessary to produce the desired information are at my disposal; I use them to generate that information. The process is entirely deliberate and planful.

Even where I do not have access to a telephone directory, and search for Smith's telephone number by rummaging through dozens of pieces of scrap paper in my trash can (on one of which I know that I jotted down the number), we would not describe a successful search as the discovery of the number. Rather we would say that, with my resources of search-labor-time, richly informative trash can, and ability to read my own hieroglyphic jottings, I deliberately produced the information I sought.

Even where, in my desperate search for Smith's telephone number, I am reduced to forlornly and pathetically asking acquaintances and strangers at random if they happen to know Smith's telephone number, we should yet describe a successful search as production of, rather than discovery of, information. All that this last scenario amounts to is a deliberate search for information in a context in which there is a definite probability of failure in the search (since I cannot, within a reasonable time, ask *everybody*, and I know in advance that only a small subset of those I might ask, in fact know the number). If search in such a scenario turns out to be successful, we will be able, *ex post*, to attribute the acquired information to prior command over the necessary resources for successful information-attainment. It is true that the strong chances, *ex ante*, for search failure in such cases, mean that my command over these information-generating resources does not give me outright assurance of success. But that command does give me assurance of success subject to some specified margin of probability. The fact that I was fortunate enough to find someone who did know Smith's phone number and gave it to me when I asked for it, means that my deliberate process for producing information happened to work. (We will return a little later to discuss the role of good fortune in such production processes.)

But if, having fruitlessly scoured my trash can, and having fruitlessly asked everyone in sight, I resign myself to not being able to phone Smith—and suddenly happen to *notice* Smith's business card lying right in front of my very eyes—we will say that I have *discovered* the needed number. It was not searching that produced the number; I was fortunately awake and alert enough to notice what was right before my eyes. To be sure, as I will emphasize a little later, most search contexts permit a significant scope for pure discovery. While searching the library stacks for a needed book, one may "come across" an even more useful and needed volume. This latter volume has been discovered as a by-product of a search process. While searching in the trash can for the scrap of paper on which I have jotted down Smith's telephone number, I may come across Smith's business card (without having realized I had it in my possession at all). I shall show later on that these cases are simply examples of the many ways in which pure discovery and pure production are intertwined in real world contexts. For present purposes it is enough that we recognize that, in principle, the deliberate search for information may be conceived as entirely free of discovery elements; and that pure discovery may be entirely free of deliberate search elements.

A useful way to distinguish sharply between search and discovery is to notice that in search there is a good deal of prior knowledge that motivates the search and makes it possible. The searcher knows what he is looking for, and he knows where to look for it. As we will be emphasizing, his knowledge need not be perfect. (In fact, were a searcher to know *exactly* where to find the object of his search, we would not call it a search at all. A man departing from the home of his dinner host may search for his overcoat among those of other guests about to depart, because he does not know precisely where it is located. But if he knows that his was the only coat in the guest closet, he simply takes it, no search being necessary.) But, while the searcher's prior knowledge is imperfect, it is, at any rate for successful searchers, fully adequate to achieve the desired objective. If I wish to know the meaning of an unusual word, and proceed to consult a good dictionary, we can see that, while I do not yet actually know the meaning of this word, I nonetheless do know exactly how to know that meaning. I know that I lack present knowledge of the word's meaning; I know that knowledge of the word's meaning is important to me; I know how to obtain knowledge of that meaning. This contrasts sharply with the case where I do not have access to any dictionary, but happen to notice the way the word is used in a newspaper story that clearly teaches me its meaning. Here I have discovered the word's meaning. (Other cases of discovery would include my discovery of a dictionary, my discovery of the very existence of this new word, or my discovery that the word, which I may have known previously, possesses a meaning I had not suspected.) In these cases of discovery the discoverer discovers something he did not know existed, or something the ready availability of which he had not realized. A discovery is always something of a pleasant *surprise*. A search that proves successful may indeed provide a pleasant ending but hardly one that is surprising. (Once again, the possibility of good fortune playing a role in search or other production processes will be taken up separately.) To put our distinction between search and discovery somewhat differently, we can focus on the kinds of ignorance which successful search and discovery respectively dispel. A successful search wipes out *known* ignorance—that is, the searcher knew exactly the nature of his prior ignorance and the procedures necessary to wipe it out. What a discoverer discovers, on the other hand, is knowledge concerning which he had not known his prior ignorance. To discover a new word is to discover a word that one did not know that one did not know. To discover the meaning of a word (whose meaning one *does* know that one does not know) is to discover that knowledge of that meaning is available in a way one had not suspected. One had not known that one did not know how easy it would have been to find out the meaning of this word. Such *utter* ignorance may be followed by serendipitous discovery; it can hardly precipitate deliberate search.

Yet another way of expressing this same distinction between search and discovery is to focus on the notion of *error*. Not to know a telephone number or the meaning of a word represents a small measure of ignorance, but it does not necessarily represent any error. We generally reserve the term "error" for activity undertaken without taking advantage of all the information which is at one's disposal. It *may* be a gross error to use a word in a way that is inconsistent with its true meaning; but then the error lies not in not knowing its true meaning. Rather the error then lies in not realizing (that which one *should* surely have realized) that this word is one whose meaning one does not know. (If one incorrectly *thinks* one knows the correct meaning of the word, then its misuse in a sentence simply expresses one's utter ignorance of the correct meaning. Such misuse may indeed bring down ridicule upon the head of the unfortunate ignoramus; those relatively less ignorant frequently find the ignorance of others to be a source of hilarity and delight. But the misuse of the word is not *itself* an *error;* after all, the only way in which we can ever deliberately use words is that consistent with the meanings we believe these words to possess. Such misuse is only an example of error if the truth is that one *should* somehow have known the word's true meaning; or, at any rate, that one should have known that one is ignorant concerning the word's true meaning.)[1] The ignorance present before its removal by search is not error, because, since one has *known* that one is ignorant, its continued presence shows that one has felt that an effort to remove the ignorance would have been too costly to be worthwhile. One has deliberately remained ignorant because to become informed would have been a wasteful use of one's time. No error is present. It follows, therefore, that the search activity that one does finally undertake to remove such ignorance does not constitute the correction of error. On the other hand a discovery does, in a definite sense, constitute the correction of error. The ignorance that is dispelled in the course of a discovery is dispelled undeliberately; no costs were assumed in order to wipe out the ignorance. In other words, the discovery yields knowledge costlessly; the knowledge was, in principle, available without any call for sacrifice. In fact the knowledge was not known, only because one had not *realized* its costless availability. Such failure to realize what is costlessly available to one, is the commission of error. Discovery constitutes the realization and correction of earlier error. These important distinctions between search and discovery need particular emphasis for the purposes of this book. I shall be arguing that standard economics and standard treatments of economic justice under capitalism have largely ignored the discovery element in capitalism. This accusation does *not* charge standard economics with assuming what amounts to omniscience. Such an accusation would be patently false and unfair, in the light of the considerable attention paid in the standard literature of economics (and of economic justice) to the existence of imperfect information. What I claim, in criticism of that literature, is not that it has no place for ignorance, but that it has no place for "utter" ignorance—and thus no place for discovery. The standard literature has indeed incorporated the economics of search, but not the economics of discovery. It will be my contention that the phenomenon of discovery entails insights relevant to economic justice that are not relevant to the quite different phenomenon of search.

DISCOVERY AND GOOD LUCK

It might be tempting to interpret much of the above as implying that discovery is merely a matter of good luck. Since discovery is by definition

---

1. For further discussion on the notion of error, see my *Perception, Opportunity, and Profit* (Chicago: University of Chicago Press, 1979), ch. 8.

not deliberate, and since it turns out that that which is discovered was in fact already costlessly available even before the discovery, it might well be concluded that only bad luck had prevented the discoverer from enjoying an earlier discovery, and that only subsequent good luck can be credited with the actual subsequent discovery. After all, if we cannot credit the discoverer with any deliberate plan that might have led to his success, it does seem natural to conclude that success can only be a matter of sheer good fortune. As has already been indicated earlier in this chapter, I do not accept this conclusion. It is my position that the temptation to treat successful discovery as the result of pure luck is to be firmly resisted. It is simply not the case, I maintain, that the occurrence of desirable events must be seen *either* as the calculated implementation of deliberate plans *or* as pure windfalls. We must, it will be my argument, recognize that many good things that enter into one's life do so through our alertness in grasping at the available opportunities that have presented themselves. The alert discovery of such opportunities is not itself a deliberately planned act—but neither is it purely a matter of chance. Discovery must, to a degree, be credited to the human being without whose alertness the good fortune would simply not have been noticed.

This contention, denying that successful discovery is purely a matter of luck, clearly holds considerable significance for the theme of this book. It makes an enormous difference, for ethical judgment on capitalist economic justice, whether a discovery can, or must, be dismissed as merely a result of good luck, or not. The fortunate beneficiary of sheer good luck stands, it is easy to see, in a far weaker ethical position (in regard to his right to enjoy exclusive title to the privileges thrust upon him by good luck) than one who alertly grasped desirable opportunities that came his way. So that my claim that discovery is far more than a matter of pure luck will hardly be accepted without at least a brief elaboration and defense. The central element underlying this claim is the insight, noted earlier, concerning the *possibility of error.* In many treatments of economics the possibility of error is, in effect, denied. The denial of error would imply that anything valuable that good fortune has placed before an individual (making it costlessly available to him), would be instantaneously perceived and grasped. The possibility of an ungrasped opportunity would, in the absence of error, be simply unthinkable. Under such assumed circumstances an improvement in one's situation could indeed never be ascribed to the correction of earlier error; such an improvement would either have to have occurred as a result of some deliberate act of production, or as a result of a stroke of good fortune. (Later on I shall discuss the possibility of good luck entering into the outcome of a deliberately undertaken process of production.) Were error never to occur, in other words, we would be compelled to see any improvement in the individual's situation as either having already been implicit in the inputs (over which he already had control) or as involving a pure windfall to that individual.

But we have already taken note of the circumstance that the phenomenon of error is alive and well in human affairs. Opportunities costlessly available to individuals (or, which is the same, opportunities for gain that far outstrip any costs of grasping them) are continually overlooked by all of us. We are all familiar with the sensation of reproaching oneself *ex post* for having failed to take advantage of a situation that had been available, but which one had thoughtlessly ignored. Looking back on such situations we see that one had had, before one's eyes, opportunities which one has spurned, as it were, for no good reason. The thoughtless rejection of these opportunities, one now acknowledges, cannot be rationalized as having resulted from any prohibitive costs (which would have been good reason for not acting). Had one behaved "rationally," it is now clear, one would have grasped, rather than rejected, these opportunities. (Indeed the denial of error with which we have charged much standard economic discussion, is simply a corollary of the standard assumption of universal, never-relaxed, rationality. Rational human beings may, it is true, be less than omniscient—presumably because the costs of deliberate learning are held to be not worthwhile. But rational human beings never err—in the sense of failing to utilize every ounce of information worthwhile acquiring.) Error, we must recognize, is widespread and important.

And once the presence of error is acknowledged, we must recognize the possibility, at least, of the correction of error. Such a correction, we have seen, must partake of the character of undeliberate discovery. Even where one's error has consisted in failing to see an opportunity for deliberately improving one's circumstances (so that error correction signals immediate initiation of that deliberate plan) the correction itself must take the form of *discovering* that oportunity for planful improvement. Subsequent initiation of deliberate exploitation of the now-perceived opportunity is a *result* of a corrected error. The error correction itself consists of an act of pure discovery. I shall argue that such error correction is *not* a matter of sheer luck.

Were the only possibility for correction of error to be a matter of sheer good luck (in which case we should presumably talk of the lucky *disappearance* of error rather than of its correction) we would have to ascribe the prior error to earlier atrocious luck. If the only thing needed and able to ensure full perception, is good fortune, it follows that only the absence of good fortune is to be blamed for the earlier oversight. But to ascribe the oversight to sheer bad luck is to exonerate our individual from any culpability—after all, he did the best he possibly could have done, given his stroke of bad luck. To take this position is clearly, once again, to deny the very possibility of error. Yet we do, surely, at least *ex post*, blame ourselves for not having seen that which was staring us in the face. We do not excuse ourselves as having been the unfortunate, innocent victims of bad luck—that somehow permitted us to gaze upon the opportunity and yet not to realize its availability.

To the extent that we do assign a measure of reproach to ourselves for having overlooked that which was costlessly available, to that extent, at least, we assign corresponding credit to ourselves when we finally do "open our eyes" and perceive the opportunity we had, for no good reason at all, ignored or spurned. We then say that we finally discovered the truth, we saw the light. What alerts us to see previously overlooked opportunities is not sheer good luck, but strong human motivation. Such motivation is not, in such instances, manifested in the careful, planful, calculation of constrained maximization. It is manifested, instead, as a generalized purposefulness so intense as to focus attention with full alertness, upon any and all available, desirable opportunities. The discovery of such opportunities is itself not a matter of luck, but of human motivation. To be sure, luck and good fortune play an important role in the *presence* of these opportunities-waiting-to-be-noticed. Someone may be described as luckier than others because he happens to be surrounded more thickly with such favorable opportunities than others are. But the *perception* of these opportunities depends on the alertness of the potential observer. The existence of these opportunities is not to be attributed (as the existence of produced output *is* to be attributed) to human agency; but the *discovery* of the opportunities originates, not in a stroke of good fortune, but in human alertness.

The temptation to attribute discoveries entirely to good luck is all the more powerful, no doubt, because it is very difficult to distinguish, in practice, between the existence and the discovery of an opportunity. (For some, indeed, there may even be serious philosophical objections to the very notion of the "existence" of an opportunity that has not yet been discovered.) So that when one contemplates the discovery by Jones of the lumber, nails, and hammer at the bottom of his hole, it becomes all too easy to merge the good fortune responsible for their prior presence at the bottom of the hole, with the discovery itself. The difficulty in distinguishing between the existence and the discovery of an opportunity is heightened by the many different degrees of existence that are possible. Lumber that is completely visible to superficial observation is more likely to be noticed than lumber that is partly concealed by useless debris. A given degree of alertness on the part of Jones might lead to discovery in the first case where it might not in the second. We would then be tempted to say that its discovery was due to the good luck that the lumber was not covered by debris. To be precise, however, we should recognize that it was the existence of the lumber in readily visible form that was lucky; its being perceived is yet to be attributed to the (given degree of) alertness of Jones. We conclude that a discovery is, in the concrete, to be attributed to the conjunction of good fortune and of human alertness—the former responsible for the availability of, and the latter for the noticing and the grasping of, that which is discovered.

GOOD LUCK AND GOOD LUCK

Our understanding of the way in which sheer good luck is intertwined with human alertness in the occurrence of discoveries, permits us to turn to consider the role of good luck in deliberate processes of production. (I have on several occasions in this chapter promised to address this question.) I have emphasized the deliberate character of production (including the production of information through search) as contrasted with the undeliberate character of discovery. This emphasis led me to note the strong element of human control governing production, as distinct from discovery, processes. The decision to engage in a deliberate process of production (including deliberate search for knowledge), I argued, is a decision to achieve an assured objective. What must be clarified is how this notion of production as the achievement of an assured objective is consistent with the presence of risk in production processes. This task is all the more important in that there exists a temptation, which I believe should be resisted, to see, in the scope which such risk accords to good fortune, an element which blurs the distinction between production and discovery. This latter temptation is especially strong in the case of deliberate search under risky conditions, where a fortunate outcome of the search may seem very close indeed to the discovery, rather than to the deliberate production, of information.

My insistence on preserving the sharp conceptual distinction I have drawn between production and discovery becomes, somewhat paradoxically perhaps, important precisely because, I shall argue later in this chapter, in practice pure discovery and pure production are almost invariably intertwined. I shall be claiming throughout this book, indeed, that production in the real world involves discovery. Our program, then, in this section is to identify the *non*-discovery character that is present in risky production—in order better to appreciate, eventually, the sense in which real world production invariably does display important discovery elements.

The point to be made in this section is that the presence of risk in deliberate processes of production does not affect the "assured" character of such processes, properly understood. Let us recall one of the examples of search referred to earlier in this chapter. I was searching for Smith's telephone number, but lacked any direct way of finding it out; in my desperation I was reduced to asking acquaintances or strangers at random if they happened to know Smith's telephone number. I argued that this, too, was search, a deliberately undertaken process through which to produce the needed information. If I am successful, and chance to ask someone who does indeed know Smith's telephone number, we should not describe this as my having discovered the number, but rather as my having produced the information through search. Now, this claim of mine may appear bizarre. Surely, it will be objected, my success is to be ascribed to my sheer good fortune in happening to ask the right person. Surely my eventually found knowledge resembles more closely the lumber Jones was fortunate enough to discover at the bottom of his hole than it does the ladder that he deliberately constructed out of that lumber. If, the objection would continue, the central feature of production consists (as argued in this chapter) in the assurance the producer has that his input bundle can, at will, be transformed into aimed-at output, then surely my desperate search for Smith's telephone number cannot be described as having produced the number; at no stage in my search was I remotely assured of ever knowing that number.

In defense of my description of this way of finding out Smith's telephone number as search rather than discovery, I emphasize the deliberate character of my desperate search. I know what it is that I am seeking; I know that the only way available to me for having even a remote chance of finding out what I need to know, is by asking people pretty much at random. It is quite true that my chances of success are very low; I have a pretty good idea of the small chance of randomly striking someone who happens to know the number I need. But in the face of these formidable odds, I choose to press ahead with this desperate search. I clearly recognize that what my efforts can assure me is definitely not certain knowledge of that number that I seek. What my efforts can assure me is merely a certain small chance of success, given the circumstances of my search. My argument is that if, against the odds, I am lucky enough to be successful, my success is to be attributed to my deliberate gamble. To be sure, my gamble did not assure my winning the prize, but it did assure me a chance of being the winner. If success indeed occurs, we will certainly recognize my good fortune in winning against the odds, but will, nonetheless, also recognize that it was my deliberate, calculated decision that, after weighing the chances of gain against the cost of the gamble, placed me in a position to be the possible winner. *There is nothing surprising about the outcome.* It is exactly the outcome for the sake of which I deliberately undertook my search. The possibility of winning was clearly perceived, and indeed served as the decisive factor in persuading me to undertake the gamble. What occurred was, admittedly, subject to the chances of the gamble, fully ensured by my actions. I cannot claim any special prescience concerning the outcomes of gambles; it was not any extraordinary "alertness" concerning my approaching stroke of good luck that inspired me to undertake this gamble. So that where, as in the telephone number search case, what the successful gamble yields is a piece of information, I cannot call it an undeliberate discovery to be attributed to my alertness to available opportunities. Rather we should see my attainment of the sought-after information as the fortunate outcome of a deliberate production gamble. At all times the results were exactly as planned. (Were the gamble not to have succeeded, we would equally well be able to say that the results were exactly as planned—since what was planned was not the certainty of success, merely the chance of being successful.)

The good luck that enters into successful discovery is thus quite different from that which enters into successfully achieved production processes (undertaken under risky conditions). In discovery, prior good fortune unexpectedly set the stage for the alert exploitation of it; in the production, good fortune, if it occurs, crowns a deliberate gamble with a success that was foreseen as a definite possibility. In discovery, alertness to unexpected good fortune generates a pleasant surprise; in production, the occurrence of good fortune is indeed pleasant, but is no surprise at all; it was, in a sense, fully anticipated.

THE DISCOVERY ELEMENT IN DELIBERATE PRODUCTION

Having spent almost an entire chapter driving home the sharp distinction between pure discovery and pure production, I turn now to smudge that clear line of distinction. I do not at all wish to be perverse, nor do I wish to retreat from anything argued thus far in this chapter. What I wish to do now is to point out that in the real world in which we live, cases of *pure* production are rarely, if ever, encountered. By far the majority of planful processes of deliberate production turn out to be embedded in an environment which sharply compromises the completeness of control which I have emphasized as being essential to the pure production concept. For deliberate production planning to be no more than the simple decision to permit output to emerge from the available inputs, we would require the guaranteed and realized absence of surprises. Only then could one say, as I have repeatedly asserted concerning the notion of pure production, that command over the necessary inputs ensures inevitable command, if this is desired, over outputs. Once we recognize that in reality a surprise-free environment is virtually unthinkable, we have irrevocably smudged the sharpness of the line of distinction separating production from discovery.

Notice that the preceding sentences do not say that the presence of *risk* compromises the purity of the deliberate production concept. We have seen in the preceding section that risk can fit quite comfortably, in principle, into the notion of pure production. But then we were able to argue that the presence of foreseen and deliberately assumed risk by no means ensured the presence of surprise. What introduces the element of surprise into the picture is not calculated risk, but rather open-ended uncertainty.

The distinction between risk and uncertainty is, of course, an old one.[2] For our purposes many of the controversies concerning the validity of

2. On the idea of "genuine" uncertainty, as developed by Frank Knight, see his *Risk, Uncertainty, and Profit* (Boston: Houghton Mifflin, 1921); see also Gerald P. O'Driscoll Jr. and Mario J. Rizzo, *The Economics of Time and Ignorance* (Oxford: Basil Blackwell, 1985), ch. 5.

this distinction can be detoured: the relevant distinction is that between open-ended and closed-ended ignorance.[3] I know that my spun coin can land either heads up or tails up. I do not know which of these landings will occur. But I do know precisely the boundaries of my ignorance. Nothing that can occur can constitute a surprise for me. This ignorance is closed-ended. As discussed earlier, the presence of this kind of "fully-known ignorance" in a process of production in no way compromises the deliberate, fully-calculated character of such a process.

Open-ended ignorance, on the other hand, is a quite different matter. This kind of ignorance exists where one entirely lacks knowledge concerning the boundaries of one's ignorance. One does not know what it is that one is ignorant about. One acts in ignorance of the true limits of one's ignorance. Here the truths, concerning which one had no inkling that one was ignorant, hit one subsequently in the nature of total surprises. They were entirely unexpected, not because the odds were against their occurrence but because the very possibility of their occurrence had hitherto escaped one's attention.

The point to be emphasized for the present purpose is simply that life is full of surprises. We live in an uncertain world—that is, a world in which we can be sure that we will be surprised. We act continually in full knowledge of the circumstance that we are quite ignorant concerning the limits of our ignorance. We act knowing that this inescapable uncertainty surrounding our planned activity drastically erodes our control over the processes we initiate. We can no longer feel confident that our command over inputs ensures our command over output.

Awareness of the ineradicable uncertainty which envelops all human activity permits us to acknowledge that the economist's model of the rational decision, in which given resources are deployed efficiently towards the maximum fulfillment of given, ranked, ends—is nothing but a model. The decisions which man makes in real life never do correspond precisely to the contours of this model. Real-life decision making, it is now widely understood, necessarily involves at the same time, a decision setting the limits that are deemed appropriate to one's conscious ignorance. In practice this means that each decision involves a specific

3. For discussion of similar ideas, see the extensive works of G. L. S. Shackle, and also B. J. Loasby, *Choice, Complexity, and Ignorance* (Cambridge: Cambridge University Press, 1976).

picture, or a specific set of alternative pictures, concerning the future state of the world, upon which the results of one's decision will impinge. One's planned course of action is oriented towards this array of envisaged scenarios. One is aware that the true state of the future may fail to conform to any one of the envisaged pictures; one is, as it were, ready for surprises, pleasant or otherwise. So that each decision depends on the perceptiveness with which one is able to see the future—the extent to which one is able to plan rationally for the future and at the same time successfully escape surprise.

In this sense we can identify an inescapable element of discovery in each successful deliberate production decision. For Jones to build an effective escape ladder out of lumber, nails, and hammer is, in a definite sense, to make a discovery not greatly different from the discovery he had made of the lumber, nails, and hammer. What Jones discovers in his building of the ladder is the existence of a gainful opportunity to be grasped by converting lumber, nails, and hammer into a ladder. This opportunity was not, in any real world scenario, clearly visible apart from the decision to build the ladder. All kinds of possibilities might render this opportunity not an opportunity at all, or not a gainful one. Perhaps the lumber will turn out to be completely useless, disintegrating at the first hammering in of a nail; or perhaps the work of building the ladder at the bottom of a hole may prove so fatiguing as to be unfeasible; or perhaps an alternative, much easier way of escaping from the hole will present itself. Had these discouraging pictures concerning the future been uppermost in Jones's mind, he might never have built his ladder; he would have missed an opportunity by not "seeing" its existence. Were it possible to live in the economist's theoretical world of pure rational decision making (where, subject to calculable risks, all elements entering into the outcome of the decision are completely known), with no room for surprise, then deciding to build a ladder would not constitute the glimpsing and grasping of an opportunity. In such a theoretical world the existence of the opportunity, with its attendant calculable riskiness, would already, prior to the decision, have been completely apparent. It would not have had to be discovered. But in the open-ended world of uncertainty the decision to produce a ladder, or to engage in any deliberate act, is an expression of one's convictions concerning the future. Such an expression of confidence is, when borne out by future events, seen to have been a prescient glimpsing of opportunities that might easily not have been seen. To proceed to build a ladder that turns out to be success-ful, or to implement any plan that turns out to have been a wise one, is to have discovered an opportunity that might otherwise have languished ungrasped. The existence of an opportunity, like the existence of lumber at the bottom of a hole, means little for human well-being until that exis-tence has been noticed and exploited. The act of noticing and grasping opportunities, or lumber, is fundamentally different from the act of devel-oping and implementing a deliberate plan. The former act is—in what-ever context—an act of discovery. Each productive decision, taken in the real world of open-ended uncertainty, reflects such a discovery element.

To be sure, a planned act of production may turn out to have been totally ill-advised. The production process itself may fail for any number of reasons; or the product may turn out to be far less valuable than antici-pated; or the costs of production may turn out to have been far higher than expected. So that the opportunity "discovered" may turn out not to have existed (or at any rate not to have been an attractive one) in real-ity, at all. (This would correspond to Jones undertaking to build a lad-der because he believes himself to have discovered lumber, when in reality what he discovered was simply old painted pieces of cardboard.) My point is not that each and every deliberate act of production consti-tutes a valuable discovery—rather that each such deliberate act includes a non-deliberate element corresponding to "noticing and grasping." Suc-cessful deliberate acts of production mean that what was noticed and grasped was a genuinely valuable discovery. Much of what I will be argu-ing in later chapters will focus on this discovery element in all economic decisions.

DISCOVERY AND CREATION

At a number of times in this and the preceding chapter I have used the terms "discovery" and "creation" interchangeably. To discover an opportu-nity, I have implied, is to create it. Sometimes I even refer to the concept of creation *ex nihilo* to characterize a successful discovery. This use of lan-guage requires some justification. The justification we set out to provide in this section will prove of considerable importance in our later develop-ment of the theme of this book.

At first glance it may appear bizarre to describe Jones as having "cre-ated" the lumber he discovers to exist at the bottom of his hole. To refer to such a discovery as creation *ex nihilo* may well appear wholly absurd and affected. Yet this use of terminology is neither imagery gone wild nor a sacrilegious use of theological metaphor; it corresponds to something very simple, yet very significant. Moreover, this terminology will help us recognize the basic unity shared by genuinely creative artistic and technological innovation on the one hand, and the more simple acts of discovery (like noticing available bits of lumber) on the other. In conjunction with the insights we have taken note of in the preceding section, our present discussion will permit us to recognize the creative element in each and every act of production undertaken in the real world of open-ended uncertainty.

It will be helpful to recall our discussion, earlier in this chapter, of the idea of pure, deliberate, production activity. Such activity, we saw, consisted in the planned transformation of given inputs into desired output. Command over the inputs, we emphasized, *ensured* command over output. Possession of inputs meant, in effect, complete access to outputs. Under such pure conditions it is clear that the decision to produce is merely the giving of permission, as it were, to the inputs to yield the potential output that they represent. The producer adds nothing; he merely gives the nod to the inputs. The output generated by the pure production process can, therefore, not be said to have *originated* in the producer. The origin of the product is to be found completely in the resources, the existence of which is entirely sufficient to ensure the emergence of the product. But a pure discovery, we saw, is quite different from a pure production case. There were no inputs that ensured the discovery. The discovery was uncaused; it originated entirely with the discoverer—who noticed and grasped the discovery without invoking the assistance of any inputs whatever.

It may, we have observed, seem odd to claim that Jones created or originated the lumber he discovers at the bottom of his hole. After all, the lumber did exist before Jones noticed it. America did exist before Columbus. There are two senses in which the assertion that Jones created that which he discovered might be defended. Let us consider them in turn.

Consider, first of all, not the physical lumber which Jones discovered, but his knowledge of its existence. That knowledge did not exist before Jones's discovery. He had no inkling of the existence of any lumber until he noticed it. If we define Jones's discovery as consisting in his acquiring knowledge of what he discovered, then it might fairly be claimed that Jones alone created that discovered knowledge. That discovery originated entirely in Jones's alert awareness of his surroundings. The knowledge that constitutes Jones's discovery was not produced deliberately from inputs (recall the distinction between search and discovery): it emerged spontaneously from Jones's alertness. It does not seem far-fetched to describe Jones as having *created* his discovered knowledge, *ex nihilo*.

But it may be objected that defining the discovery of lumber as consisting in the knowledge concerning the lumber rather than in the lumber itself, does not avoid the real difficulties surrounding the "creation" metaphor. Just as the lumber itself existed before it was discovered, so did the information concerning its existence. After all, the objective existence of the lumber at the bottom of the hole, even if this existence was not known to any human being, is a source of information (regarding the existence of the lumber) no different from the information stored in the memory of a computer, or as an entry in a printed telephone directory. The entry in the telephone directory may not have been read yet by a single soul. I would hardly wish to say that the first reader of that entry has created the knowledge contained in that entry. Noticing the lumber at the bottom of the hole creates no information that was not waiting to be "read" at the bottom of the hole—just as reading a phone directory entry creates no information that was not already present on the printed page. To be sure the knowledge I subjectively possess after absorbing the information from the printed page did not exist in my mind previously. But it seems quite uninteresting to describe myself as having *created* that subjectively possessed knowledge; and, in light of the prior existence of the printed information which I read, there appears no justification at all to describe myself as having created anything *ex nihilo*. The assertion that Jones independently originated his knowledge concerning the lumber may yet be defended on the grounds that unnoticed objective information guaranteed no discovery of it. Jones's undeliberate discovery was not ensured by the existence of that objective information; it was his own alertness that grasped it. This defense is, in my view, valid. However, we find ourselves pushed substantially in the direction of the second of the two senses which I referred to earlier as possible interpretations of the assertion that Jones created his discovery. Let us consider this second interpretation.

The second interpretation is that Jones may in an important sense be held to have created the very lumber that he notices. True, the lumber was physically in existence long before Jones fell into the hole. But unnoticed lumber is, in a very practical sense, non-existent lumber. This is not any abstruse philosophical point involving trees crashing unheard in the primeval jungle, or any poetic pathos concerning the blush of full many an unseen flower. Objects whose existence has not been suspected have, after all, been utterly irrelevant to human history. They have played no role in the sequences of cause and effect that make up the tapestry of history. Their injection into history occurred only at the moment of their discovery.

To express the same idea in somewhat more narrowly economic terms, we may say that, until its discovery, the lumber lacked economic value. Jones's discovery of lumber transformed it from an economically valueless—and therefore practically non-existent—entity into an item of considerable human value. That created value must be attributed *entirely* to Jones's alertness. The newly created value cannot be imputed to any contributing group of complementary inputs (as the value of a deliberately produced ladder can be imputed to the lumber, nails, and hammer that produced it). The value created by the discovery of the hitherto valueless lumber was created *ex nihilo*.

In the preceding section I drew attention to the discovery element inevitably present, in the real world of open-ended uncertainty, in each deliberate act of production. The insights developed in the present section imply, then, a creative element in each real world process of production. The pure notion of deliberate production contained nothing within it that corresponded to either discovery or creation. That which is produced is produced simply by transforming given inputs, in which the aimed-at product is already fully implicit. But deliberate production in the real world always is, we saw, also the expression of an alert discovery and exploitation of a hitherto ungrasped productive opportunity. The grasping of a hitherto unnoticed opportunity for gain is, we now understand, the *creation* of that opportunity. So it is true that Jones's ladder was produced, not *ex nihilo,* but out of lumber, nails, and hammer, but the finished ladder contains within it, nonetheless, an element of a purely created entity. In creating the opportunity to convert lumber into ladder, Jones was acting creatively; he was adding something to the lumber, a something which originated wholly in his own alert creativity.

Consideration of this creative element in deliberate production processes permits us to link the notion of creation I have emphasized in this section, with the kinds of artistic or engineering creativity more conventionally recognized in production processes. A gifted architect, artist, or engineer creates a new structure; we ascribe creativity to these authors on the basis of the inspired novelty of their designs. These producers *use* inputs to create something that was not at all already implicit in those inputs. The marble and chisel from which the gifted sculpture is created, are by no means enough to ensure the emergence of the sculpture—even with the help of a skilled artist. The creativity of the sculptor is needed to put these necessary ingredients to work to produce something wholly new. Our discussion has shown how, in each and every act of production in the real world, no matter how mundane and routine that production process may appear, there is present a trace, at least, of a very similar creative element. What every producer does is to *use* the inputs which he identifies, to produce the product he decides to produce. It is the producer's creative decision to recognize, among the inputs to which he has access, a profitable opportunity to produce something valuable. This decision involves, we now understand, precisely the same *kind* of creative discovery—if not to the same degree—as does the artist's vision of converting stone and chisel into inspired and sublime art. Both expressions of creativity are of the same pattern as the pure discovery of lumber-at-the-bottom-of-the-hole by Jones.

3. SEARCHING FOR DISCOVERY IN THE LITERATURE OF ECONOMIC JUSTICE

Our discussion of the meaning of the concept of discovery has shown how sharply different it is from the idea of deliberate production (in the context of given goals and resources) which is central to standard analysis. We have also seen that in real world production processes (as distinct from the economics textbook models of such processes) we can invariably identify some element of discovery. My contention in this book is that for many ethical observers the presence of a discovery element in economic decision making (and in the incomes that may be received as a result of such decision making) definitively affects one's evaluation of economic justice under capitalism. I also maintain that the presence of this discovery element has not been recognized in the literature of economic justice. The present chapter sets for itself the somewhat daunting task of proving this negative proposition; of establishing the absence, in a large literature, of appreciation for the circumstance of discovery, and for its relevance for economic justice. The reader may be reassured to learn that it is not my intention patiently to examine each contribution to the literature and to establish that it fails to pay attention to the idea of discovery. Instead my principal strategy will be to consider a small number of landmark contributions and scrutinize their treatment—in regard to the ideal of justice—of the concept of *pure economic profit*. My position will be that if discovery were recognized at all as being relevant to economic justice, we should expect to find such recognition in the treatment of pure economic profit. If, as I shall show, such treatments fail to reveal any appreciation for the concept of discovery, I shall feel entitled to conclude that the literature of justice has indeed ignored the relevance of this notion. A brief examination of several additional discussions in the literature will further confirm this conclusion. Before embarking on this search for discovery, it may be helpful to devote a few paragraphs to address a possible misunderstanding that might quite easily arise. The point arises from our identification, in the preceding chapter, of discovery with creation.

THE JUSTICE OF CREATION

It would certainly be unfair to the literature on economic justice to accuse it of ignoring the circumstance that the output which is to be justly distributed has been created.[1] Certainly the literature has frequently approached the question of economic justice by asking "who produced the economic pie?" or "what fraction of the pie has been produced by a specified resource?" Moreover, it has certainly been widely understood that the size of the pie to be shared out may itself be crucially dependent upon the pattern adopted for its distribution. The literature has thus indeed understood that the very justice of a distributive scheme may be determined, in part, by the effect this scheme may have on the size of the pie that is being created.[2] But none of this represents any recognition of the insights central to this book's theme.

Although my argument is based on the insight that an act of discovery is, in an important sense, an act of creation, and although I have emphasized the corresponding discovery-creation element in all real world productive processes, the novelty I claim for my thesis is certainly not simply that an act of production is an act of creation. My thesis is, rather, that the creative aspect of production is to be found *only* in the discovery element within it. My dissatisfaction with the literature consists, in large part, not over whether production is or is not creative, but over how one should perceive the creative aspect of production. The literature of economics, and of economic justice, sees production as creative in the simple sense that the product is physically different from the resources from which it originates. My own view on the matter is that the product has been created in the sense that the entrepreneurial decision to produce constitutes a discovery, a creation *ex nihilo*. From my perspective, therefore, a determination that the literature of justice recognizes that the pie to be distributed must first be created, is by no means relevant to our concern. What we will be searching for is not evidence of recognition

1. Discussions of income distribution that ignore the circumstance that in the real world output emerges only as a result of the actions of people, have been termed "manna-from-heaven models." See R. Nozick, *Anarchy, State, and Utopia* (New York: Basic Books, 1974), pp. 198, 219.

2. See further, Arthur M. Okun, *Equality and Efficiency: The Big Tradeoff* (Washington: Brookings Institution, 1975).

of the created character of the pie, but rather evidence of recognition of the *discovered* character of that pie. We will be searching for hints that the just claim which an economic agent may possess in respect to his income may derive from his having, somehow, created that income *ex nihilo* through an act of discovery.

THE FOCUS ON PURE PROFIT

As indicated earlier, I shall be paying particular attention to the treatment of pure economic profit. It is relatively easy to overlook the possibility of discovery in regard to other kinds of income. Mainstream economics has been eminently successful in doing so. Mainstream economics has proceeded, especially in its less sophisticated versions, by filtering out any scope for discovery from its analysis. It has approached the formidable task of bringing the seething agitation of the real world within analytical grasp, by a series of mental experiments and heroic abstractions. The analytical models yielded by these simplifications are peopled, in effect, by efficient decision makers each of whom is supremely untroubled by any doubts or uncertainties concerning the future, knowing, in particular, exactly what decisions other market participants are making, and moving in unerring fashion to select the respective best positions made available by the relevant environment. In these models there is no possibility for pure profit—since omniscient market participants cannot be imagined to have irrationally permitted unexplained and unjustified price differentials to have prevailed. Incomes, in such models, are confined to revenues received by resource owners in perfect markets for the sale of resource services (with interest incomes treated in these models as revenue received for the productivity services of investment).

These economic models have been very useful. They have elucidated important features of economic reality. They have, in particular, clarified the market forces that operate to determine resource prices—and thus resource incomes. Since these models have been carefully designed to exclude the vagaries introduced by uncertainty and surprise, it is only to be expected that the explanations they provide for resource pricing and resource incomes are couched in terms which are incapable of embracing any element of discovery whatsoever. Within the scope of these mainstream models, therefore, questions relevant to considerations of economic justice inevitably invite treatment from a perspective inherently incapable of encompassing discovery. Pure profits simply do not exist in these models; other incomes can and are fully explained in terms of models that simply cannot accommodate the phenomenon of discovery. We shall indeed find that the literature on economic justice, steeped, as it had to be, in mainstream economics, evaluated resource incomes from a perspective to which the concept of discovery was utterly foreign. But the real world phenomenon of pure profit, it might seem, is too important and palpable a presence to have been wholly swept under the analytical rug in such fashion.

And, indeed, mainstream economic theorists have, for over a century now, grappled with the phenomenon of pure profit, endeavoring somehow to make room for it in their theoretical interpretations of the market system. It is to these theories, therefore, that one would reasonably look for glimmers of recognition of the possibility of pure discovery; and it is in the use made of these theories by thinkers on economic justice that one might hope to find consideration of the ethical implications of discovery. After all, the phenomenon of pure profit corresponds to prices paid for outputs which exceed the sums of prices paid for *all* necessary inputs. The difference between these sets of prices is grasped by the entrepreneur as pure profit. This profit can clearly not be explained as revenue received in exchange for sale of any input, since by definition *all* inputs were already taken account of in the sets of prices from which the pure profit was calculated. Presumably this profit-difference has been present because its existence had not hitherto been anticipated by anyone; its having now been grasped constitutes, one would surely conclude, an entrepreneurial discovery. The reason why discovery elements in wages of labor, or in the prices paid for other resource services, are easy to overlook, is that it seems so natural to relate every penny of income so received to the resource services supplied. The income received is seen simply as the sales proceeds of the resource services supplied. The source of the incomes is seen, very naturally, in the productive contribution which these services have rendered. Nothing needs, at least on the surface, to be described as having been discovered; every penny of income received has been generated directly by the input service for which it has been paid. So long as results can be attributed to inputs, the idea of discovery can be dispensed with. But pure profit, by its very definition, is not to be attributed to inputs. Its source is not to be identified with anything possessed by the entrepreneur; it is, as it were, uncaused. It has simply been discovered. So, at any rate, one might reasonably argue, and might consequently reasonably expect profit theorists to identify the discovery concept in the course of their theoretical discussions.

Moreover, precisely because pure profits cannot be explained ("justified") as reward for services rendered, one would expect ethical questions to be raised concerning the legitimacy of pure profit incomes. Surely, one might expect, theorists of justice in focusing on the justice or injustice of pure profits, would come to consider possible justification on the grounds of discovery.

The kind of ethical questioning concerning the justice of pure profit I have in mind is exemplified nicely in a brief passage in which Professor Samuelson once questioned the justification for the winning of pure speculative profit. Samuelson was considering the case where a crop failure generates profits for successful speculators.[3] Samuelson recognizes that the speculators have provided a useful social function. They have curtailed relatively less urgently needed consumption at earlier dates, in order to permit some more urgently needed consumption at later dates. He therefore considers the possibility of justifying the large profits won by the successful speculator, by referring to the social benefit his activity has produced. But Samuelson finds himself compelled to reject this possible justification. After all, a successful speculator need be only a trifle quicker than his rivals in order to make his fortune. And we may assume that if this successful speculator *had* in fact been just a little slower, other speculators would, perhaps minutes or seconds later, have grasped at precisely those speculative opportunities which were in fact grasped earlier by their successful rival. Even on an ethic that justifies incomes received in return for productive service rendered, it seems difficult to justify the capture of *all* the profits by the speculator who saved society from no more than a few seconds of unwise consumption. Here we have the ethical problem posed by the phenomenon of pure profit. It corresponds to nothing additional produced. The difference between the low price at which the speculator bought up grain, and its subsequent price, has been caused by no production activity, by no services rendered by resources. A view on the ethical justification for incomes that insists on finding a productive counterpart to that income, must find pure speculative profit

3. P. A. Samuelson, "Intertemporal price equilibrium: a prologue to the theory of speculation," *Weltwirtschaftliches Archiv,* 79 (December 1957), p. 209.

to be without justification—as Samuelson did. My own position on the matter will of course be that pure speculative profit is an example of a discovered gain, a kind of gain to which "productivity" justifications are essentially irrelevant. My focus on pure profit in this chapter is motivated by the possibility of finding some recognition of the discovery character of pure profits, and some related recognition, possibly, of the special ethical significance of the discovery concept. I shall examine the four principal approaches to entrepreneurial profit theory traditionally identified in the literature. These approaches are those associated respectively with the names of J. B. Clark, F. B. Hawley, F. H. Knight, and J. A. Schumpeter.[4]

J. B. CLARK, PROFIT AND JUSTICE

It seems particularly useful to focus on Clark's treatment of pure profit because he is widely known for his explicit consideration of distributive justice under capitalism. Although Clark does not appear to have dealt directly with the justice of pure profit, his views on the matter seem to flow rather naturally from his general theory of justice and from his observations concerning the nature of pure profit.

For Clark pure profit is an analytical category that emerges from consideration of the difference between the full reality of the dynamic market, and the static state of imagined market equilibrium. In the imagined static state men "might conceivably produce to the end of time the same kind of goods. . . . Their tools and materials might never change; and they might not alter, either for the better or for the worse, the amount of wealth that industry would yield."[5] The so-called "normal rates" of wages, interest, and profits are those "which would be realized if a society were perfectly organized but were free from the disturbances that progress causes. . . ."[6] Although these rates are those relevant to an imagined state, they are nonetheless "the standards about which the rates of pay for labor and capital are always hovering in actual mills, fields, mines, etc."[7] This is because although the static state is imaginary, "static laws

4. The order of the discussion will not be strictly chronological.

5. J. B. Clark, *The Distribution of Wealth* (New York and London: Macmillan, 1899), p. 28.

6. Ibid., p. 29.

7. Ibid.

are nevertheless real laws. The forces that would work in a world that should be held in fixed shape and made to act forever in a fixed manner still operate in the changing world of reality. We can always see them working in connection with other forces, but we have to imagine them working alone. We study them separately, in order that we may understand one part of what goes on in dynamic society."[8]

In the imagined static state each unit of productive resource is paid a price for its contribution to production—identified as the value added to total output by virtue of the presence of that unit of resource. "In other words, free competition tends to give to labor what labor creates, to capitalists what capital creates, and to *entrepreneurs* what the coordinating function creates."[9] This is the celebrated marginal productivity theory of distribution, which Clark developed in painstaking detail in a book over four hundred pages in length.[10] It is abundantly clear that Clark saw in this theory the fullest vindication of the economic justice of capitalism, and it seems clear that it was this that provided the motivation for his book. In stating his thesis at the outset of the work Clark wrote that "more hinges on the truth of it than any introductory words can state. The right of society to exist in its present form, and the probability that it will continue to so exist, are at stake."[11]

But in this static state of perfect Clarkian justice there is no room for pure profit. "Profit has no place in such static conditions. The two incomes that are permanent and independent of dynamic changes are the products, respectively, of labor and of capital. Each of them is directly determined by the final productivity law."[12] It is only under dynamic conditions that profit can emerge. Although Clark is, within the static scope of his study, not directly concerned with the phenomenon of pure profit, he nonetheless makes it clear as to how he views it as occurring under dynamic conditions.

For Clark pure profit emerges as the joint result of two circumstances, "dynamic change" and "economic friction." As an example of dynamic

8. Ibid., p. 30.
9. Ibid., p. 3.
10. Ibid.
11. Ibid.
12. Ibid., p. 201.

change Clark cites "an improvement in the methods of production" such as an invention. The final result of such an improvement will be higher wages. "Wages now tend to equal what labor can now produce, and this is more than it could formerly produce."[13] But, until this tendency has been completed, wages are lower than their new higher, static level, and the entrepreneur grasps temporary profit. "The interval between actual wages and the static standard is the result of friction; for, if competition works without let or hindrance, pure business profit would be annihilated as fast as it could be created—entrepreneurs, as such, could never get and keep any income. . . . Dynamic theory has to account for the whole of that friction on which *entrepreneurs'* shares depend; while static law determines what wages will be, when the friction shall have been completely overcome, and what they would be at this instant, if friction were immediately to vanish."[14]

Clark also adds several sentences in which he sees social utility in the friction that permits pure profit to exist. Were it not for this friction entrepreneurs "would have no incentive in self-interest to make any improvements, and it is clear that additions which are difficult and costly would be in danger of not being made. Profit is the lure that insures improvement. . . . To secure progress, this lure must be sufficient to make men overcome obstructions and take risks."[15]

Clark's view of pure profit thus appears fairly clear. It occurs as a result of dynamic changes, at least part of which are in fact inspired by the entrepreneur's response to the lure which profit offers. That the profit generated by change is not instantaneously ground down to zero by competition, is the result of "frictions." Profit, although it may serve as a lure to overcome obstructions and take risks, is not seen (as wages and other resource incomes were seen) as a settled return to a resource owner in return for that resource's productive contribution. The invention that raises the productivity of labor is not seen as something produced by the entrepreneur. Clark has no qualms concerning the justice of the circumstance that, after frictions have been overcome, it is wages that will be

13. Ibid., p. 405.

14. Ibid., pp. 410–11.

15. Ibid., p. 411. See F. H. Knight, *Risk, Uncertainty and Profit* (Boston and New York: Houghton Mifflin, 1921), p. 35 and fn., for a critique of Clark's theory of profit.

permanently higher, with nothing permanently left for the entrepreneur who introduced the invention. The difficulty and costliness of introducing improvements, to which Clark has referred, is somehow not seen by him as justifying any but the fleeting opportunity of grasping profit. On the other hand, Clark nowhere suggests that the profits temporarily won by the innovative entrepreneur have somehow been exploited away from the permanent factors, labor and capital. Apparently Clark views the enormous social benefits generated by entrepreneurial innovation as sufficient justification for the capture of pure profit by entrepreneurs, since without it we can hardly expect entrepreneurs to overcome obstructions and take risks. (I presume this is what N. Scott Arnold meant when he recently[16] referred to Clark—without citing his specific source location— as believing that "entrepreneurs deserve their profits as a reward for bearing uncertainty"—although one might wish to quibble about the wording of Arnold's interpretation.)

Nowhere in Clark's discussions do we find any explanation how, by overcoming obstructions and taking risks, it is possible to innovate new inventions and improvements in productive techniques. Nor does Clark elaborate on the nature of the frictions that prevent the immediate disappearance of the profits so generated. If we pursue Clark's theory of justice in the functional distribution of incomes, we are confronted with a puzzle. For Clark, an income is justified when it is received in return for productive service rendered, at the full market value of such service. On the one hand, Clark does not appear to recognize any productive service rendered by the entrepreneur, even under dynamic conditions. Yet Clark appears content not to challenge the justice of the grasping of entrepreneurial profit—in light of the social usefulness of permitting entrepreneurs to respond to the lure of profit. We are not called upon to seek any new interpretation of Clark that might resolve these paradoxes. For our purposes the important point to be emphasized is that nowhere does Clark identify the entrepreneur's innovation as a discovery. Nowhere does he refer to a possible justification for pure profit as arising out of the entrepreneur's discovery—either of the possibility for improvement or of the temporary gap between prices and costs which that improvement has brought about.

16. N. Scott Arnold, "Why profits are deserved," *Ethics* (January 1987), p. 395.

To be sure, Clark's self-imposed discipline limiting his work to its exclusive static focus, made it unnecessary for him to explore the nature and the ethical status of pure profit, since profit is a strictly dynamic phenomenon. So that it may be objected, as against my negative conclusions in the preceding paragraph, that Clark's silence should perhaps not be interpreted as making any definitive statement at all. Nonetheless, it seems fair to conclude that Clark's silence is indeed eloquent. Clark's exclusive concern with the static state, we have seen, was based on his conviction that it is the forces that govern that imaginary state which are in fact dominant and the most significant in the real world of dynamic change. "In the midst of all changes there are at work forces that fix rates to which, at any one moment, wages and interest tend to conform. However stormy may be the ocean, there is an ideal level surface projecting itself through the waves, and the actual surface of the turbulent waters fluctuates about it. There are, likewise, static standards with which, in the most turbulent markets, actual values, wages and interest tend to coincide."[17] It was for this reason that Clark felt that his static study provided an adequate framework for defending the economic justice of income distribution in the real, dynamic capitalist economy. Given this weight that Clark placed on the justice of static, permanent income shares accruing to labor and capital, it does not seem illegitimate to read significance into his failure to identify the discovery element in pure profits.

FREDERICK HAWLEY AND HIS RISK THEORY OF PROFIT

Frederick B. Hawley is usually cited—when he *is* cited—as a half-forgotten profit theorist of the turn of the century. Yet at the time he wrote his work his profit theory was taken very seriously indeed. In his survey of the literature that preceded his own *Risk, Uncertainty and Profit*, Knight saw Hawley's theory as one of the principal earlier contributions with which he himself took issue (and also as one of those principal earlier contributions from which the elements of what Knight considered the correct theory, could be taken). Hawley appears not to have had normative, ethical considerations uppermost in his mind. He was concerned that economists should correctly characterize the phenomenon of normal profit, and he felt that existing economic theory, especially that of

17. Clark, op. cit., p. vi.

J. B. Clark, failed to do this. Yet, although ethical considerations were not foremost in Hawley's mind, his conceptualization of the entrepreneurial function and of the profit income share held clear implications for a theory of economic justice. Whatever flaws existed in Hawley's positive theory had correspondingly erroneous implications in regard to concepts of economic justice. Although it is not my primary concern to explore the flaws which economists have seen in Hawley's theory of profit, my concern with the justice of pure profit does require that we briefly consider Hawley's work. Hawley's theory of profit is all the more important in that it not only appears to have influenced many American textbook writers of the early decades of this century, but also inspired a post–World War II attempt at reviving the basic thrust of that textbook tradition.[18]

Hawley's central thesis was that the "distinguishing function of the *entrepreneur*" is the "assumption of risk" and that economic profit is "the economic reward for services rendered by the assumption of industrial risk."[19] Without someone assuming this industrial risk, production will simply not occur, in our uncertain world. It is the entrepreneur who initiates the productive process by assuming this necessary risk. Economic profit, the *reward* for risk-assumption, is at the same time the *inducement* to the entrepreneur persuading him in fact to assume the risks involved in producing.[20] This reward and inducement is not at all identical with the amount paid by an unwilling risk-bearer to insure himself (and thus shift the risk to the insurer). This latter insurance payment ("a sum sufficient to cover the actuarial or average losses incidental to the various risks of all kinds necessarily assumed by the entrepreneur and his insurers"[21]) is included among the costs to the entrepreneur. Hawley's contention is that production will not occur unless the entrepreneur is persuaded to assume risk by the prospect of a surplus over and above all costs, *including* the cost of insurance. The need for an inducement being offered to the prospective entrepreneur in order to persuade him

18. On this, see M. Bronfenbrenner, "A reformulation of naive profit theory," *Southern Economic Journal* (April 1960), pp. 300–309.

19. F. B. Hawley, "Enterprise and profit," *Quarterly Journal of Economics*, 15 (November 1900), p. 75.

20. F. B. Hawley, "Reply to final objections to the risk theory of profit," *Quarterly Journal of Economics*, 15 (August 1901), p. 613.

21. Ibid., p. 610.

to assume risk arises from "the irksomeness of the uncertainty,"[22] that is, the circumstance that a businessman, even where he has confidence in the validity of his actuarial judgment over the long run (during which time losses and gains tend to balance each other[23]), will not assume the risk attached to a *particular* project, unless he is compensated for that irksomeness (". . . industrial risks will not be assumed without the expectation of a compensation in excess of the actuarial value of the risk."[24]).

It was Frank Knight who put his finger on the damning weakness in Hawley's theory. It is in this weakness, in fact, that we can most clearly see how Hawley's approach made it difficult for him to recognize the central role of discovery in understanding pure profit. (As I shall argue below, it is noteworthy that Knight, who clearly identified the flaw in Hawley's theory, was nonetheless led to yet another theory of profit in which discovery plays no role.) The problem with Hawley's approach, Knight points out, consists in a confusion (shared both by Hawley and his earlier critics, most important among whom was J. B. Clark) "in assuming that the 'actuarial value' of the risks taken is known to the entrepreneur."[25] Hawley and his critics had all ignored "the fundamental distinction between the reward for taking a known risk and that for assuming a risk whose value itself is not known."[26] Knight was to reserve the term "uncertainty" for that which is inherently indeterminate and immeasurable due to the utter unpredictability of future change. The flaw in Hawley lies in his idea of "irksomeness" in bearing risk the value of which is known: "a little consideration will show that there can be no considerable 'irksomeness' attached to exposure to an insurable risk, for if there is it will be insured; hence there can be no peculiar income arising out of this alleged indisposition."[27]

For our present purposes it is sufficient for us to note that, if the actuarial value of all risk is known, there is little of economic relevance remaining for the entrepreneur to discover. For Hawley, it is true, the profits

22. Ibid., p. 604.

23. Ibid.

24. F. B. Hawley, "The risk theory of profit," *Quarterly Journal of Economics*, 7 (July 1893), p. 460.

25. F. H. Knight, op. cit., p. 43.

26. Ibid., pp. 43–44.

27. Ibid., p. 46.

won by the entrepreneur in a specific industrial venture are an "unpre-determined residue," but over a sufficient number of ventures there is, as Knight pointed out, nothing that Hawley recognizes as undetermined. Nor does Hawley link the profit made on a specific venture with any superior entrepreneurial forecasting that might have been exercised. The unpredetermined residue that is won as profit on the specific venture is, somehow, simply there; it has to be there, on average, or else entrepreneurs would not assume the necessary risk. There is no hint, in any of Hawley's lengthy expositions of his theory of profit, of the entrepreneur grasping profit by virtue of any uniqueness of vision. Profit is justified, it is being suggested in Hawley's theory, not because the entrepreneur has independently found that profit, but because it is needed in order to provide the incentive necessary to overcome the irksomeness of risk-bearing. Despite Hawley's emphasis on uncertainty, suggesting a central place for the entrepreneurial dissipation of ignorance, his theory of profit decisively places it outside the scope of any discovery criterion for economic justice.

FRANK KNIGHT AND THE
UNCERTAINTY THEORY OF PROFIT

Building on ideas introduced by Clark and by Hawley, Frank H. Knight constructed his own uncertainty theory of profit. Clark had seen the source of profit in dynamic change. Hawley identified profit with the residual bearing of risk. In rejecting both these theories, Knight emphasized that, nonetheless, "there is a principle of truth in both the 'dynamic' and the 'risk' theories, and the true theory must to a considerable degree reconcile the two views. On the one hand, profit is in fact bound up in economic change (but because change is the condition of uncertainty), and on the other, it is clearly the result of risk, or what good usage calls such, but only of a unique kind of risk, which is not susceptible of measurement."[28] Knightian profits are the uncertainty-bred differences between the anticipated value of resource services and their actual value. Profit increments are the "differences between incomes in disequilibrium and at equilibrium, or between incomes *ex post* and *ex ante*, rather than . . . compensations for uncertainty-bearing."[29]

28. Ibid., p. 48.

29. Bronfenbrenner, op. cit., reprinted in W. Breit and H. M. Hochman (eds.), *Readings in Microeconomics*, 2nd ed. (New York: Holt, Rinehart and Winston, 1971), p. 413.

It is my complaint that Knight's theory of profits sees them as somehow falling into the entrepreneur's lap merely because he has luckily been inspired to put himself into a position to grasp these windfall gains—not because he has been alert enough to see where and how these gains can be grasped. From Knight's perspective a successful entrepreneur is successful not because he has presciently noticed where he can take advantage of changes that may be in the making, but because he is the fortunate beneficiary of changes which no one could have foreseen.[30] This is not to assert that Knight is not fully aware of the incentive to entrepreneurial activity that the *prospect* of profit provides;[31] it is merely to point out that for Knight the realization of a prospect for profit has not very much to do with the entrepreneur's superior ability at noticing such prospects. "Both profit and loss arise in many cases from circumstances entirely apart from human foresight."[32] It is not at all accidental that Knight was "strongly of the opinion"[33] that aggregate entrepreneurial losses exceed aggregate profits. There is little recognition in Knight of the possibility for the entrepreneur to *initiate* profitable change (as Schumpeter had emphasized); still less of the possibility that he can successfully notice opportunities that others have missed. It is true that Knight speaks of the difficulties arising out of the interplay of "judgment and luck" in entrepreneurial activity.[34] But it appears, upon a careful reading, that the entrepreneurial judgment of which Knight speaks has primarily to do with the task of successfully carrying out the routine managerial tasks in the face of an uncertain world—rather than with judgment of how and where to grasp pure profit opportunities.

Knight does not appear to have spent much time, either in *Risk, Uncertainty and Profit,* or in later writings, analyzing the justice of pure profits. In his well-known 1922 ethical critique of the laissez-faire economy, Knight found much with which to be unhappy in the ethics of its

30. Such a Knightian view seems also to underlie the defense of entrepreneurial profit in H. B. Acton, *The Morals of Markets* (London: Longman, 1971), pp. 29–32.

31. See Knight, op. cit., p. 363.

32. F. H. Knight, "Profit," in *Encyclopedia of the Social Sciences,* vol. XII, reprinted in W. Fellner and B. F. Haley (eds.), *Readings in the Theory of Income Distribution* (Philadelphia and Toronto: Blakiston, 1949), p. 546.

33. Knight, *Risk, Uncertainty and Profit,* p. 365.

34. See, e.g., ibid., pp. 278ff.

distribution,[35] but did not directly address the question of the justice of pure entrepreneurial profit. No doubt this had much to do with his conviction that profits are in general outweighed by losses. "Both in abstract ethics and from the standpoint of social interest in adequate motivation, a proposal to reduce high profits raises the question of using the proceeds to reduce losses."[36] One presumes that Knight would see pure profit as fundamentally undeserved. This seems to be the case not only because he does not recognize any ethical validity to the results of discovery—he was in fact explicit in recognizing only effort as having ethical validity[37]— but also because for Knight realized pure profit is not, indeed, to be seen as the successful outcome of any act of discovery at all.

THE PROFITS OF THE SCHUMPETERIAN ENTREPRENEUR

Schumpeter's view of the entrepreneurial role is well known. His understanding of profit is derived directly from his theory of entrepreneurship. Schumpeter defined the entrepreneurial function as consisting in the "carrying out of new combinations," in innovating new methods of production and new products.[38] The emphasis is not upon *inventing* the new, it is upon *introducing the new into practice,*[39] "in getting things done."[40] Where the Knightian entrepreneur endeavors to perform his managerial functions in a world of uncertainty generated by unforeseen change, Schumpeter's entrepreneur is the business leader whose initiative and vision introduced the innovations responsible, in their totality, for the continuous change that characterized Schumpeterian capitalism. These entrepreneurial innovations make up "the perennial gale of creative destruction"[41] continually pushing aside existing products and techniques in favor of the new.

35. See F. H. Knight, *The Ethics of Competition* (New York: A. M. Kelley, [1935] 1951), pp. 54ff.

36. Knight, "Profit," op. cit., p. 546.

37. Knight, *Ethics of Competition,* p. 56.

38. See Joseph A. Schumpeter, *The Theory of Economic Development* (Cambridge: Harvard University Press, 1934), pp. 74ff.

39. Ibid., pp. 88f.

40. J. A. Schumpeter, *Capitalism, Socialism and Democracy,* 3rd ed. (New York: Harper and Row, 1950), p. 132.

41. Ibid., p. 87.

The profits won by Schumpeter's entrepreneurs are not windfall gains; they are deliberately created by the entrepreneur's "new combination." In carrying out his new combination the entrepreneur creates a divergence between his revenues and his costs, reaping the difference as profits—for as long as it takes the army of competing "imitators" to compete away that profit-difference to zero. The capitalist process consists in the continual series of innovations, accompanied by rounds of new profits won, with each of them being eroded by the competition of imitators. Samuelson translated the Schumpeterian vision into an apt metaphor. "The violin string is plucked by innovation, without innovation it dies down to stationariness, but then along comes a new innovation to pluck it back into dynamic motion again. So it is with the profit rate in economic life."[42] When competition has restored the violin string to stationariness, the economy is once again in the state of circular flow (the Schumpeterian counterpart to Walrasian general equilibrium). In the circular flow, costs and revenues are equal; the "value of the original means of production" has attached itself "with the faithfulness of a shadow to the value of the product."[43] There are no profits to be made by pursuing existing production activities. The entrepreneur's innovation pulls the economy away from this state, by producing a given product with a new, less costly bundle of inputs, or by using given inputs to produce a new, more lucrative, product. Schumpeter leaves no room for any suggestion that profits so won should be seen as the reward for risk-bearing. It is strictly the capitalist who bears the risk of any entrepreneurial venture.[44] Entrepreneurial profits are won in the course of innovating new productive combinations. Profits are won by jolting the economy out of the equilibrium state. Uncertainty has nothing to do with the matter.

No doubt Schumpeter would not deny that the entrepreneur's activity must expose him to uncertainty. No doubt he would concede that the successful entrepreneur is the one who in fact has the more accurate vision concerning the future. But there is also no doubt that Schumpeter did not see profit as being that which the entrepreneur has discovered. This emerges very clearly from his discussion of the qualities required

42. P. A. Samuelson, *Economics*, 8th ed. (New York: McGraw-Hill, 1970), p. 729.
43. Schumpeter, *Theory of Economic Development*, op. cit., p. 160.
44. Ibid., pp. 75, 137.

for leadership—in which he sees the essence of entrepreneurship.[45] Schumpeter emphasizes that the difficulty involved in leadership activity, and the circumstance that makes leadership a scarce commodity is not that of discovering opportunities, but that of actually grasping them once they have been perceived. It is, Schumpeter remarks, no part of the function of leadership "to 'find' or to 'create' new possibilities. They are always present, abundantly accumulated by all sorts of people. Often they are also generally known and being discussed by scientific and literary writers. In other cases there is nothing to discover about them, because they are quite obvious."[46] The difficulty of leadership in general, and of "economic leadership" (that is, entrepreneurship) in particular, is that of breaking away from established, familiar ways of activity. What is needed is not so much superior vision as superior *will*. "In the breast of one who wishes to do something new, the forces of habit rise up and bear witness against the embryonic project. A new and another kind of effort of will is therefore necessary in order to wrest, amidst the work and care of the daily round, scope and time for conceiving and working out the new combination. . . ."[47]

It is true that much of Schumpeter's notion of entrepreneurship-as-leadership could fairly easily be translated into the idea of entrepreneurship-as-vision-and-discovery. Presumably one's intensity of will in pursuing what appears to be a profitable opportunity, is an expression of the clarity with which one "sees" that opportunity. So that the central ingredient in Schumpeter's economic leadership need not be identified exclusively as the determination to pursue possibilities that are visible to all; it can, altogether equivalently, be identified as the superior vision to see as profitably attainable that which others see only as an abstract possibility. But the point is that Schumpeter, as we have seen, was explicit in insisting that innovation, not discovery, is the essential contribution and identifying feature of the entrepreneur.

This means that any consideration of economic justice that remains faithful to the Schumpeterian vision of the entrepreneurial process, cannot treat profit as a *discovered* gain. For this view, the profit won by the entrepreneur

45. Ibid., pp. 84ff.
46. Ibid., p. 88.
47. Ibid., p. 86.

was, in principle, fully visible to all. What inspired the entrepreneur's successful activity was not that he saw what others failed to see, but that he possessed the will, determination, and leadership qualities needed to grasp that which was seen, but not grasped, by all. One may or one may not, in the Schumpeterian scheme of things, impute the profits gained to these leadership qualities.[48] But Schumpeter was, in principle, prepared to see profit as generated by these entrepreneurial qualities in a way similar to that through which, in neoclassical terms, the product of labor is imputed to labor. There is no discovery element in neoclassical wages; and there is no discovery element in Schumpeter's entrepreneurial profit.

SOME REMARKS ON MISESIAN PROFIT

The one economist whose theory of profit can be unequivocally described as a discovery theory, is Ludwig Mises. It is Mises' theory of the entrepreneurial market process which is at the heart of the discovery view of the market upon which this book is based. Mises presents his theory of profits very simply. "What makes profit emerge is the fact that the entrepreneur who judges the future prices of the products more correctly than other people do buys some or all of the factors of production at prices which, seen from the point of view of the future state of the market, are too low. Thus the total costs of production—including interest on the capital invested—lag behind the prices which the entrepreneur receives for the product. This difference is entrepreneurial profit."[49] The emphasis is on the superior judgment of the profit-making entrepreneur. This draws attention to the circumstances which are responsible for the errors which manifest themselves as opportunities for pure profit. "The ultimate source from which entrepreneurial profit and loss are derived is the uncertainty of the future constellation of demand and supply. If all entrepreneurs were to anticipate correctly the future state of the market, there would be neither profits nor losses. . . . An entrepreneur can make a profit only if he anticipates future conditions more correctly than other entrepreneurs."[50] Because human foresight is imperfect, opportunities

---

48. Ibid., p. 143.

49. L. Mises, *Planning for Freedom and Other Essays and Addresses*, 2nd ed. (South Holland: Libertarian Press, 1962), p. 190.

50. L. Mises, *Human Action* (New Haven: Yale University Press, 1949), p. 291.

for profit emerge; input prices can be lower than the prices which output will in fact be able to command. The superior entrepreneur, moving to take advantage of his own perception of these discrepancies, grasps these profit opportunities. He has discovered gaps generated by market errors.

But although, as I have shown, Mises' theory of profit can certainly be described as a discovery theory, the fact is that Mises did not emphasize this aspect of his theory. No doubt this has something to do with Mises' strictly utilitarian approach to issues of economic justice. In most of his work Mises never did confront the challenges of those who would question the *moral* justifiability of pure profit. It was enough to point to the wealth-and-welfare-enhancing consequences of the entrepreneur-driven market process. On the rare occasions when he did examine these ethical challenges to pure profit, Mises dismissed them. "There is no other standard of what is morally good and morally bad than the effects produced by conduct upon social cooperation."[51] Obviously, given such an ethical perspective, Mises did not feel called upon to argue the justice of entrepreneurially-won profits on the basis of any conceivable ethics of discovery.

Yet we must recognize that Mises' profound understanding of the market process points ineluctably to the identification of *all* market-earned incomes as discovered incomes. For Mises there is an inescapable strand of entrepreneurial function in each and every market action undertaken. And, as noted, entrepreneurial gain is, in the Misesian view, *discovered* gain. My claim, in this book, is that the Misesian perspective, therefore, transforms (or at any rate should transform) discussions on the economic justice of capitalist distribution.

SOME OBSERVATIONS ON RAWLS

My purpose in this chapter is not to survey the literature of economic justice. Rather, I am searching for evidence of attention to discovery elements in the incomes generated by market processes. The preceding sections in this chapter have shown how (except for Mises) the literature of profit theory failed to recognize the discovery character of pure entrepreneurial profit. In the concluding portion we examine some of the more important recent contributions to the theory of economic justice. In these

---

51. L. Mises, *Planning for Freedom,* op. cit., p. 145; see also his *Human Action* (New Haven: Yale University Press, 1949), pp. 715ff.

contributions, too, we shall find clear evidence of failure, or unwillingness, to recognize the discovery character of market-generated incomes. My emphasis, as in the preceding sections, continues to be on the *economic* understanding embodied in the contributions discussed.

John Rawls's theory of justice is celebrated as a philosophical contribution of the first order. It is a magisterial body of work which has—regardless of the merits of its conclusions—succeeded in establishing its topic as one of prime interest among the philosophers, economists, and political scientists of our time. My own interest in this theory has to do, not with its moral foundations, nor with its substantive conclusions, but with the understanding of economic processes and relations which informs its discussions.

Rawls's understanding of markets is solidly in the neoclassical tradition of welfare economics. "Under certain conditions competitive prices select the goods to be produced and allocate resources to their production in such a manner that there is no way to improve upon either the choice of productive methods by firms, or the distribution of goods that arise from the purchases of households. . . . No further mutually advantageous trades are possible; nor are there any feasible productive processes that will yield more of some desired commodity without requiring a cutback in another."[52] As Rawls fully understands, this understanding of markets presumes already attained general equilibrium (the prerequisite for competitive prices throughout the economy, in this usage of the term). Moreover, and most importantly, Rawls prominently accepts the doctrine "that, theoretically at least, a socialist regime can avail itself of the advantages of [the market economy]."[53]

Rawls's acceptance of this doctrine can serve almost as a copybook example of the understanding of capitalist incomes from which this book wishes to depart. We may distinguish two erroneous—or, at least, highly dubious—related elements supporting Rawls's belief in the "consistency of market arrangements with socialist institutions."[54] First, this belief rests on the mistaken view that the market process under capitalism is

52. J. Rawls, *A Theory of Justice* (Cambridge: Harvard University Press, 1971), pp. 271f.

53. Ibid., p. 271.

54. Ibid., p. 273.

not driven, in any essential way, by private profit-motivated entrepreneurial activity. Second, this belief rests on the mistaken or highly dubious view that it is possible to draw a sharp distinction "between the allocative and the distributive function of prices." Let us examine these two underlying views in turn.

That Rawls assumes that private, profit-motivated entrepreneurial activity is not essential for the capitalist market process, is evident in his belief that under socialism, with private profit-making entrepreneurship ruled out, the market could, in principle, operate as under capitalism. In fact this assumption underlay the position (associated in particular with contributions dating to the thirties by economists Oskar Lange and Abba P. Lerner) that socialist planners can simply announce prices and permit managers of socialized enterprises to treat these prices as "parameters," leading to the same production decisions that such prices would inspire capitalist producer-entrepreneurs to make under capitalism. As both Mises and Hayek understood, this Lange-Lerner view simply assumes that active entrepreneurial competition (innovating new prices, new products, or new methods of production) plays no essential role in the capitalist market process. In fact it was around the truth or falsity of this view that the celebrated inter-war controversy concerning the possibility of socialist economic calculation revolved. As has been made clear in recent scholarship, the cardinal issue separating the Mises-Hayek denial of the possibility of socialist calculation, from the Lange-Lerner affirmation of this possibility, was the role played in capitalist markets by active entrepreneurial competition.[55] For Mises and Hayek the idea that capitalist markets could work without profit-seeking entrepreneurs was a sheer illusion. As discussed at a number of points in this book, I follow Mises and Hayek fully in this position. For me, therefore, Rawls's implicit acceptance of the Lange-Lerner view not only invalidates his belief that socialism can incorporate the market process, it also illustrates my contention that he failed to recognize the discovery aspect of market-generated incomes. To imagine away the need for entrepreneurial discovery in market processes, is to imagine away the uncertainty and the errors which it is in fact the function of capitalist market processes to dispel. It is no accident that while Rawls

55. See D. Lavoie, *Rivalry and Central Planning* (Cambridge: Cambridge University Press, 1985).

discusses uncertainty in a number of places in his theory of justice (particularly as it relates to setting up a framework for justice in advance, from behind the Rawlsian "veil of ignorance"), nowhere does he display awareness of how deeply uncertainty and error pervade and characterize real world economic activity.

The second (related) highly dubious view (underlying Rawls's belief in the consistency of markets with socialism) is that which argues a sharp distinction between the allocative and the distributive functions of market prices. This view reminds us of, but should not be confused with, the older view that alternative distributive patterns may be discussed as if the size of the total pie to be distributed is not affected by the choice among such distributive patterns. Thus, to cite perhaps the most famous instance of this older view, J. S. Mill distinguished sharply between the laws of the production of wealth and the question of the distribution of wealth. "The laws and conditions of the production of wealth partake of the character of physical truths . . . [T]here are ultimate laws, which we did not make, which we cannot alter, and to which we can only conform.[56] It is not so with the distribution of wealth. That is a matter of human institution solely. The things once there, mankind, individually or collectively, can do with them as they like. They can place them at the disposal of whomsoever they please, and on whatever terms."[57] Clearly for Mill, the discussion of distribution could be conducted by treating the pie to be distributed as already "there"—in Nozick's terminology, as "manna-from-heaven." Rawls is certainly not guilty of this view. He understands fully how the size of total output may be highly sensitive to the distributive pattern adopted. But he believes, nonetheless, that one can isolate the efficiency function of market prices from their distributive function.

Socialist "market" prices "are indicators for drawing up an efficient schedule of economic activities. Except in the case of work of all kinds,

56. This last sentence is from the first (1848) edition of Mill's book; see reference in next footnote, p. 200, fn. 1.

57. John Stuart Mill, *Principles of Political Economy with Some of Their Applications to Social Philosophy* [1848], Ashley ed. (London: Longmans, Green, 1909), pp. 200f. Hayek considers this the "silliest sentence ever penned by a famous economist" (F. A. Hayek, "The origins and effects of our morals: a problem for science," in C. Nishiyama and K. Leube (eds.), *The Essence of Hayek* [Stanford: Hoover Institution Press, 1984], p. 323).

prices under socialism do not correspond to income paid over to private individuals. Instead, the income imputed to natural and collective assets accrues to the state, and therefore their prices have no distributive function."[58] Rawls cites the eminent British socialist economist James Meade as the source for his view that for "the consistency of market arrangements with socialist institutions, it is essential to distinguish between the allocative and the distributive functions of price." For me this Meade-Rawls doctrine exemplifies perfectly the blind spot which I argue has characterized the standard view of capitalist income-distribution process.

Meade devoted a (very short) book to an examination of alternative institutional arrangements with which to cope with "the problem of the possible clashes between the 'efficiency' and the 'distributional' aspects of prices and, in particular, of the real wage rate."[59] Meade considers a variety of schemes, such as "the trade union state," "the welfare state," and alternative systems restricting ownership rights in private property. He examines the effects upon efficiency that would be caused by these various efforts at achieving greater distributive equality. He is, emphatically, aware that modifying the distributive implications of capitalist market prices may certainly alter the incentive structure in possibly inefficient ways. But this awareness is, in effect, *confined strictly to incentive effects upon market choices assumed to be made with full awareness of all other choices being made elsewhere in the market*—in other words Meade assumes entrepreneurial alertness so complete and instantaneous as to render any entrepreneurial market process unnecessary and irrelevant. This assertion calls for some elaboration.

A market participant, offered a choice between known alternatives (say, a day's leisure or 10 dollars) will choose the alternative he prefers (say, a day's leisure). An alteration of the relative attractiveness of the offered alternatives (say, an increase in pay offered, to 20 dollars for the day) may induce an alteration in the choice made (he may now prefer to work). Here we understand the change in relative attractiveness as having provided a changed incentive structure. This kind of incentive refers to the incentive to grasp an *already-perceived* alternative (the opportunity to work for pay). But

58. Rawls, op. cit., p. 273.

59. J. E. Meade, *Efficiency, Equality and the Ownership of Property* (Cambridge: Harvard University Press, 1965), p. 23. See also Okun, op. cit., above fn. 2.

consider now a market in which market participants are not fully aware of all alternatives actually available. A laborer working for 10 dollars a day may not yet be aware that a nearby employer has recently expanded his operations and, urgently needing more labor, would gladly pay him as much as 20 dollars. Here the gap between the present wage of 10 and the possible wage of 20 offers an incentive for alert entrepreneurship. This gap is not needed to overcome the attraction of leisure since we have posited that the laborer was willing to forgo leisure for as little as 10 dollars. But it does serve to spark the attention of an entrepreneur (possibly the worker himself) who can win a profit (a "finder's fee") by redirecting the worker's energies towards the higher-paying job. This incentive of pure profit plays a key role—in fact the key role—in the ability of markets to work. This entrepreneurial profit incentive is so central to the operation of the capitalist market that it should be obvious that its effect upon distribution really cannot be divorced from its effect upon efficiency—meaning its effect upon the ability of the market to coordinate market decisions. Both Meade and Rawls ignore this inescapable linkage between the distributive and the efficiency effects of market prices.

My conclusion is that the Rawlsian discussion of justice—whatever its substantive strengths and weaknesses—is unable to take into account any possible ethical implications of the discovery character of capitalist incomes.

NOZICK AND CAPITALIST DISCOVERY

I postpone for later in this book a discussion of the implications of an ethics of discovery for Robert Nozick's entitlement theory of justice.[60] The present brief section merely points out that the economic insights underlying Nozick's own theory of justice and his critique of alternative theories, while not at all inconsistent with a discovery approach to capitalist incomes, did not in fact lead Nozick to take note of the possibility of such an approach.

Nozick's brief references to the theory of profit explicitly reveal his familiarity with the view of pure profit as generated by differential awareness among entrepreneurs of available opportunities.[61] This

---

60. Nozick, *Anarchy, State and Utopia*, op. cit., chs. 7, 8.
61. Ibid., p. 262, and p. 349, fn. 18.

familiarity could certainly have permitted Nozick to recognize that capitalist incomes represent entrepreneurial discoveries. Nozick does not, however, do so. It can plausibly be maintained that this has much to do with the circumstance that Nozick's own entitlement theory permitted him, from his own perspective, to perceive the possible justice of capital incomes without reference to any conceivable discovery character which they may display. (And of course Nozick may in fact be convinced that any such discovery character is of no relevance for a theory of justice.) At any rate, it might be argued that Nozick's understanding of economic processes should, in spite of his silence on the matter, be seen as at least entirely consistent with the discovery perspective emphasized in this book. Nozick is not, it can be held, unaware of the discovery aspect of capitalist incomes; he is merely not prepared to assign ethical significance to it.

I need not deny the tenability of this reading of Nozick's economic views. Yet I may also confess to a sense of such a reading being not quite plausible. Nozick's book devotes many, many pages to discussions of the foundations for private property rights. He discusses the notion of just acquisition from nature, and of just acquisition from an earlier just owner. Nowhere, despite ample opportunities for doing so, does Nozick even suggest that discovery might conceivably offer a basis for ethical discussion. It is difficult to avoid the conclusion that Nozick has simply not perceived the discovered quality of capitalist incomes. Recognizing that pure profit may arise out of superior perception as to where unexploited opportunities for gain are to be grasped, does not of itself ensure an understanding of the discovery aspect associated with all incomes under capitalism. (Nor does it even ensure an understanding of the economic and the moral aspects of discovery that set it distinctly apart from non-discovery.)

ECONOMICS AND ECONOMIC JUSTICE

This chapter has examined the economics upon which existing discussions of economic justice have been based. We have searched for hints of recognition for the discovery character of capitalist incomes. Our search was directed, in particular, to the way in which pure entrepreneurial profit had been understood. Except for Mises, we found, none of the writers, neither the economists nor the philosophical theorists on justice, displayed the recognition we were looking for.

It is this negative finding which underlies my contention that the literature on economic justice is deeply flawed. If, as I shall argue in the following chapter, the capitalist economic process is indeed one made up of continual discoveries, and if, as I have argued in the preceding chapter, discovery does radically alter the character of economic activities and outcomes, then it is only reasonable to expect the assessment of capitalist distributive justice to take note of these circumstances. The next chapter develops in some detail the economic understanding of the capitalist economy for which we are demanding attention. Subsequent chapters will then draw out some of the more significant implications for economic justice.

4. THE MARKET AS A DISCOVERY PROCESS

Central to the thesis of this book is the claim that the market is a process of discovery. Only if this discovery character of the market is recognized, I argue, can one properly begin to assess the justice of market-generated incomes. This chapter sets out to establish this discovery character of the market process. Unlike subsequent chapters, therefore, the present one does not itself explore any normative implications of discovery. Its purpose is simply to persuade the reader of the validity of my assertion that each price paid in the market, each income received, constitutes a part of a complex system of discovery procedures. Each market transaction is the outcome of simultaneous discoveries by the parties involved. But, in addition, the total pattern of income distribution, and the total output of the market society, must both be recognized as being *discovered* outcomes. I begin with a small example of what is meant when I assert that a market transaction represents a set of simultaneous discoveries by the parties involved. Careful consideration of this most trivial example will be helpful when I attempt, a little later on, to argue the more general claim of this chapter in regard to *all* transactions, taken separately and taken as a whole.

THE SIMPLE TWO-PERSON EXCHANGE CASE

Jones has 20 apples; Smith has 10 grapefruit. Jones would prefer, let us imagine, to have 10 grapefruit rather than his 20 apples (in fact he prefers even 7 of the grapefruit to his 20 apples). Smith would prefer, on the other hand, to have 20 apples rather than his grapefruit (in fact he would prefer even 15 apples to his 10 grapefruit). Clearly, the conditions for mutually gainful exchange (between Jones and Smith) do exist. Smith, let us further imagine, indeed offers Jones his grapefruit in exchange for Jones's 20 apples. Jones accepts the offer, gives up the 20 apples, and acquires the 10 grapefruit instead. Both Smith and Jones have gained, in their respective prospective estimations, from this transaction.

Superficially, it might seem that no element of discovery is to be discerned in this little story. Jones gained from the transaction because Smith offered him a deal that was obviously attractive. Even Smith, whom we imagine to have initiated the deal, does not seem to have discovered anything. All that he did was to act to take advantage of the given situation that we hypothesized. Given the preference rankings postulated, Smith simply acted to grasp the gain clearly obtainable by engaging in trade with Jones. Given the assumed initial endowments, the source of the respective gains which Smith and Jones enjoy clearly lies in the hypothesized inverted preference rankings. Given these inverted preference rankings, it was clear, both the apples and the grapefruit were initially in the "wrong hands"—i.e., each of these was in the possession of the person who ranked them lower than he ranked the other. It was these initial circumstances, the structure of preferences and the pattern of ownership, that rendered exchange profitable to both parties. If one were to ask what *justifies* Jones's enjoyment of his gain from exchange, one would presumably answer that he was the fortunate owner of an item in high demand. The eager buyer of his apples gladly *offered* the grapefruit. There would seem no need (and no possibility) to argue that Jones is entitled to his gain because he discovered that gain.

Yet a moment's thought should assure us that discovery is indeed at the heart of this story. Let us consider: although we did hypothesize the conditions for mutually beneficial exchange, we certainly did not hypothesize that both Jones and Smith—or anyone else for that matter, *knew* that these conditions were fulfilled. Suppose that, at first, no one knows these conditions are fulfilled. Jones may not know that Smith is holding any grapefruit; or he may not know how much Smith prefers apples to grapefruit. And so on. Then it is clear that no apple-grapefruit trade is likely to occur. Like ships in the night Jones and Smith might pass each other in the street, each totally unaware of the other's economic situation. The mere fact that the conditions for mutually gainful exchange are satisfied does not at all guarantee that the exchange will ever take place. So that if, as it turns out, exchange does eventually occur, it will hardly do to ascribe the gains derived from that trade simply to the initial presence of the conditions for exchange. In order for the gains from this trade to have been won, both Jones and Smith must, somehow, have discovered something that each had not known to have been waiting to be discovered. (Notice that I do *not* say that the eventual trade called for research to have been deliberately undertaken, as a result of which Jones and Smith learn that a trade would be mutually beneficial. My assumption that no one was aware that the conditions for gainful trade were fulfilled could well have meant, after all, that Jones and Smith had no inkling that there was anything to look for. Jones passes hundreds of persons in the street; he might well have thought it quite pointless to interrogate *any* of them as to whether they could offer something that might attract him to give up his 20 apples. If the discovery that led to the realization of the exchange did follow a deliberate search, this must then have been preceded by the discovery that such a search might indeed prove fruitful and worthwhile. The eventually consummated exchange transaction could not have occurred without prior discovery of information both Jones and Smith had not known that they lacked.)

Notice further that the initial discovery leading to the realization of the exchange transaction might well have been made by some third (entrepreneurial) party. Perhaps Brown, noticing Smith's and Jones's initial endowments, sensing their respective preference rankings, offered simultaneous deals to both of them that permitted all three to improve their situations. Perhaps Brown offers Smith 15 apples for his 10 grapefruit, and offers Jones 7 of the grapefruit for his 20 apples. But whether the initial entrepreneurial step is taken by Brown or by Smith or by Jones, *both* Smith and Jones must have "made discoveries" for the exchange to be consummated. In other words each of the participants in this exchange transaction must have come to realize that he had, up until now, been laboring under a damaging misconception. Each of them has failed to realize that an opportunity for gain has been within his grasp. The finally consummated transaction has come to pass only because both participants have, somehow, succeeded in penetrating the initial fog of their own ignorance that had prevented them from even asking one another whether some trade was at all feasible.

It is clear, in the light of these considerations, that when Jones (or Smith) subsequently looks back on the gain he has derived from the exchange transaction, he will have to recognize that the gain is to be attributed, in the final analysis, to his finally realizing his earlier error. Without that discovery, he would never have enjoyed the gain. (Even if it was Smith whose offer opened Jones's eyes to the situation, it was only the fact that Jones paid serious attention to Smith's offer that brought him to the realization of the true state of affairs. So that while Smith's discovery—or perhaps Brown's!—was pivotal in triggering Jones's discovery, Jones did nonetheless himself come to discover the truth, and only *this* discovery finally moved him to enter the deal.)

To be sure, the initial set of conditions (of pattern of ownership and of inverted preference rankings) *constituted* the opportunity for mutual gain which both Smith and Jones had initially overlooked. But a gainful opportunity that languishes unnoticed does not constitute gain, any more than undiscovered available lumber can build a ladder. When, in chapter 2, Jones noticed lumber at the bottom of his hole, he made a discovery. It was to that discovery that he can, after having built the ladder with the lumber, attribute his having the means necessary to have built the ladder. His possession of lumber resulted from his discovery of it. To be sure, the prior physical existence of the lumber waiting-to-be-discovered was, most importantly, the necessary precondition for the discovery. But the critical difference was made, chronologically speaking, by the discovery. Similarly, the gain from exchange which Jones won must, chronologically speaking at least, be credited to the discovery which made it all happen.

We very often take knowledge for granted. Where the objective conditions exist for a gainful opportunity, we very often unthinkingly assume that all relevant parties are aware of these conditions. So that we jump to the conclusion that the gain in fact enjoyed as a result of grasping that opportunity is indeed to be attributed simply to the fulfillment of those conditions. But we have seen how this may not at all be the case. Gainful opportunities are, very often indeed, simply not seen. Before these opportunities can generate gain, they must somehow be noticed. When they are finally noticed, surely, the gain so generated must be recognized as a *discovered* gain—with whatever ethical implications that description entails.

It is true that some discoveries may not appear very exciting. Perhaps Smith's discovery of Jones's ownership of apples was something that "must" have occurred sooner or later. And once Smith made his offer to Jones and showed him his seriousness by dangling his grapefruit before Jones's fascinated eyes, it seems almost unimaginable that Jones should fail to realize his earlier error. So that Jones's "discovery," and perhaps even Smith's, may not appear as much of a discovery at all. This must certainly be acknowledged—and this may certainly entail corresponding qualifications concerning the ethical implications of these discoveries. But my point has been made. The transition from a state of affairs where a mutually gainful exchange opportunity has not been grasped, to one in which the exchange has been consummated, must have come about as a result of discoveries.

What my very trivial example should have driven home to us is the insight that gains from transactions *may* not necessarily be explicable (either in the sense of positive explanation or of moral justifiability) strictly in terms of the objective economic realities on the basis of which the transactions are gainful. It may be necessary to recognize a possible stage in the sequence of events that led up to the grasping of gain, at which crucial discoveries were made. In analyzing the market process, then, we must ask ourselves whether it is possible that similarly crucial discoveries might, as an essential characteristic of that process, be made in the course of the unfolding of that process. My position will, indeed, be that the market process *is* a series of discoveries. The gains made in the course of the transactions that constitute the steps in that process will, therefore, be seen indeed to be discovered gains. It will be useful to illustrate this thesis by carefully considering the most simple market one can imagine, the single-commodity market under competitive conditions.

SUPPLY AND DEMAND

Consider a competitive market for fresh fish. Each day many competing vendors of fish offer fish to the market. Each day a large number of homemakers enter the market with a view to the possibility of buying fish for the family evening meal. When fish prices have been expected to be high, more fish is available; when fish prices have been expected to be low, a smaller supply of fish is forthcoming. On the demand side, on the other hand, low fish prices spur consumers to seek to buy more fish; at higher fish prices only smaller quantities are bought. This is the classic situation depicted in the standard supply-demand diagram (figure I). Because quantities supplied are

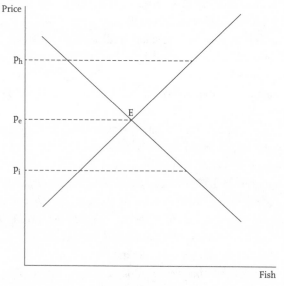

FIGURE 1

positively related to price, the supply curve slopes up; for symmetrically opposite reasons the demand curve slopes down. At the intersection of these two curves, point E marks the position of equilibrium. At the price p_e all those wishing to buy fish will be successful in buying the quantities they seek; all those offering fish for sale will be successful in finding buyers for all the fish they wish to sell.

Standard economic analysis proceeds to show that, given the conditions of supply and demand shown, the market will rapidly gravitate towards the equilibrium price and quantity combination. The story told in elementary economics classrooms and textbooks runs something like the following. Let us suppose that the price in the market is initially higher than p_e, say p_h. At this high price the quantity supplied exceeds the quantity demanded. Sellers, realizing they will be left with unsold fish, cut their prices in competition with other would-be sellers. Prices move downwards towards the equilibrium level. Suppose, on the other hand, that the market price for fish is below equilibrium. At this low price the quantity of fish demanded to be bought exceeds the quantity vendors are prepared to sell at the price. Buyers finding it impossible to obtain all the fish they seek, begin to compete with one another, offering higher and higher prices. Prices move up towards equilibrium. The upshot of the story is that, should the price be either higher or lower than the equilibrium level, competition will soon tend to force a price correction towards equilibrium.

For our purposes we can, for the most part, go along with this story supporting the idea of the equilibrating market. What I wish to do is to point out that this story illustrates how each market transaction expresses discoveries made by buyers and sellers. Unless we assume perfect initial market omniscience on the part of buyers and sellers—which would entail that equilibrium must be instantaneously attained—the process by which fish prices drift towards the equilibrium level is, we argue, a process of learning by discovery.

Let us reflect on what it would mean to suppose that fish prices are above equilibrium. To suppose this is to suppose that both buyers and sellers are making costly errors. Buyers who buy at the high price do so, presumably, because they mistakenly believe that there are enough buyers willing to buy at the high price to make it unnecessary for sellers to cut their price. Sellers who have been left with unsold fish because of the high price have presumably held out for the high price because they mistakenly believed that buyers would be available at that high price. Both buyers and sellers mistakenly overestimated the willingness of buyers to buy fish at the high price. As a result of this series of errors on the part of both buyers and sellers, it is not only the case that those who bought paid a price that is "too high" (in light of the true, less eager state of demand); more seriously, perhaps, it is also the case that many potential buyers fail to buy because of the mistaken high price upon which sellers are insisting. Had sellers been aware that their high price would leave them with unsold fish, they would have been happy to sell at a lower price, attracting additional buyers who are not sufficiently eager fish buyers to wish to buy at the high, above-equilibrium price. In other words, the above-equilibrium price means that fish remains unsold *in spite of the circumstance that with respect to this unsold fish the conditions for mutually beneficial trade between the sellers and the (additional) buyers may well exist.*

What has happened when sellers lower their prices as a result of finding themselves left with unsold fish, is that they have discovered their earlier error. The invisible hand of the market has not mysteriously pushed prices down; it has revealed to alert sellers that their earlier assessment of market conditions had been over-optimistic, leading them deliberately to offer more attractive terms.

Quite similar discoveries are involved where prices have been initially below equilibrium, generating unsatisfied demand. Here the buyers, finding it impossible to obtain fish at the price at which they had expected to buy, realize that they have been over-optimistic. They realize that in order to obtain fish it will be necessary to attract sellers and buyers who had, in the beginning, passed each other by. (The buyers had simply been uninterested in buying fish at higher prices since they believed enough would be forthcoming at the lower price; potential sellers had not bothered to announce their willingness to sell at the higher prices, because they too had believed that there were sufficient numbers of sellers satisfied to sell all that buyers might wish to buy at the lower price.)

So that the process whereby the law of supply and demand nudges market price in the direction of equilibrium, is indeed a process of spontaneous discovery. At each moment the price of fish expresses the lesson learned, thus far, by buyers and sellers. It is true, of course, that the discoveries made thus far may not be sufficient. Perhaps sellers have even now not lowered their prices sufficiently. The point, however, is that the buyers who *have* been enabled to buy as a result of the market-enforced price reduction, enjoy their purchase (as the sellers enjoy their revenues) only as a result of the discoveries triggered by the market's experience. If some fish still remains unsold, it may inspire still further discoveries.

What I have described as the discoveries generated by the forces of the market, do satisfy the definition I have given in chapter 2 of the idea of discovery (as distinct from the idea of deliberately acquired knowledge). The earlier ignorance which prevented sellers from lowering their prices in the first place was ignorance of which these sellers were unaware. They had charged the higher price simply because they believed—with enough confidence to permit them to act on their belief—that sufficient numbers of buyers would be forthcoming at the higher price to make it unnecessary to accept anything less. The lessons which the market has taught were not lessons deliberately learned; the market has taught lessons by abruptly disappointing the expectations of sellers (who had expected to sell at high prices) or buyers (who had expected to buy at low prices). Once noticed, these messages conveyed by the market can hardly be ignored.

In concluding this discussion of the forces of supply and demand in the single commodity market, it appears useful to supplement the textbook story concerning this market, to which we have been referring. The story we have been interpreting in terms of discovery is not quite satisfactory. It will be recalled that the story told how an initially high, above-equilibrium, market price is lowered as a result of the excess supply generated by the high price. That story made it seem as if, at any given moment during the market day, all fish is being sold at a single price throughout the market. According to that story, then, as if in concert, all sellers, realizing that they have unsold fish, lower their prices in unison. This story, even allowing for the deliberate simplifications sought for the sake of didactic effectiveness, is disturbing. To assume that everyone is, at each instant, asking and receiving the same price is to assume away the possibility of price competition—or, alternatively, to assume that competition achieves its results instantaneously. If we wish to understand the competitive process of supply and demand more adequately, we must amplify the textbook story to recognize that different sellers and different buyers may be charging different prices. In fact, by supplementing the textbook story in this fashion we will be able to notice yet another dimension along which discoveries are made in the course of the market process.

When we recognize that, at any initial point of time, buyers and sellers may be offering, asking, and accepting different prices (for the same quality of fish), we are recognizing a new array of possibilities for market ignorance. Not only may sellers and buyers overestimate the eagerness of buyers (leading them to agree to "erroneously" high prices); not only may sellers and buyers overestimate the eagerness of sellers (leading them to agree to "erroneously" low prices); buyers may, in addition, agree to pay prices that are higher than the prices at which fish is now available from other sellers; sellers may agree to accept prices for fish that are lower than the prices that other buyers are now paying for fish. A buyer who pays a higher price than was in fact necessary (since other sellers were selling for less) has clearly done so as a result of ignorance of which he was unaware. Had he been aware of the lower prices (or aware of availability of information concerning possible lower prices) elsewhere, he would clearly not have paid higher prices. And the same is clearly the case for sellers who accept lower prices than other buyers have actually paid. These kinds of unwitting ignorance on the part of buyers and sellers are present wherever fish is sold at different prices in the same market.

Now the market does not automatically signal this latter kind of unwitting ignorance by abruptly disappointing the expectations of buyers or sellers (as it did when too-high prices led sellers unexpectedly to find themselves left with unsold fish; or when too-low prices led to buyers unexpectedly finding themselves unable to obtain fish). There is nothing that *ensures* that buyers buying at high prices do not continue to do so indefinitely day after day, even though others continue to buy at lower prices. There is nothing to ensure that the first set of buyers shall become aware of the second set of sellers (or that this second set of sellers, continuing to sell for lower prices, shall become aware of buyers paying higher prices). But we may appreciate that, nonetheless, it is strongly to be anticipated that prices will tend to converge, that buyers and sellers will no longer err, that buyers will discover the cheapest sellers, sellers will discover the highest-paying buyers (in this way bringing about the tendency towards price convergence). The point is that wherever prices are different in different parts of the market, clear-cut opportunities for pure gain are being unwittingly overlooked. Buyers, who value fish highly (and in fact pay the higher prices), could have obtained same fish for less. Sellers, who would be happy to sell fish for low prices (and in fact do so), could be obtaining higher prices for the same fish; third parties, who neither possess fish nor wish to eat it, could be obtaining pure entrepreneurial profit by buying fish from the sellers who sell for low prices, and selling that fish to the buyers who are paying high prices for it. Such opportunities for pure gain are likely to attract attention. As attention is attracted, prices tend to converge, reflecting, once again, discoveries made in the market. These discoveries, too, are essential parts of the market process. Together with the discoveries noted earlier (in which the market abruptly disappoints over-optimistic expectations held by buyers or sellers) these discoveries do drive the market process, in the single commodity market, towards a single price for fish throughout the market, at a level at which no surpluses nor shortages are generated. During this process each step consists of revised opinions on the part of potential participants concerning the market situation which they face. These revisions consist, as we have seen, either in a rude awakening to the fact that one has been, up until now, over-optimistic, or in the realization that one has in fact, until now, overlooked an attractive opportunity that is available. It is these discoveries that are expressed in the continually changing arrays of bids and offers being made in markets.

Each quantity of fish sold, during the course of the market process, represents essentially discovered fish to buyers; each such sale presents the seller with discovered revenue. For a buyer who succeeds in buying fish, the fish has been discovered in the sense that somehow it was brought to his attention that it was available, at this particular attractive price. The initial possession of the money paid for fish was simply not enough to ensure acquisition of the quality of fish purchased. Only discovery made this purchase possible. For the seller who succeeds in selling fish, revenue has, similarly, been discovered in the sense that initial possession of that fish was in itself not sufficient to generate the revenue received. It was necessary, in addition, for the seller to discover the availability of the buyers prepared to pay this particular sum of money for this quantity of fish.

THE MARKET OF MANY MARKETS

We have taken note of the element of discovery that enters into the isolated exchange transaction. We have examined the role of discovery in the market process imagined as confined to the single market. It remains briefly to recognize the now-obvious and altogether pervasive character of discovery as it enters into the multi-market economy.

In the multi-market economy activity is not confined to the buying and selling of one commodity; it consists in buying and selling in the markets for many different commodities. The equilibrating market process takes the form, then, not simply of many market prices of fish converging towards a single price, and of that single price tending towards the market-clearing level—but of analogous, simultaneous movements in the prices of many commodities. It is abundantly clear that each of these movements is the expression of discoveries by prospective buyers and sellers—discoveries made, in this complex context, along many different commodity dimensions. For example, a buyer allocates his income among a variety of commodities, depending on their qualities and on their prices. In making such an allocative decision the buyer is acting on his perception of what commodities are available, and of what prices he must bid to secure them. These perceptions are likely to be, in part, incorrect. The course of the market process consists of revisions in such perceptions. The possession of an initial stock of purchasing power is by no means sufficient to ensure command of the optimal bundle of commodities attainable with that sum of money. The prospective buyer must, in addition, discover what, in fact, is the spectrum of prices that must be paid, and what the commodities are with respect to which he may make buying choices. As discoveries are made concerning hitherto overlooked commodities and hitherto unsuspected price opportunities, the arrays of buyers' bids become progressively modified. The market process consists in the succession of ever-changing sets of transactions that emerge as a result of the interplay of these changing arrays of bids and offers. The particular commodities acquired by buyers, and the particular revenues received by sellers at any given time, thus represent the respective discoveries made up until that date. They also express, of course, errors currently being made by these buyers and sellers (and by others who *might* have been buyers or sellers had they been aware of actual market possibilities). Scope for market discovery is present as long as unexploited opportunity for mutually gainful exchange exists between any pair of market participants, in regard to any pair of commodities they respectively possess. In the multi-commodity market the discovery of any such opportunity can be expected to cause ripples of further changes in buying and selling decisions. Under the impact of these changing plans, fresh opportunities for mutually gainful exchange are likely to be generated. The market process consists in the succession of discoveries so inspired. We can conceive this process to run out of steam, in the absence of exogenous changes, only in the utterly imaginary state of affairs in which mutual awareness on the part of market participants has attained completeness—that is, when all opportunities for mutually gainful exchange are being exploited, so that no scope for further market discovery remains.

Although my account of the multi-market discovery process has paid no explicit attention to production decisions, it will be apparent that production itself opens up the door to a host of additional dimensions for discovery. Not only may production offer scope for discovery of new products worthwhile producing, and new methods of producing known products. Producers may discover, in addition, new sources of supply for given input services, and new attitudes on the part of known suppliers of given input services (permitting their acquisition at lower prices). All of these discoveries continually modify not only the prices of products, but also the prices of inputs. The series of such modifications are all part of the market discovery process. We can conceive of the cessation of this complex market process only in the altogether imaginary case where the pattern and structure of each production process is such that no conceivable change in production (i.e., of input utilization or output sale) could possibly lead to a Pareto-preferred position. (A Pareto-preferred position is one which, when compared with some initial state of affairs, improves the well-being of some market participants without lowering that of any others.) In the absence of such a state of affairs, each market day experience represents the implementation of discoveries made. The availability of each of the specific items produced, at the prices that have in fact prevailed, is a result of complex mutual discoveries made by entrepreneurs, owners of input services, and consumers. The income earned by each owner of input services is similarly the result of a similarly complex series of mutual discoveries. In particular the pure profit won by alert entrepreneurs during the market process (during which, for example, input services may be bought at prices lower than the respective revenues they can generate at the margin) is clearly the outcome of these entrepreneurs' alert discoveries of such discrepancies and market opportunities.

COMPETITION AS A DISCOVERY PROCEDURE

It was Friedrich A. Hayek who pioneered the explicit insight that the driving force of the market process is dynamic competition—and with the recognition, moreover, that this process takes the form of the continual discovery of information that was initially simply not at *anyone's* command.[1] It is, following Hayek's breakthrough, not difficult to grasp how each step in the market process can be understood as an expression of dynamic competition. And we have already seen that each such step consists in a market discovery. So that Hayek's thesis that the competitive market process continually generates a flow of knowledge otherwise simply not within grasp, is one that we can readily accept.

This notion of dynamic competition is sharply contrasted with the static concept of competition that dominates the economics textbooks. The textbook notion of competition refers to the state of affairs in which the number of market participants (buyers and sellers) is so great, and knowledge of market possibilities so widespread, that it is inconceivable for any one market participant to obtain a market deal not obtained, at the same time, by countless others. It is now well recognized that this static textbook notion of competition requires that the market has *already* somehow attained full equilibrium. This static notion of competition can clearly generate no genuine discoveries at all (since equilibrium is a state inconsistent with scope for any as-yet-unknown opportunities for mutually gainful exchange). The static notion of competition thus marks out a state of affairs in which no process of market discovery is thinkable.

In contrast, the dynamic notion of competition emphasized by Hayek refers to no settled state of affairs at all; it refers to the potential for a

1. F. A. Hayek "The meaning of competition," in *Individualism and Economic Order* (Chicago: University of Chicago Press, 1948); "Competition as a discovery procedure," in *New Studies in Philosophy, Politics, Economics and History of Ideas* (Chicago: University of Chicago Press, 1978).

market process of discovery. During the course of this market process it is continually revealed that earlier stages were expressions of erroneous decisions. Each later stage expresses new insights discovered. Competition, in this process, takes such forms as new products introduced in the market (expressing the discovery that it is possible and worthwhile to produce an item hitherto explicitly or implicitly rejected) or new productive techniques innovated in production processes (expressing the discovery of the technical or economic feasibility of techniques whose worthwhile availability was hitherto not recognized). What is required for the dynamic process of competitive discovery is not the presence of large numbers of buyers and sellers, but only complete freedom of entry for prospective buyers and sellers, whether producers, resource owners, or consumers.

Freedom of entry serves both as a wholesome threat, spurring market participants to keep on their toes, and also as the effective implementation of that threat. Incumbent producers are under constant pressure to serve the public more efficiently, by noticing the availability of hitherto overlooked opportunities which they must introduce in order to forestall newcomers—while newcomers in fact do introduce new opportunities that were hitherto not noticed. Freedom of entry for newcomers tears away any kind of privileged status from the incumbents. They cannot rest somnolently on their laurels, relaxing their alertness towards newly available opportunities which they might set before the market. It is this dynamically competitive pressure that generates the incessant series of discoveries—what Schumpeter[2] called the "perennial gale of creative destruction"—that makes up the market process. What producers, resource owners, and consumers decide to do at any given time is decided under this competitive pressure to discover, to notice, to be alert to hitherto overlooked possible courses of action. What they decide to produce, the incomes and profits they earn, and the consumer goods they secure, are all, to greater or lesser extent, the outcomes of discoveries spurred by competitive pressure. We turn now to reinforce these insights by briefly taking notice of the *entrepreneurial* character of the dynamic competition opened up by freedom of entry.

2. J. A. Schumpeter, *Capitalism, Socialism and Democracy,* 3rd ed. (New York: Harper and Row, 1950), p. 87.

COMPETITION AND ENTREPRENEURSHIP

Our understanding of the discovery character of each step in the competitive market process can be deepened by recognizing the nature of entrepreneurship and its centrality to dynamic market competition.[3] The difference between entrepreneurial decision making and the economist's model of non-entrepreneurial decision making is a sharp and profound one. In the textbook analysis of non-entrepreneurial decision making the agent is presumed to enter the analysis already fully equipped with a clear perception of what alternative goals he wishes to pursue (including clear perception of their relative marginal importance to him) and also of what means and resources are at his disposal for the possible attainment of his objective. His decision making consists of an essentially mathematical chore, namely, the allocation of his scarce resources among his competing arrays of sought-after objectives, so as to maximize his degree of goal-achievement. While this formal conception of non-entrepreneurial decision making need not presume omniscience (since the decision may well turn out to be a resolve to obtain needed information), it does presume a surprise-free framework. Non-entrepreneurial decision making assumes that the objectives now believed—with whatever degree of sketchiness—to surround the availability of means have been correctly perceived. (Information that may be yielded by subsequent deliberate search can, in this model of the decision, certainly fill gaps in the sketchily perceived framework, but cannot turn out to reveal error in that perception.)

As contrasted with the model of the non-entrepreneurial decision, the decisions made by entrepreneurs are essentially speculative ones. Entrepreneurial decisions are those made in a world whose uncertainty is such as to render all deliberate action inevitably subject to surprises, both welcome and unwelcome. In the context of such uncertainty the entrepreneurial decision embraces, centrally, the mental identification of the present and future context within which speculative action is being taken. Entrepreneurial activity represents, then, not the pursuit of the optimal course of action marked out by given circumstances and given objectives, but the pursuit of objectives revealed *by the entrepreneurial decision itself* as

3. On this section see further my *Competition and Entrepreneurship* (Chicago: University of Chicago Press, 1973), pp. 2, 3.

being worthy and capable of pursuit. In the terminology we have adopted in this book, entrepreneurial activity expresses pure discovery.

In the Crusoe context, entrepreneurial decision making takes the form of pursuing one's realization that a new, desirable objective is capable of being attained. Crusoe entrepreneurially discovers such new opportunities. In the market context, entrepreneurial decision making takes the form of perceiving discrepancies in the structure of market prices. The entrepreneur believes he can buy an item at a price lower than the price at which he can sell it. In particular, he may believe that he can buy input services at a total cost lower than the revenue he can obtain by producing and selling output. In these situations the opportunity he entrepreneurially perceives and pursues is one which he has discovered—in fact one which he has, in a sense, created. Until now these arbitrage opportunities had not been seen, by others or by himself (otherwise they would have *already* been exploited and eliminated); entrepreneurial action to grasp such pure profit market opportunities represents their discovery. An important claim made in this book is that each and every market action taken in our uncertain world contains an ineradicably speculative, entrepreneurial element. For present purposes it is enough to emphasize that the dynamically competitive market process we have been discussing is driven by an incessant series of entrepreneurial market discoveries. Ludwig von Mises expressed this as follows:

> The driving force of the market process is provided . . . by the promoting and speculating entrepreneurs. These are people intent upon profiting by taking advantage of differences in prices. Quicker of apprehension and farther-sighted than other men, they look around for sources of profit. They buy where and when they deem prices too low, and they sell where and when they deem prices too high . . . Profit-seeking speculation is the driving force of the market as it is the driving force of production.[4]

The course of the entrepreneur-driven market is seen by Mises as being one of benign social discovery:

> The entrepreneur is the agency that prevents the persistence of a state of production unsuitable to fill the most urgent wants of the

---

4. L. Mises, *Human Action* (New Haven: Yale University Press, 1949), pp. 325f.

consumers in the cheapest way . . . The mentality of the promoters, speculators and entrepreneurs is not different from that of their fellow men. They are merely superior to the masses in mental power and energy. They are the leaders on the way toward material progress. They are the first to understand that there is a discrepancy between what is done and what could be done. They guess what the consumers would like to have and are intent upon providing them with these things . . .[5]

The competition among the entrepreneurs is ultimately a competition among the various possibilities open to men to remove their uneasiness as far as possible by the acquisition of consumers' goods . . . It reflects in the external world the conflict which the inexorable scarcity of the factors of production brings about in the soul of each individual . . . The pricing process is a social process. It is consummated by an interaction of all members of the society . . . Competing in cooperation and cooperating in competition all people are instrumental in bringing about the result, viz., the price structure of the market, the allocation of the factors of production to the various lines of want-satisfaction, and the determination of the share of each individual.[6]

Mises' unambiguous statement of the entrepreneurial character of the market process places emphasis on the role of specialist-entrepreneurs. But this is a simplification deliberately introduced to facilitate exposition. In fact, as the concluding sentences of these quotations imply, market phenomena reflect the competitive—and thus entrepreneurial—activities of *all* market participants. Mises himself put the matter very clearly. "Action is always speculation. . . . In any real and living economy every actor is always an entrepreneur and speculator."[7] My insistence, in this book, on the element of discovery inherent in *each and every* market transaction, is based on this insight concerning the entrepreneurial element in each and every real world market decision.

The congruency that exists between the exercise of creative entrepreneurship on the one hand, and the dynamic force of competitive freedom of entry on the other, should be immediately apparent. In my discussion

5. Ibid., p. 333.
6. Ibid., p. 335.
7. Ibid., p. 253.

of free entry I emphasized that the threat of entry, and its realization, combine to generate an incessant flow of market discoveries. We can now see that each of these discoveries is of an entrepreneurial character. With free entry, with complete freedom to grasp profit opportunities perceived, prospective entrepreneurs are inspired to notice market price discrepancies from which they may profit. Grasping the profitable opportunities thus perceived means, in the more important cases, acting to innovate new production possibilities where the expected revenues sharply exceed the relevant input costs. Even where the profitable opportunities perceived consist, more modestly, in the discovery of more lucrative ways of buying inputs and/or selling outputs for existing lines of production, these competitive discoveries generated by free entry (or the threat of it) are, clearly, entrepreneurial. They involve transcending the existing ways of doing things.

Conversely, we notice, entrepreneurial discoveries are to be expected only in areas of activity into which entry is not blocked (by institutional barriers, or, possibly, by monopolized exclusion from resource availability). Blocked entry not only precludes entrepreneurial innovation on the part of newly competing potential entrants, it also removes the force of such competitive pressure upon incumbents, inevitably congealing their entrepreneurial juices.

My insistence, as the central theme in this book, on the discovery element present in each and every market transaction, rests on the insight that, by definition, a market society involves at the very least a significant measure of freedom of entry, and thus of scope for entrepreneurial potential. While the degree of freedom of entry may indeed vary widely among different market societies (or among markets in a given society) it remains the essence of the market that it offers scope, in some measure at least, for competitive price and product innovativeness. It is this circumstance which assures us that market transactions necessarily retain a measure of speculative and discovery character.

MARKET PRICES AS A COMMUNICATION NETWORK

As a result of work by Friedrich A. Hayek it has become widely understood in economics that markets and market prices fulfill a highly important communicative function. Because a market society is one of decentralized decision making, in which countless independent decisions are constantly being made without the benefit of deliberate coordination by central planning authorities, the redoubtable achievements of the market economy constitute a highly significant example of what has been called *spontaneous order*. Often identified with Adam Smith's "invisible hand," the achievement of spontaneous order is now understood to depend upon spontaneous generation of information flows to decentralized decision makers, permitting them to make independent decisions that are, nonetheless, effectively, efficiently, and "rationally" linked.[8] What dispels the specter of market chaos—in which countless independent decisions clash with one another in frustrating and utterly wasteful discordance—is the spontaneous flow of information of which the market process itself continuously consists. Although the decisions of each market participant are constrained directly only by the limits of his or her property rights, nonetheless each decision tends to take account of the decisions of other market participants by virtue of the limited set of market opportunities which these other decisions mark out. But it is, of course, not sufficient to note that a decision can be made only within the set of opportunities marked out by the decisions of others. Market chaos can be avoided only if decision makers are correctly and completely *aware* of these respective limits and parameters. In claiming that market participants do tend appropriately to take account of the decisions of others, I am drawing attention to the property which the market possesses, of communicating relevant information to its participants. Our contention in this book is that this process of generating information flows is made up of an endless series of entrepreneurial discoveries made incessantly by each and every decision maker. This claim requires some careful elaboration.

It is sometimes asserted that market prices communicate information, that market prices serve as "signals" guiding independently made decisions into a coordinated pattern. Merely by taking existing market prices as reference points, it is possible for decision makers to rest assured that their independently made acts of purchase and sale dovetail substantially with the decisions being made by others. There is much validity in this assertion. But my contention that the market process is the ceaseless generation of information flows made up of countless

8. Adam Smith, *An Inquiry into the Nature and Causes of the Wealth of Nations*, ed. E. Cannan (New York: Modern Library, 1937), p. 432; see also E. Ullman-Margalit, "Invisible hand explanations," *Synthese*, 39, no. 2 (October 1978), pp. 263–91.

discoveries by entrepreneurial market participants goes beyond the assertion that market prices constitute a coordinated network of signals. It is one thing to imagine a system of coordinated price signals already in place. It is a quite different thing to see the market process as continually modifying the pattern of prices in the possible direction of greater coordination. It is the latter modification process—a process of spontaneous learning—that I am describing as being made up of acts of entrepreneurial discovery. And I am asserting that if market prices are, at any time, able to serve as reasonably useful signals guiding independently made decisions into a coordinative pattern, we must understand this as reflecting the prior course of this modification process of spontaneous learning and discovery.

All this is directly relevant to my claim that market incomes are discovered incomes, and that in fact all market transactions express discovery elements. Were given, known, market prices already to be signals flawlessly reporting decisions being made by others, they would provide no scope for further entrepreneurial discoveries. I could then hardly claim that transactions completed at these market prices inevitably express elements of discovery. (I would then have to recognize that market outcomes are simply the "inevitable," "automatic," consequences of the given, flawless, system of signals.) But, I wish to point out, real world market prices never have, at any given date, become modified so sufficiently in regard to one another that their pattern offers a flawlessly dovetailing system of signals. Further, the potential of the market process to generate spontaneous learning and discovery stems precisely from this circumstance that real market prices always are substantially different from what would make up a flawless signalling system. What motivates and inspires entrepreneurial discovery is the prospect of winning pure profits—a prospect utterly dependent upon identifying gaps and imperfections in the signalling system provided by current market prices. So that my contention that market transactions consist of acts of discovery rests on this insight that market transactions invariably involve price bids and offers which *subsequent* stages of the market process will reveal to have represented, at least partially, false and misleading signals. The point is that prices agreed on in any market transaction emerge from speculative offers and bids by entrepreneurial market participants who (correctly) understand that their decisions may be able to take advantage of "gaps" in the market.

By taking advantage of these gaps, market participants are exploiting their discoveries of ways to make profit (in so doing possibly nudging the structure of prices closer to a pattern that might serve as a fully coordinated signalling system).

MARKETS, DISCOVERY, AND CENTRAL PLANNING

The emphasis in this book is on the discovery character I am claiming for all transactions completed in the market system. This is because I am concerned with the question of the economic justice of market systems, and believe that the discovery character of market transactions is of great relevance for that question. But it will perhaps be helpful for us to take note of the wider relevance of the notion of discovery, for economic systems quite different from market capitalism. This may be particularly important to the extent that real world capitalist systems typically contain very substantial elements of non-market, governmental control.

I have argued, earlier in this chapter, that all market transactions express discoveries, since it is the essence of the market economy that it offers scope, in some measure at least, for competitive price and product innovativeness. In other words each market transaction offers scope, to greater or lesser extent, for the exercise of entrepreneurial vision, within a speculative context. We should recognize that this entrepreneurial and speculative aspect of decision making is a feature of true decision making as such, within *all* types of social frameworks, rather than being found exclusively under market capitalism.[9]

What is unique in regard to market capitalism is the widespread scope it offers for such decision making, since the essence of market capitalism is the decentralized decision making it consists of, as permitted by a system of widespread private property rights. By way of contrast, a *purely* centralized decison making system, in which one might imagine *all* decision making to be centralized and concentrated within the authority of a central planning agency, is a system within which scope for entrepreneurial, speculative decisions is available only for that central planning agency. I certainly do not wish to submerge recognition of the discovery character of such central planning. (A Crusoe economy is certainly a

9. See the works of G. L. S. Shackle (e.g., *The Nature of Economic Thought* [Cambridge University Press, 1966, part II]) for careful development of the idea that (what I have called) entrepreneurship is an essential element in all decision making.

centrally planned one, yet each of Crusoe's decisions is made in a speculative context!) Within real world systems of central planning, of course,
scope for entrepreneurial discovery exists for all agents in the system
for whom the central planning system permits a degree of discretionary
choice (with that choice including responsibility for identifying the relevant present and future factual environment).

My claim that each decision—market or non-market—involves an
element of speculative entrepreneurship, is merely an echo of the claim
made in chapter 2, that each decision, made in an "open-ended" context,
involves a discovery element. This remains true for decision making
wherever it occurs; pure capitalism, pure socialism, or whatever mix of
these "pure" systems we wish to imagine. What renders the speculative
and discovery character of *market* decisions especially relevant for issues
involving economic justice is the following set of circumstances. First, it
is only under market capitalism that decision making is so widespread,
since the essence of the system is its decentralization of decision making.
Each institutional modification made to the degree of decentralization
permitted to exist, necessarily attenuates the extent to which speculative entrepreneurship is permitted to enter. Second, it is only under
market capitalism that incomes can be unequivocally described as being
obtained by their recipients as a result of their own entrepreneurial-
speculative discoveries. Under centrally planned systems incomes are, to
a greater or lesser extent, assigned as a result of central direction. It is
true that speculative elements must enter such central decision making;
I have already emphasized that it is not incorrect to describe central planners as acting entrepreneurially (in terms of whatever goals—social
or personal—enter into the motivation of central decision making). But the
resulting incomes, to the extent that they flow from such centrally made
decisions, cannot be seen as accruing to income recipients by virtue of
their own entrepreneurial discoveries. In centrally planned economies
arguments for the justice of any given pattern of income distribution cannot make reference to the discovered character of income shares: to the
extent that incomes are centrally assigned (rather than won by the speculative choices of income recipients) they cannot be described as discovered incomes.

Gains accruing to economic agents can thus fail to be described as
discovered gains, under each of two sets of circumstances: (1) in the
centrally planned economy with incomes assigned (either in direct

income assignment, or through rigidly controlled closed-ended incentive systems); (2) in the decentrally-planned economy with imagined full equilibrium in all price and quality variables. In the centrally-planned economy, as we have seen, individual income recipients cannot be said to have discovered their gains, since it was not their own choices which generated these gains. In the decentrally-planned economy in imagined full equilibrium, on the other hand, gains won by market participants are indeed the outcome of their choices, but these choices, occurring under equilibrium conditions, necessarily lack speculative and entrepreneurial character. Equilibrium conditions imply that so much essential market data are *already* known to all relevant market participants, that their actions can be described as being wholly determined by the surrounding circumstances, leaving no scope for imaginative, entrepreneurial vision.

So the thesis of this book (criticizing standard discussions of capitalist economic justice on the grounds that they ignore the discovery element in capitalist incomes) rests on two parallel insights. The one insight is that standard discussions of economic justice under capitalism often treat this system as if, in regard to the requirements for just distribution, it can be fairly compared with the centrally planned economy. Principles of justice developed for the centrally planned economy are held to be directly relevant for appraisal of capitalist economic justice. We have seen how this view ignores a fundamental distinction between the two systems: capitalism does, but the centrally planned economy does not, offer opportunity to all for discovered gains.

The second, parallel, insight is that standard discussions of economic justice under capitalism often treat this system as if it operates, at all times, under the conditions of full general equilibrium. We have seen how such treatment necessarily causes one to overlook a crucial feature of real world capitalism that is absent from the general equilibrium model, namely, the discovery character of capitalist incomes.

This chapter has emphasized the discovery character of capitalist incomes. Chapter 2 explored the meaning of discovery. It remains for me to demonstrate the possible ethical implications of these insights—insights concerning the economics of speculative decisions under capitalism, and insights concerning the philosophical character of discovered gain. To this task I turn in the following two chapters.

5. THE FINDERS-KEEPERS RULE

The central thesis of this book is that thoughtful understanding of the capitalist system, and especially of its mode of income assignment, strongly suggests the relevance of an ethical criterion which the literature of economic justice has, unfortunately, ignored. Once the capitalist system is recognized as a continual process of spontaneous discovery, I argue, the justice of its assignments of income must surely be judged against criteria appropriate to the context of discovery. Because the standard literature of economic justice has overlooked the discovery character of capitalist incomes, it appears to me that this literature has, to a significant extent, missed the point. In order to set matters straight I turn, then, to examine an attractive candidate criterion for economic justice in the context of discovery, the criterion that is popularly expressed by the colloquialism, *finders, keepers*. The examination will be divided into two quite distinct discussions, the first making up the present chapter, the second constituting the chapter immediately following this one. In the present chapter I avoid ethical and philosophical appraisal of the finders-keepers rule. The purpose of this chapter is not to evaluate the finders-keepers rule from the economic perspective. Rather it seeks to define the finders-keepers rule with some care, and (on the basis of the discussions in chapters 2 and 4) to establish its *potential relevance* for the capitalist economy. It goes without saying that establishing the potential relevance for capitalism of any candidate criterion for economic justice is not at all sufficient to elevate the criterion into *the* standard of capitalist economic justice. To anoint any criterion to serve as the standard of economic justice under capitalism requires, of course, that one should persuasively argue the compelling ethical merit of such a criterion. The present chapter attempts no such ethical foray. The purpose of this chapter, in establishing the potential relevance to capitalism of the finders-keepers rule, is simply to show how wide a scope, in the appraisal of capitalist economic justice, there exists for application of the finders-keepers rule to the capitalist income-assignment process—should this rule be judged to constitute an ethically significant criterion. It will then be left for us in the next chapter (chapter 6) to consider the finders-keepers rule from the purely ethical perspective. It will be in that chapter that I shall argue as persuasively as I can that this rule, if it does not quite compellingly and unequivocally establish itself as *the* philosophical standard for economic justice, yet appears to satisfy widely shared ethical intuitions concerning justice in the context of discovery. Taken together, I shall argue, the present chapter and the next offer a reasonably strong case for a radical reworking of our assessment of capitalist justice, a reworking in which finders-keepers intuitions can play a very substantive role.

THE FINDERS-KEEPERS RULE AND
THE RIGHT TO PRIVATE PROPERTY

The finders-keepers rule asserts that an unowned object becomes the justly owned private property of the first person who, discovering its availability and its potential value, takes possession of it. It might appear, at first glance, that this rule has quite limited scope—a scope confined largely to acquisition of unowned objects from nature, like seashells on the beach. Certainly this rule seems to have little relevance to the "big" questions concerning capitalist justice in income assignment, the questions concerning the legitimacy of capitalist pure profits and interest, the questions concerning possible exploitation of labor, and so forth. In this chapter I will show how widely, in fact, the finders-keepers rule does apply to the evaluation of the justice of capitalist incomes, once the full scope of the rule is properly grasped. My first task in this regard, however, must be to relate this rule to the broader issue of the legitimacy of private property in general. Clearly, before any discussion can begin concerning the justice of capitalist income assignment, the legitimacy of capitalism's defining characteristic—its complete dependency upon the individual's exclusive right to property ownership—must be accepted, if only for the sake of argument. From this perspective a finders-keepers rule applied to first acquisition from nature may indeed have a fundamentally important role to play. Its role in this regard is obviously parallel to that played by the Lockean theory of private property.

Both the finders-keepers rule and Locke's principle (that property in hitherto unowned objects originates through mixing one's labor with them) offer possible grounds for legitimacy for private property insofar as that property ownership can be legitimately traced back to original acquisition from nature. To be sure, the finders-keepers rule and the Lockean principle are to be distinguished from one another. Despite a certain ambiguity in his discussion, there is rather limited basis for reading Locke's principle of original acquisition as rooted in any finders-keepers ethic.[1] It is true that *any* principle of first acquisition from the unowned state is likely to overlap substantially with a principle based on the right of discovery. After all, the first to mix his labor with the unowned object is very likely to be its first discoverer. But it seems clear that Locke was primarily depending not on the circumstance of first discovery but upon the circumstance of first applied labor effort.[2] First possession not accompanied by labor-effort confers no Lockean title, despite its following on original discovery. The ethical basis for Locke's principle is (as we shall see in chapter 6) quite different than that undergirding a possible finders-keepers rule. (In particular, as we shall see, the limitations upon original acquisition that rest on the famous "Lockean Proviso" do not apply, it can be argued, in regard to finder-based original acquisition.) Nonetheless, despite the differences between the Lockean principle and the finders-keepers rule, both appear able (within their respective ethical frameworks) to serve similar roles in legitimizing the private property system central to the capitalist system.

Of course, it is by no means the case that theories of economic justice are in general satisfied with a defense of capitalist justice grounded in nothing more than some Lockean-type legitimization of original acquisition. But an *entitlement* theory of capitalist justice, such as that expounded with such persuasive verve by Robert Nozick,[3] would appear to be capable of resting on a finders-keepers basis for original acquisition in exactly similar fashion, at least, as the way in which Nozick rests his own case on Lockean original acquisition. (In fact I shall argue in chapter 6 that "finders-keepers" offers an even firmer footing in this regard.) In other words, *if* one is sufficiently convinced of the ethical legitimacy of finders-based original acquisition, then it would be possible to argue, as Nozick does, that *all* subsequent, voluntary, and non-fraudulent, market transactions, with all the assignments of income which these capitalist market

1. For some discussion of this point, see H. M. Oliver, *A Critique of Socioeconomic Goals* (Bloomington: Indiana University Press, 1954), p. 42; Israel M. Kirzner, *Perception, Opportunity and Profit* (Chicago: University of Chicago Press, 1979), pp. 195ff.

2. See above, chapter 1, pp. 19–20, for the distinction between the notion of finders-keepers as used in this book, and the quite different rule of original acquisition from nature based on being the "first claimant."

3. Robert Nozick, *Anarchy, State, and Utopia* (New York: Basic Books, 1974).

transactions entail, enjoy a strictly derivative legitimacy. Provided no subsequent injustices (which for Nozick can consist only of failure to respect the full integrity of original-acquisition-based property titles) are permitted to contaminate the networks of capitalist exchanges, the outcomes of capitalist assignment of incomes cannot be criticized, on grounds of strict justice. So that, from such an entitlement theory perspective, a finders-keepers ethic, once accepted, does indeed hold a possible relevance for judgments concerning the justice of capitalist incomes that covers the entire field of economic justice. Yet, I shall argue in this chapter, the finders-keepers ethic holds a potential relevance for judgments on capitalist justice that extends far beyond the scope of an entitlement theory. Whether or not one subscribes to an entitlement theory, I shall maintain, acceptance of a finders-keepers ethic is capable of substantially altering one's judgment concerning the justice of capitalist incomes. The relevance of the finders-keepers ethic extends substantially beyond the strict implications of the legitimacy of original acquisition from the state of nature. To show this I must first subject Nozick's entitlement theory of capitalist justice to critical examination.

ENTITLEMENT AND ERROR

Nozick's entitlement theory defense of capitalist justice rests substantially on the *voluntary* character of market exchanges.[4] Once we confine attention to a society with initially just title to all property holdings, all results of market transactions are themselves just insofar as they are the outcomes of voluntary market interaction. To be sure, not all real world transfers fit these guidelines: "Some people steal from others, or defraud them, or enslave them, seizing their product and preventing them from living as they choose, or forcibly exclude others from competing in exchanges. None of these are permissible modes of transition from one situation to another."[5] But, again, none of these has any place in an ideal free market capitalist system with complete respect for the integrity of property rights and complete freedom of entry for all potential competitors. Within such an ideal market system all transactions are,

---

4. This section draws on ideas developed by the author from a somewhat different perspective in *Perception, Opportunity and Profit*, op. cit., pp. 201–5.

5. R. Nozick, op. cit., p. 152.

by definition, completely voluntary. "Whether a person's actions are voluntary depends on what it is that limits his alternatives. If facts of nature do so, the actions are voluntary. (I may voluntarily walk to some place I would prefer to fly to unaided.) Other people's actions place limits on one's available opportunities. Whether this makes one's resulting action non-voluntary depends upon whether these others had the right to act as they did."[6] In the ideal market all actions are limited by the possibilities rooted in one's justly owned property; no market actions, therefore, in any way erode the voluntariness of the actions of others, with whom one deals. If, as in Nozick's example, Wilt Chamberlain earns an exceptionally large income by selling his unique talents to a basketball team, he is justly entitled to that income because "each of these persons" (who paid to watch him) "*chose* to give twenty-five cents of their money to Chamberlain. They could have spent it on going to the movies, or on candy bars, or on copies of *Dissent* magazine, or of *Monthly Review*. But they all, at least one million of them, converged on giving it to Wilt Chamberlain in exchange for watching him play basketball."[7] But this line of reasoning, based substantially on the voluntariness of market transactions, seems vulnerable to possible criticism.

It is one thing to recognize that those who paid Wilt Chamberlain to watch him play basketball did so without having been coerced; it is quite another thing, it might be insisted, to argue that Chamberlain is therefore justly entitled to these payments. The mere fact that spectators spontaneously offered to pay to watch Chamberlain does not, it may be held, necessarily satisfy the criteria for justice in transfer of the money they paid. After all, spectators may have been deceived: perhaps they were falsely told that this was their only remaining chance to see Chamberlain this season; perhaps they have been misled as to Chamberlain's degree of excellence. Had spectators known the full truth, perhaps some might *not* have paid to watch the game. It is true that no one forced them to pay at the point of a gun; spectators paid to watch of their own accord. And it may even be true that no one deliberately deceived these spectators— or was even aware of the misunderstanding. So that Chamberlain or his representatives may not have consciously *defrauded* these spectators.

6. Ibid., p. 262.
7. Ibid., p. 161.

Nonetheless, once the full truth has become apparent to all, these spectators, or disinterested ethical observers, may feel quite strongly that the money so paid was in fact paid on the basis of a misunderstanding so substantial as to effectively erode the legitimacy of the transfer—or even, it may be held, to cast a shadow over the very voluntariness of the payment. The spectators, it may be held, did not *really* wish to pay to watch that which it turned out to be the case that they watched. Justice requires that those payments be returned, yet the law of capitalist exchanges (citing *caveat emptor*) may let the transaction stand.[8]

A Nozickian defense of the justice of market transfers might attempt to deflect this criticism by refining the definition of a legitimate market transaction. Such a defense might thus beg the *critic* to define the degree of "fullness of awareness" that would render a market transaction immune, to the critic's satisfaction, to ethical challenge on the basis of mistake—and then proceed to define a market transaction in terms of that degree of full awareness. The *ideal* capitalist legal system, it will be insisted, should and will ensure that mistaken transactions—defined by reference to *this* standard—be voided. The only remaining transfers of title will be those that are indubitably made without mistake. Nozick's point about the justice of Wilt Chamberlain's high income will still stand because presumably much of that income was derived from payments made by fans who knew exactly what they were paying for—and were excitedly happy to do so. But this defense of the entitlement approach may itself be further questioned.

This defense takes it for granted that, once we have filtered out all cases of mistaken transactions, the bulk of capitalist exchanges will still stand, so that the broad outlines of capitalist income assignments and of property titles, remain immune to charges of injustice based on transaction error. But supposing it could be shown that virtually all market transactions are, to greater or lesser extent, flawed by mistake? Supposing it could be shown that, were all such transactions to be conceded to be questionable, the legitimacy of virtually *all* market-generated property

---

8. See also *Perception, Opportunity and Profit,* op. cit., pp. 207–9, on the significance of the law of mistake for discussions of the morality of capitalism. For an early and fascinating treatment of these issues see Gulian C. Verplanck, *An Essay on the Doctrine of Contracts: Being an Inquiry How Contracts Are Affected in Law and Morals by Concealment, Error, or Inadequate Prices* (New York, 1825).

titles would be subject to challenge? Let me show how such challenges to the meaningful voluntariness of virtually all market transactions—challenges rooted in claims of error and mistake—might be raised with some measure of plausibility.

The grounds for such challenges are to be found in the circumstance that market processes are, in a crucially essential way, fuelled by ignorance and by the profitable discovery of ignorance. As outlined in chapter 4, a sensitive understanding of how a market economy works reveals the central role played by market error under disequilibrium conditions. The capacity of markets to approach equilibrium conditions, with prices moving towards market clearing levels and with opportunities for mutually profitable exchange tending to be successfully exploited, is derived, we have seen, precisely from the circumstance that errors create pure profit opportunities that attract entrepreneurial discovery. In other words, what confers upon markets the degree of social efficiency they possess, is the dynamic generated by market errors. The problem, for an entitlement defense of capitalist justice, is that such errors might be held substantially to rob market transactions of meaningful voluntariness—if a voluntary transaction is taken to mean one entered into willingly with full knowledge of all relevant facts. The problem is that the crucial role played in market processes by error suggests that the voluntariness of the bulk of market transactions may reasonably be questioned.

As we have noted in chapter 4, market error may take the form of offering to buy at a price higher than the prices others are buying at elsewhere in the same market. Or error may take the form of buying (selling) at a high (low) price unaware that (as a result of this price) a surplus (shortage) of goods is developing that makes it wise for sellers (buyers) to cut (raise) prices. Or these errors may consist of producing products that are in fact in such low demand as not to be worthwhile producing at all, or (which is ultimately the same thing) of failing to produce products for which the potential demand is so strong as to more than justify costs of production. Or these errors may consist in using unnecessarily costly methods of production. The point is that each of these errors is responsible for market transactions that would not have been made were knowledge and awareness more complete. No one, in all of these errors, may necessarily be liable to be accused of deliberately defrauding or deceiving anyone else. Yet in the case of each of these mistaken transactions one of the parties may feel that, in a real sense, the transaction was not entirely voluntary—consent was given in a flawed fashion, on the basis of a mistaken belief concerning the relevant facts. Were these errors somehow peripheral to the central contours of market activity, the challenge they pose for an entitlement defense of capitalist justice would be less serious. But, as we have seen, these errors are crucially central to the way in which the market economy works.[9] These critical considerations are among those which render a finders-keepers rule relevant to issues of capitalist justice that go far beyond the legitimacy of original acquisition of scarce resources from nature.

FINDERS-KEEPERS AND MARKET ERROR

The key to the matter lies in the following circumstance. Precisely to the extent that error might, in the eye of the critic, be held to erode the meaningful voluntariness of market transactions, a finders-keepers rule may be held to neutralize the ethical problems so raised. The error held to invalidate capitalist transfers may invariably be seen to be, in fact, nothing but the other side of the finders-keepers coin. Wherever a seller may (upon realizing the full truth) wish he had not, in his unawareness, agreed to a sale, the buyer's title can be shown to be buttressed by a finders-keepers rule. Wherever a buyer (upon realizing the full truth) may wish he had not, in his unawareness, agreed to a purchase, the seller's title to the agreed-on payment can be shown to flow from a finders-keepers rule. This circumstance does not, in itself, offer a defense against challenges to the justice of error-ridden transfers—since we have not yet argued that justice demands adherence to any finders-keepers rule. But this circumstance does, nonetheless, indicate how wide a scope exists for a finders-keepers rule—should such a rule be held to be required on grounds of economic justice. Our present discussion refers strictly to this question of scope. Let us consider afresh the problems raised by error for capitalist justice.

We have seen that, even in the absence of fraud, even in the absence of the kinds of fundamental mistake which the law conventionally

---

9. We will deal, a little later on in this chapter, with the "hard-boiled" *caveat emptor* position that argues, in effect, that each market participant agrees, in regard to each transaction in which he is involved, to an implicit clause providing that surprise not be considered grounds for revoking a transaction already completed.

recognizes as invalidating transfers, market exchanges are invariably and pervasively affected by errors. I raised the possibility that critics may therefore conclude that the justice of market transfers is typically capable of being challenged on the grounds of such errors. One rebuttal to such critics might be to point out that market transactions are entered into with full awareness of at least the *possibility* of error, so that a transactor hardly has strong grounds in justice to invalidate an erroneous transaction. After all, the transactor *knew* that he might be making a mistake; by entering nonetheless into the deal he consciously assumed the risk of such a possible mistake. If a vacationer at the beach resort finds his vacation ruined by unseasonably bad weather, he can hardly consider it injustice of the hotel keeper not to refund the money paid in advance for his accommodation. He can hardly argue that, had he known it would be raining for days, he would not have reserved the room. After all he *did* know that it *might* rain. By booking and paying for the room nonetheless, he consciously assumed the risk of bad weather. No error, no unanticipated event, in the last analysis, invalidated the hotel reservation that he made.

But the critics might stand their ground. They might distinguish between error the discovery of which engenders no genuine surprise, and the quite different kind of error the discovery of which does generate genuine surprise. While one may indeed consider several days of rain to be highly unlikely (in the sense of its occurrence being a possibility held to have a very low probability) one will presumably not maintain that the rain was an occurrence totally unforeseen. As Professor Shackle has taught us, a low-probability event may be quite unsurprising—if the event is one the occurrence of which has been fully imagined and judged possible. If I win the lottery, an event has occurred to which I have attached extremely low probability; yet the event can hardly be described as astonishing or surprising—after all, *somebody* wins the lottery, always. "Surprise is that dislocation and subversion of received thoughts, which springs from an actual experience outside of what has been judged fully possible, or else an experience of a character which has never been imagined and thus never assessed as either possible or impossible: a *counter-expected* or else an *unexpected* event."[10] The expected event—even if

---

10. George L. S. Shackle, *Epistemics and Economics* (Cambridge: Cambridge University Press, 1972), p. 422.

expected to occur only with very low probability—need occasion little surprise if it does occur. While it is true, the critics will readily concede, that error unaccompanied by genuine surprise need not invalidate the justice of market transfers, it may yet be held that error resulting in a genuinely surprising event *does* invalidate the justice of error-ridden transactions. The transactor who erred may insist that he did *not* consciously assume the risk of this event's occurrence; he can insist on this because he never imagined its possibility at all. Moreover, even if it be argued, against the critics, that transactors know they live in a world of surprises (so that they presumably accept even the hazards of total surprise), the critics may still remain unsatisfied. Even if transactors have accepted the hazards of possible surprise, does this really mean that these transactors were in fact *aware* of the true facts? May not a transactor after all honestly pronounce his payment or his purchase *not* to have been made entirely voluntarily— if a voluntary transaction is defined in terms of willingness to transact in full awareness of all relevant circumstances? To be sure, one may believe that, by consciously (even if perhaps stupidly) accepting the hazards of unanticipated surprise, the transactor renounces all ethical claims to have the transaction revoked. But the *voluntariness* of the transaction is nonetheless open to question. Is there not an ineradicable logical contradiction contained in the notion of "expecting a surprise"? If a true surprise turns out, as it must, to have been unexpected, could the transaction have been made "with full awareness"? If the relevant circumstances turn out, then, to have been totally unexpected (in Shackle's sense) surely the resulting surprise does, after all, becloud the legitimacy of the transaction— if legitimacy is seen as rooted exclusively in its voluntariness?

But once we have compelled the critic to narrow down the case (against the justice of error-ridden market transactions) to examples of error which are revealed through surprise, the relevance of a finders-keepers rule comes clearly into focus. It now becomes obvious that the market participants who have gained as a result of these errors (made by others) may, surely, claim that their gain (grasped at the apparent expense of those surprised others) represents a *discovery*, to which justice, as defined in a finders-keepers rule, assigns them full title. Those surprised by these discoveries can hardly claim to have suffered injustice. Suppose a resource owner sells a unit of it at a low price and discovers, to his complete surprise, that the entrepreneur to whom he sold it used the resource innovatively in a highly profitable line of production. The seller regrets his error in selling the resource for less than (what he now realizes is) its "true" value. And the critic of capitalist justice therefore challenges the legitimacy of the gain made by the entrepreneur through his imaginative and innovative use of the resource, questioning the entrepreneur's title to the resource he bought. The entrepreneur's response, if we assume a finders-keepers rule, will be to avoid resting his claim to the gain he has made, upon an exclusively entitlement basis. Rather he will point out that the gain, measuring the difference between the "true" value of the resource and the low value accepted by the erstwhile resource owner, is a wholly *discovered* gain and thus belongs, in justice, to its discoverer. The very reason for questioning the integrity of the entrepreneur's title to the resource—namely, the circumstance that its true higher value through being deployed in the innovative line of production was a total surprise, implying sharply limited awareness on the part of the seller at the moment of sale—indicates that this gain was in fact discovered entirely by the entrepreneur whose innovativeness and initiative generated the higher value. *The additional value now seen by all to have resided in the resource was in fact found by the innovative entrepreneur.* If we follow a finders-keepers rule we can no longer countenance any simple revocation of the resource sale. Simply to revoke the sale will be to assign to the seller a gain which someone else, not he, discovered. Precisely because the seller had no inkling of the "true" higher value residing in his unit of resource he must recognize that the gain to be derived from the discovery of the higher value, justly belongs to another under a finders-keepers rule. Precisely the circumstance which might render it plausible to invalidate the sale on grounds of flawed voluntariness, suffices under a finders-keepers rule, it thus turns out, to make it pointless for the seller to invalidate it (because the rule insists that the discovered gain shall inure to the benefit of its discoverer). Let us examine more carefully how a finders-keepers rule would justify the general phenomenon of pure profit under capitalism.

FINDERS-KEEPERS AND PURE ENTREPRENEURIAL PROFIT

In our examination in chapter 3 of the economic literature dealing with pure entrepreneurial profit, we noticed how incomplete the conventional treatments of capitalist justice have been. For example, we noticed that John Bates Clark's celebrated marginal productivity defense of justice under capitalism did not provide any defense of the legitimacy of pure profit. Pure profit, I pointed out, cannot be rationalized as having been "produced" by the entrepreneur; he may simply have bought an item at a low price and resold it subsequently at a higher price. My discussion, in the preceding sections of this chapter, of certain problems with the Nozickian entitlement approach, suggested that this approach, too, may not be adequate as a defense of the entrepreneur's claim, in justice, to pure profit (since the very phenomenon of pure profit implies incomplete awareness on the part of those who sell to the profit-making entrepreneur and of those who subsequently buy from him). We now see how a finders-keepers rule, if accepted, provides the missing theory of justice needed to confer legitimacy upon the phenomenon of pure profit.

Every case of pure profit, we have noted in earlier chapters, constitutes a case of pure discovery. Pure profit is what is grasped as a result of being able to buy and sell in different markets, to buy where the price is low, and to sell, now or in the future, where or when the price is higher. No matter whether the pure profit is grasped as a result of simple arbitrage-like activity (in which the item sold is physically identical with that bought) or whether it is grasped as a result of a complex series of industrial and financial decisions (in the course of which input services are acquired at a *total* cost which is exceeded by the revenues obtained by selling the resulting fabricated output), pure profit represents the gap between price paid and price received. The existence of such a gap presents serious conceptual difficulties.

How is it possible, one wonders, for sellers to sell at a low price that which the buyers will shortly sell for a higher price? (It will not do to answer that they cannot afford to wait until the higher prices occur, or to undertake the costs of delivery, and the like, because the notion of pure profit implies that it exists over and above any implicit interest cost of waiting, or of delivery costs, or whatever.) And again, why do those who buy from the profit-making middleman at these higher prices, pay him these higher prices? Why do not *they* buy at lower prices? One cannot, it must be emphasized, rationalize the gaps by reference to the cost of obtaining information. One cannot, that is, explain that those who sell at the low price (or those who buy at the high price) do so in order to save the cost of finding out where to find buyers offering higher prices (sellers willing to sell for less). Such an explanation would imply that the profit-making middleman *did* incur the cost of finding out this information, in which case his pure profit turns out to be *zero*, since the difference between his buying price and his selling price is equal to his expenditure on information. (Or at least—for cases in which the middleman somehow costlessly acquired this information—we would have to concede that his gain is no more than the fair market value of the information which he put to use, so that this gain is simply the competitive market value of a resource which he happens to possess, again placing the gain outside the category of pure profit.) The phenomenon of pure profit, based as it is on this problematic gap between the prices accepted by the (first) sellers and those paid by the (second) buyers, cannot be imagined to occur except as a result of sheer ignorance. Sheer ignorance, it will be recalled from discussion in earlier chapters, is ignorance which one cannot—at any cost—dispel through diligent search, because one is ignorant of one's ignorance (or, which is the same thing, one is ignorant of the possibilities for search). It is in fact the unwillingness of economists to grapple with the phenomenon of sheer ignorance which has led them, so often, to imagine that pure profits simply never occur. Sheer ignorance on the part of sellers concerning their ability in fact to sell for higher prices than they are now being offered, sheer ignorance on the part of buyers concerning their ability in fact to buy at lower prices than those which they are now paying, permit the gaps between prices which emerge as pure profits to their discoverers. (If we are not explaining away pure profit as merely the implicit market value of the profit-making entrepreneur's superior information, we must imagine that he too, was, before he noticed the profitable opportunity, utterly ignorant of it.)

The nature of pure profits, therefore, is such that pure profits can never be won except through an act of pure discovery. All of the earmarks of discovery that we discussed in chapter 2 apply with great precision to the winning of pure profit. Sheer ignorance cannot become transformed into a profitable action except through the pure discovery of that concerning which one was utterly ignorant. The alert entrepreneur who notices the price differential and moves to grasp the profitable opportunity thus presented, has produced nothing. He has discovered an opportunity for net gain.

All this suffices to explain how a finders-keepers rule might provide the missing justification for pure profit. The alert entrepreneur has discovered an opportunity to which no one else has hitherto laid claim, an opportunity, in fact, of which no one was even aware (otherwise that opportunity would *already* have been snapped up). By discovering and grasping this pure profit opportunity the alert entrepreneur is in exactly the same situation as one who finds and grasps an unowned object before it has been found by anyone else. According to a finders-keepers rule, he is fully entitled to what he has found.

THE CENTRALITY OF A FINDERS-KEEPERS RULE

All this surely points to the truth of what I have asserted: the relevance of a finders-keepers rule extends far beyond the legitimacy of original acquisition from nature, it extends far beyond the claims that may be made for capitalist justice on the basis of a Nozick-type entitlement approach. A finders-keepers rule, if accepted, could radically transform one's perspective on the justice of the capitalist market process, not on matters peripheral to the workings of the system, but in regard to its central mode of operation. As argued at length in chapter 4, the economic achievements of capitalism arise in an essential way from the ceaseless competitive process of entrepreneurial discovery. The incentive that drives this process, the spark that switches on the entrepreneurial alertness central to its operation, is the incentive of winning pure economic profit. It is the prospect of discovering and grasping pure profit which spurs entrepreneurs to buy and sell, to innovate and to produce—in this way generating those equilibrating tendencies so much emphasized in conventional expositions of the roots of capitalist efficiency. It is this ceaseless drive after pure profits which agitates markets at each moment.

Yet it was precisely the phenomenon of pure profit which we found, in chapter 3 and in the present chapter, to be left untouched by existing theories of economic justice. A theory defending the justice of capitalist income assignments which offers no justification for pure profit would appear to be not merely an incomplete theory, but one which seems almost incoherent, since it fails to address the ethical dilemmas which swirl around the central driving force of the capitalist system. The acceptance of a finders-keepers rule, we now see, is entirely able to address these questions. If accepted, then, this rule turns out to be of critical relevance to the very mainspring of the capitalist process. It does not merely fill a gap left by earlier approaches; it addresses perhaps *the* root issue in capitalist justice.

It is true that criticisms of capitalist income distribution, offered on grounds of justice, have traditionally focused more emphatically upon other issues than that of the justice of pure profit. The central focus of traditional criticisms has been on the way in which capitalism assigns incomes to capitalists on the one hand, and laborers on the other. The "profits" of capitalists which Marxist criticism, for example, saw as exploited away from labor, were not pure profits at all, of course, but a conglomerate of analytically disparate income categories, chief among which was interest on capital. What was being primarily attacked was the justice of an interest-income share, enjoyed by a class held to make no personal contribution to the production of output. The volume of *pure* profit won by entrepreneurs surely refers to only a small fraction of capitalist "profits" in the broad sense of the word used by the classical economists (and especially by Marx). It is no accident, it could be conjectured, that pure profit did not loom more importantly in the classic discussions of capitalist justice; the phenomenon was simply not important enough. If the major significance attached to a finders-keepers rule is that derived from its relevance to the justice of pure profit, a critic may argue, then that significance is hardly central to the broader question of capitalist justice, after all.

My insistence on the centrality of importance, for capitalist justice, of a finders-keepers rule does rest substantially, nonetheless, on its relevance for the justice of pure profit. The truth surely is that the most vexing questions regarding the justice of capitalist income distribution have always challenged not any given analytical category of income as such, but rather all kinds of payments received by participants in the capitalist process *not in return*, in the critics' judgment, *for productive service rendered*. The critical point of such challenges derived from the ethical intuition (the coherence of which is not now the topic of discussion) that only those who participate actively and personally in production are justly entitled to share in the produced output. The central injustice seen as pervading the capitalist system is that it assigns to participants in the system income shares which bear no relation to the effort these participants have contributed to production. Not only is it the case that this kind of challenge holds direct relevance for pure entrepreneurial profit; it became clear, through the decades of literature debating the validity of these challenges, that ultimately it is *only* in regard to pure profits that these challenges retain a modicum of cogency. The profits on capital which non-Marxian economists have, for over a century now, called interest, can be, and have been, quite successfully defended against these challenges. For productivity theorists interest is paid out of additional output made possible only by the productive contribution of capital; it must be paid if consumers are to benefit from the availability of these capital resources. While critics may not agree that the capitalist is required to make a personal sacrifice comparable in rigor to those made by laborers in working for capitalists, they can at any rate not insist, on this theory of interest, that it is unrelated to productive contribution. For an entitlement theorist of justice the justice of interest income derives simply from the circumstance that market participants (borrowers and lenders) voluntarily agreed to the making of interest payment on borrowings (with the *grounds* for such payment—pure positive time preference, or whatever—being matters treated as of no consequence for the purpose of ethical discussion). Only pure profit, it appears, seems to be truly threatened by the productivity-ethic criticisms of capitalist justice. For pure profit really is an income share for which no productivity justification can conceivably work. Pure profit really is, by its very definition, the amount left in the hands of the capitalist entrepreneur after *all* costs of production, explicit and implicit, have been deducted from gross revenues received. Nor, as argued earlier in this chapter, does an entitlement approach offer an obviously acceptable case for the justice of pure profits. The central ethical challenges hurled at capitalist justice do, it turns out, have primary relevance to pure profit payments, after all. But I wish to show the system-wide breadth of scope and relevance of a finders-keepers rule also by additional considerations, beyond those directly pertinent to pure profits.

FINDERS-KEEPERS AND THE JUSTICE
OF RESOURCE INCOME

Thus far our discussions on the scope and relevance of a finders-keepers rule have focused (apart from the issue of original acquisition from nature) upon the category of pure profit. This might quite naturally be seen as supporting the traditional view that has treated other kinds of income, notably incomes received through the sale of productive resource services, as completely understandable and defensible without reference to any finders-keepers insights. But I shall argue that resource incomes, too, display features to which a finders-keepers rule would have clear relevance, and that, in fact, the justice of resource incomes is hardly established with completeness in the absence of such a rule.

The grounds for the standard view upon resource incomes that sees them as neither requiring any finders-keepers rule nor as being within the scope of such a rule are fairly straightforward. Economic analysis

of resource incomes has been pursued on the basis of a sharp analytical distinction between resource ownership and entrepreneurship. The
resource owner is for the main part perceived, in standard economic theory, as
choosing whether or not to sell the services of his resource on the basis of
given resource prices equally available to all owners of similar resources.
In other words, it is assumed that resource markets are "perfectly
competitive"—cast in a market model notorious for its neglect of any
entrepreneurial role. Economic theory has certainly taken account of the
case of resource monopoly; but it has done so in a manner which in effect
assumes that the parameters of the resource market are fully known to all
market participants. Neither in the perfectly competitive resource markets
nor in the monopolistic resource markets treated in mainstream theory
has any room been left for any entrepreneurial behavior on the part of
the resource owner. The resource owner is confronted with a given—and
entirely obvious—demand curve for the services of his resource; he must
decide merely on which point of that demand curve to place himself. Questions concerning the justice of resource incomes have therefore traditionally been addressed in terms of the legitimacy of resource ownership and
the rights of the just owner to the productive fruits of his resource. Nothing
is "found"; therefore no question of finders-keepers arises.

It should be observed, moreover, that from a diehard traditional perspective, the emphasis laid in this book on the category of pure profit,
and on the entrepreneurial function to which pure profit is to be traced,
need not be seen to alter very much in regard to the treatment of resource
incomes. It is true, it may reasonably be argued, that the standard theory
was flawed in its neglect of the entrepreneurial role. It is true that the
standard theory should not have treated *all* incomes, in effect, as resource
incomes in the state of entrepreneurless equilibrium. But all that we need
now to do, the argument could run, is to introduce the long-neglected
entrepreneurial function, and with it pay explicit attention to the category
of pure profit. This can be done, surely, without giving up the view that
sees resource owners as entirely non-entrepreneurial.

What I wish to point out in this section is that, while at the level of pure
analysis such a position might certainly make a good deal of sense, at a
somewhat lower level of abstraction matters appear rather differently. In
the real world, after all, resource owners never are exempted from having to encounter substantial entrepreneurial opportunities and responsibi-
lities. To insist that finders-keepers insights hold no relevance for resource

incomes, is to maintain a position which, while strictly valid at the analytical level, is likely to be a misleading one in regard to practical questions (including, especially, such as concern economic justice). The scope of a finders-keepers rule may, as a matter of pure analysis, be confined to the realm of pure entrepreneurial profit, but, from the perspective of the social observer concerned with the justice of the capitalist system, the insights underlying a finders-keepers rule must surely be seen to hold relevance for virtually every single income receipt in the system.

Were the labor market typically to be in full equilibrium, with a single wage rate clearing the market for each kind of labor service, then it would be correct to treat wages as a category of income to which entrepreneurial discovery has no reference. Under such conditions each laborer knows exactly what his labor is worth and exactly how to obtain that value in the market. He must simply choose between a day's leisure and a day's wages. No uncertainties need cloud his brow, and the wages he receives by the sweat of that unclouded brow are justly his simply by virtue of his self-ownership and the willingness of employers to pay him the going wage. No element in his wages or working conditions is a discovery; he wins no discovered profits and can suffer no losses; there is simply no scope for error on his part. But the labor market in the real world never is at equilibrium.

In the real world no resource owner can avoid fulfilling some measure of entrepreneurial function. No laborer is, in practice, in a position where his market opportunities in the labor market are given and obvious. Inevitably the laborer must determine for himself—in an open-ended world fraught with inescapable uncertainty, pervaded by the sheerest of utter ignorance—which job to apply for, which job to accept, and what wages and working conditions to hold out for. This means that the more successfully "entrepreneurial" laborer will in fact enjoy a job offering wages, working conditions, prestige, and prospects for advancement, which may substantially exceed those won by a fellow laborer with equal talents *qua* laborer, but with less potential as entrepreneur.

When a resource owner announces his willingness to sell quantities of resource services for specified amounts of money, under specified conditions of employment, he is taking a daring entrepreneurial gamble. He has no guarantee that his offer will be accepted. Perhaps he has priced himself out of the market. And, on the assumption that his offer to sell *is* accepted, he has no guarantee that he is obtaining the "true" market value of his resource service. Perhaps his resource could have displayed far greater productivity in a different industry, or in the hands of manufacturers other than those to whom he is making his offer. Had these other potential employers been made aware of the availability of his stock of resources, they would be prepared to offer higher prices. So that his present offer may be the expression of error, of sheer ignorance; it may be, in an entrepreneurial sense, an embarkation on a *losing* venture, since it will yield less than the true value of what he is surrendering. Every penny which the resource owner in fact obtains in exchange for his resources is thus a "find." A finders-keepers rule would have to be brought into any attempt at judging the justice of resource incomes so received.

Nor should it be imagined that the entrepreneurial element in resource owners' decisions can be somehow dismissed as so peripheral to the essential function of resource ownership as to permit it to be safely ignored in appraising the justice of resource incomes. It should not be imagined, that is, that in the same way that economic theory treats the real world laborer as able to be modelled as a pure non-entrepreneurial resource owner, a theorist of economic justice may quite similarly treat his labor income as if the entrepreneurial component in the laborer's makeup were negligible. There is no harm at all, in positive economic theory, with the view that a worker's real world wages can be treated as the sum of two analytically distinct components: a pure wage (corresponding to the equilibrium wage for the particular labor service he offers) and a pure entrepreneurial profit (or loss), being the *difference* between the actual wage received and the equilibrium wage for this quality of labor service. So that, on the assumption that this profit/loss difference is reasonably small, it can plausibly be ignored, for the purposes of much applied economic theory. But in regard to judgments concerning the justice of wage receipts, things are quite different. In regard to questions of justice it is reasonable to argue that even a very small component of pure profit or loss in fact transforms the *entire* sum received as wages into a thoroughly entrepreneurial income.

That this is the case can perhaps most easily be seen by thinking of the case of the entrepreneur who uses his *own* labor to produce a product or service offered for sale to consumers. Think of Mr. Jones who borrows capital to buy a taxicab which he then drives himself. Analytically the economist will think of Jones's total "profit" (after deducting from gross revenues all out-of-pocket expenses, including interest on the borrowed capital) as in fact made up of (1) an implicit wage (envisaged as equal to the wage for which he could have driven a taxicab for a fleet owner), and (2) the residual pure entrepreneurial profit attributable to his entrepreneurship in pursuing this particular taxicab business venture. But from Jones's own perspective, surely, things must appear rather differently. By working for himself, rather than for a taxicab fleet, he has exposed himself to entrepreneurial uncertainties in regard to his entire operation. While he may not treat *all* his net revenue (after deducting out-of-pocket expenses) as pure profit, since he is aware that he could have earned a wage driving for other fleet owners, nonetheless he will surely insist that no penny out of the net revenue that he in fact takes home, was the kind of assured, steady wage flow that we think of as typical resource owner's income. By combining his pure entrepreneurial function together with his resource owner's (labor) function, Jones has effectively transformed his *entire* income into one attributable to his entrepreneurial success. It is simply not in accordance with the real world facts to say that Jones-the-laborer received a resource-owner's equilibrium-rate income, without any entrepreneurial risk or uncertainty, while Jones-the-entrepreneur enjoyed the difference between that equilibrium rate income and net revenue received. Nothing that Jones received came to him without shouldering entrepreneurial uncertainty in an essential way.

But things are not greatly different for Jones's friend Smith, a cab driver who prefers the relatively quiet life of working for a wage for Brown, a fleet owner. It is true that Brown the fleet owner, not Smith, now bears the entrepreneurial risk associated with sending Smith out in the streets with a cab. But, as argued earlier, Smith is an entrepreneur nonetheless. Just as Jones, who sells his driving services directly to the consumer (as part of the cab rides which he provides) sees the earnings he makes from his driving services as attributable to his entrepreneurship, so Smith who sells his driving services to Brown the fleet owner, will see the earnings he makes from his driving services as attributable to his own entrepreneurship (in the sale of his labor). This is so because Smith never was *assured* of anything at all. He was never in the position of someone choosing between two simple, clear-cut alternatives, a day's leisure or a day's wage income. As already noted, any number of "entrepreneurial" doubts must in fact beset Smith's decision to work for the fleet owner—including the doubts Smith must have as to whether he has been complete in his mental listing of these doubts. Brown may go bankrupt; Smith may never collect his wage. Or it may turn out that competing fleet owners were, just today, in special need of additional drivers, and prepared to offer Smith substantially higher wages than he now agrees to accept from Brown; and so on. In selling his driving services to Brown, the fleet owner, Smith is not simply transforming these services into their fully known cash value, he is taking a step into the dark, uncertain entrepreneurial future, guided entirely by his entrepreneurial hunches. Even when, *ex post*, it becomes apparent that the wages Smith has received were in fact identical with those paid elsewhere, this does not alter the circumstance that, *ex ante*, Smith's entrepreneurial sense was certainly called into play.

So that when the justice of a laborer's right to his wage payment—or any resource owner's right to the income from his resource—is being scrutinized, there is every reason to recognize the relevance of a finders-keepers rule. Smith's successful and productive employment in Brown's taxicab fleet is the result not only of the discovery by Brown of Smith's potential. If discovery is held to be crucially relevant to questions of justice—as a finders-keepers rule would maintain—then the scope of the finders-keepers rule must be recognized as extending far beyond the area of pure entrepreneurial profit. Real world resource incomes, too, fall within its scope. The point warrants some additional discussion, from a somewhat different starting point.

DISCOVERY IN PRODUCTION, ONCE AGAIN

It will be recalled that in chapter 2, after developing a sharp distinction between discovery and production, I proceeded, somewhat perversely perhaps, to muddy the line of distinction. After discussing the notion of pure discovery, and carefully contrasting it with the notion of pure production activity, I pointed out that in the real world, examples of such pure cases are simply not to be found. Every real world act of production, I showed, invariably and inevitably displays elements of pure discovery. It is this insight that we now find illustrated afresh in the circumstance that every decision by a resource owner to translate his resource services into resource income, is inescapably pervaded by entrepreneurial elements.

Pure discovery differs from pure production, it will be recalled, in that what is discovered can in no sense be attributed to the discoverer's deliberate decision to achieve a goal the attainment of which was fully within his control (by virtue of his control over the relevant factors of production). An act of discovery, we saw, was an act that originated the existence of something that had, before the moment of discovery, been entirely outside one's grasp. An act of pure production, on the other hand, is simply the deliberate decision to transform inputs into outputs. In the act of pure production nothing new is introduced at all; the output achieved "existed" fully even before it was produced. The output existed in inchoate form, in the guise of inputs, the availability of which sufficed to guarantee the output, at will. In pure production, control over the future is guaranteed by current control over inputs. In pure discovery nothing in the future is guaranteed by anything that existed prior to the discovery.

In the real world, however, we found, cases of pure production simply do not occur. Control over inputs never does guarantee inevitable attainment of output goals, whenever desired. In the real world of open-ended uncertainty, productive activity occurs in an environment in which the opportunities for useful production are not self-evidently known to all, but must be presciently seen by the prospective producer. In grasping these opportunities that he sees, he is expressing his convictions about the open-ended future. Nothing in any resource complex over which the producer has control guarantees the perception of the particular productive opportunity which he in fact grasps. So that when he does actually produce output with the inputs at his disposal we cannot claim that that output *already* existed, in embryonic form, in the inputs already under his control. The output produced was, in a sense, *originated* by the perceptive vision of the producer in recognizing, in this uncertain world, the worthwhileness of this particular act of production.

I remind the reader of these discussions in chapter 2 in order to reinforce my claim that each and every resource income can, in the real world, be seen as entrepreneurially generated. In a world of equilibrium the generation of resource income from owned resources is a process that parallels pure production activity. Ownership of the resource is sufficient, under conditions of market equilibrium, to guarantee receipt of this resource income, which can therefore be traced back historically to the possession of the resource. No trace of discovery has any part in the generation of this income. The contrast between pure resource income on the one hand, and pure entrepreneurial profit on the other, is complete. Pure entrepreneurial profit emerges from pure discovery; it cannot be traced back to anything possessed by the entrepreneur (since the entrepreneur, *qua* entrepreneur, owns no resources whatever). The origin of pure profit is to be seen entirely in the entrepreneur's discovery of an opportunity to buy and sell at different prices. Pure resource income, on the other hand, originates entirely in the resources already owned. These resources sufficed entirely to ensure this income. The pure resource owner needs simply to express his desire to transform resources into income, in precisely the same fashion as the pure producer needs simply to express his desire to transform input into output.

But in the real world, as we have seen, no pure resource ownership occurs. No owner of a resource is in a position to guarantee its transformation into income. Possession of a resource still leaves its owner subject to the uncertainties of an ever-surprising world. To transform an owned resource into income calls for decision making in the context of possible surprises and disappointments; it requires from the resource owner an expression of conviction regarding the future which he perceives. Such an expression of conviction constitutes an act of perception, an act of discovery. The income thus grasped through such an act of entrepreneurial discovery cannot be seen as justly belonging to its recipient simply by virtue of his resource ownership (any more than the output of an entrepreneurial producer can be seen as simply the automatic transformation of the inputs over which he had control).

All this supports, surely, my contention that theories of justice which recognize none of these aspects of discovery in capitalist incomes— aspects which form the grist for any finders-keepers rule—are ignoring not only the category of pure entrepreneurial profit, but also the true character of all capitalist incomes, including resource incomes as they occur in fact under real world conditions of open-ended uncertainty.

THE DISCOVERY ELEMENT IN PRODUCTION— SOME FURTHER REMARKS

Our discussion of the discovery element inevitably to be found in every real world production decision may perhaps help us to understand why the literature of economic justice has unfortunately ignored the broad relevance of a finders-keepers rule. Why is it, one wonders, that production is treated as if each decision to produce is made in a clockwork-like world without surprises? Why is it that resource incomes are treated as if the proper niche for each unit of each productive resource is clearly identified and apparent to all, as if its appropriate market value is somehow a self-evident fact obvious to all? Much of the answer to these questions is perhaps to be found in the distinction between an *ex ante* and *ex post* perspective on market activity.

When one observes the flow of economic events it is extraordinarily easy to overlook the *ex ante* uncertainty that surrounds each market decision. From an *ex post* perspective, the context of past decision making may appear far less problematical than it appeared at the moment of decision. *Ex post* it seems easy to ascribe output to inputs. After all, the truth was that inputs did produce output. So that, with the benefit of hindsight, it may well seem obvious that earlier control over inputs did indeed guarantee the emergence of output. Thus, *ex post* it may well appear to be the case that a decision to produce was nothing more than the "pressing of a go-button," the granting of permission for the input-embryo to mature costlessly into the output into which it has effortlessly become transformed. One may not realize, from this *ex post* perspective, how uncertain the future in fact appeared at the moment of decision, how unsure one was of being able to achieve a desired goal with the inputs to which one had possible access, how unsure one was concerning the value of such a possible goal, how unsure one was over whether one indeed had access to the necessary inputs, and so on.

Quite similarly, once a resource owner has indeed converted units of his resources into resource income, it may be easy to forget the doubts which had earlier befogged the resource owner's vision (or which *should* have befogged that vision!). After all, an employer has, it can now be clearly seen, paid a definite wage for a day's work. It seems obvious that, at the beginning of the day, the laborer was confronted with the simple option of either enjoying a day's leisure or working for this definite wage. But, again, what can now be seen to have occurred was not always the obvious course which the (then) future must inevitably take. At the beginning of the day the possibilities were numerous and not always precisely perceived. The choice actually made was by no means the only wise choice that could have been made. What appears wholly non-entrepreneurial from the perspective of today, may have been thoroughly conjectural from yesterday's perspective.

So that that which was grasped yesterday in an insightful and imaginative expression of entrepreneurial alertness and conviction, may today appear to have called for no foresight and vision at all. Looking back at resource incomes, these appear to have involved not a single ounce of discovery; looking back at pure profits won in the course of buying and reselling, these appear to have been won only by the entrepreneur somehow misleading both the buyers and sellers with whom he has been dealing. It is perhaps understandable that so much of the literature of economic justice has thus simply overlooked the discovery element, not only in resource incomes, but even in the winning of pure entrepreneurial profit.

Yet our discussions should have shown that a narrowly *ex post* perspective may be profoundly misleading. If a finders-keepers rule is considered to be meaningful at all, it should now be clear that such a rule holds relevance for virtually every single income receipt under the capitalist market system. It is by broadening one's vision to comprehend the *ex ante* uncertainty that envelops decision making of all kinds, that one can grasp the discovery character of virtually every action taken, and every outcome achieved. From the point of view of the ethical observer seeking to appraise the justice of capitalist incomes, all this may be of extremely high significance. From such a point of view the realities of the market must be appreciated in their complete fullness, rather than in terms of models which find it analytically useful to abstract from certain features of reality. What may, for the purposes of positive economic theory, be an efficient simplifying assumption, may turn out, for the purposes of ethical appraisal, to be highly misleading distortion of reality. Surely the open-ended uncertainty which has been excluded from equilibrium models of markets, has had the effect of deflecting attention from the discovery character of just about every income receipt in the market system.

WHAT A FINDERS-KEEPERS RULE WOULD MEAN FOR THE JUSTICE OF CAPITALISM

As announced at the outset of this chapter, I postpone all discussion of the ethics of finders-keepers to chapter 6. In this chapter we have confined our attention to the meaning and scope of a finders-keepers rule—were such a rule to be held ethically meaningful and acceptable. We are now, after the rather prolix examination of these matters in the present chapter, in a position to review the importance of a finders-keepers rule (if accepted) for any appraisal of capitalist justice. Acceptance of a finders-keepers rule must, it is now apparent, entail extensive implications for capitalism. Acceptance of the rule could sharply modify the degree of reliance which a defense of capitalist justice need place upon entitlement arguments. Moreover, acceptance of the rule can permit more than reinforcement of entitlement arguments where these latter appear vulnerable to challenge; the rule would offer a defense of capitalist income assignments at levels where an entitlement approach has no relevance at all, or where an entitlement approach, taken on its own, could in fact serve to challenge the justice of capitalist assignment of income. A reasonable pairing of an entitlement approach and a finders-keepers approach appears to offer a powerful case for capitalist justice.

First, a finders-keepers rule provides a fresh basis for original acquisition from nature. As such the rule can figure as one of the foundation stones upon which an entitlement approach can be constructed. A finders-keepers approach can nourish the fundamental private property ethic upon which the capitalist system must ultimately depend.

Second, the rule provides a direct defense of the legitimacy of pure entrepreneurial profit. The rule effectively defends such profit against claims of mistake which might plausibly be raised to question the justice of title to pure profits.

Third, the rule provides a rationale for the justice of resource incomes which parallels that provided by the entitlement approach, but which goes significantly beyond it. As discussed at length, each receipt of income through sale of resource service can be perceived to partake of the character of a discovery. Not only, therefore, may the resource owner claim just title to that income by virtue of his private property entitlement to that resource (and thus to the market quid pro quo offered in exchange for its productive services), he may, on the finders-keepers rule, argue that his title to the income is reinforced by that rule; he is entitled to the market proceeds resulting from the sale of his resource services because it was he who in fact discovered the opportunity (both for those to whom he sells and for himself) constituted by such possibility of sale. The entrepreneurial element, great or small, present in the sale of resource services thus finds its justification in the application of the finders-keepers rule to such sale.

Taken together these three implications of the finders-keepers rule go far towards revolutionizing discussion in regard to capitalist justice. Moreover, a finders-keepers rule can be seen as offering the market incentives for making socially valuable discoveries at all levels.

It is not only the case, then, that a finders-keepers rule provides a defense of the manner in which capitalism slices and distributes the pie which it produces; this rule can be seen to be responsible, in significant measure, for the size of the pie available for distribution. As argued briefly in earlier chapters[11] the point here is more than the (widely under-stood) circumstance that the size of the total pie depends on its mode of distribution. Rather, my point here is that the very *concept* of a pie-waiting-to-be-distributed turns out, from a discovery perspective, to be fundamen-tally flawed. The pie which, from the *ex post* perspective, will have been shared out in the capitalist income distribution process is a pie which in no sense can be held to have "existed" in the factors of production in prin-ciple known to be available to society. Society's pie turns out to be one the size and composition of which are discovered, "created," in the course of the entrepreneurial capitalist process itself. A finders-keepers rule is not a distributive incentive procedure cleverly devised to draw the most out of given resources with given productive capacity; it is a procedure with the incentive potential of stimulating discoveries that could other-wise in no way be predicted. The rule can be counted upon to reveal the availability of resources that might otherwise never have been noticed; it can be counted upon to reveal valuable uses of known resources that might otherwise have gone unglimpsed. The rule can be counted upon not only to uncover unsuspected resources and unsuspectedly produc-tive engineering uses for these resources; the rule can also be counted upon to reveal social configurations of supply and demand, of need, and of availability, that, taken together, can radically enhance the social value of society's known resources, even in regard to their already-known engi-neering productive capabilities.

THE FINDERS-KEEPERS ETHIC AND THE LONG RUN

Although I have been at great pains to draw attention to the discovery ele-ment in every sale of resource service (as in every deliberate real world act of production) this has of course not meant that resource incomes are to be seen as *pure* discoveries. The only income that corresponds to pure dis-covery is the analytical category of pure profits. Resource incomes present aspects both of discoveries and of simple entitlement-generated resource proceeds, depending on the significance of the disequilibrium and the uncertainty that characterize particular resource markets. My criticism earlier in this chapter, of the way in which the standard literature on jus-tice has treated resource incomes as simply the market value of owned

11. See above, ch. 1, pp. 17–19, and ch. 3, pp. 67–69.

resource services, was focused on that literature's failure to see *any* discovery element in these incomes. But, I conceded readily, where market conditions have achieved a stability so pronounced and well-recognized that resource owners do feel themselves virtually assured of a given, uncertainty-free income obtainable in exchange for their resource services, the traditional literature may be fully justified in abstracting from possible residual elements of discovery. In typical real world cases the theorist of justice must recognize both those features of resource incomes that are relevant for a finders-keepers ethic, and those that are relevant for a pure entitlement ethic. It would be as serious an error to ignore the entitlement-relevant features of real world resource incomes, as I have argued it to be to disregard their important discovery features. Any defense of capitalist justice will certainly be able to appeal to ethical principles besides those that stem from the discovery features of real world capitalism.

I wish to point out, in concluding this chapter, that the extent to which discovery elements (and consequently a finders-keepers rule, if accepted) are to be considered significant in an ethical appraisal of capitalist justice, may vary over time. At one particular time the degree of instability, disequilibrium, and open-ended uncertainty prevailing in markets may be so great as to make a finders-keepers rule overwhelmingly relevant; at other specific times, particular markets may have evolved to so stable a state as to render a finders-keepers rule of only marginal relevance in the appraisal of capitalist justice. The direction of likely change can hardly be systematically predicted without strain or ambiguity.

On the one hand, economic theory has placed great emphasis on its conclusion that typical markets, upon receiving an external shock, tend to gravitate more or less rapidly to a new equilibrium in response to the external change. This would suggest that different markets, at different times, will exhibit varying degrees of discovery relevance and consequently of finders-keepers relevance—but that there are constant forces at work to erode and curtail the importance of these finders-keepers-relevant features.

On the other hand, it seems reasonable to point out what may well be a fairly systematic long run tendency in precisely the opposite direction. Historically, the development of capitalist economies has consistently been in the direction of greater economic wealth, higher income, and more complex structures of production and interrelationship of markets. The proliferation of new production, new technologies, and newly discovered sources of input services has, quite typically, occurred at an increasingly rapid pace. The business environment generated by this character of markets has tended to be one more and more suggesting, not stability, but opportunity; not equilibrium, but open-ended uncertainty. Not only has this historical trend generated an environment and a climate that has set entrepreneurial juices to running at increasing rates of ingenious innovation, it has tended sharply to increase the range of options available to owners of resources, and has opened up for them new possibilities of creating or discovering new uses for their services. A young person who is finishing high school these days must surely exercise a capacity for entrepreneurial discovery, in order to develop his or her productive capacities to the utmost, to a degree far more complicated and fraught with unknowns than would have been the case for earlier generations.

So that, from the perspective of this book, a plausible case can be made that as capitalism progresses, an appraisal of the justice of its income assignments must more and more take note of the discovery elements that surround all decisions made in the system. If there is some justification for the traditional neglect of the scope of a finders-keepers rule in treating the justice of capitalism, it is to be found, just possibly, in the circumstance that the capitalist system, in earlier times and particularly in the nineteenth century, tended to demand far less, entrepreneurially speaking, from resource owners' decisions than is the case today. The more affluent the market economy becomes, the greater the variety of its productive offerings, the richer the arrays of possible employments that might be found for given resource services, the greater the significance of discovery insights—and the greater the relevance of a finders-keepers rule, were such a rule to be accepted.

It is against the background of this understanding of the scope of finders-keepers considerations, that we must now turn, in chapter 6, to examine widely shared ethical intuitions in order to assess the plausibility and acceptability of a finders-keepers ethic.

6. THE ETHICS OF FINDERS-KEEPERS

Throughout this book I have endeavored to highlight the discovery element that, in my view, provides the dynamic force to market processes. And I have repeatedly promised to show that acceptance of the discovery character of market processes permits, or even entails, appreciation for a hitherto ignored ethical dimension of the market. I have again and again suggested that the discovery character of market processes points to the ethical feasibility of a finders-keepers rule in assessing the economic justice of capitalist income assignment. The present chapter has the task of fulfilling these promises and of elaborating on these suggestions. It will be useful to pause and reflect on what I do and what I do not expect to achieve in this chapter.

The first and foremost responsibility is to make clear that I will *not* be claiming that recognizing the entrepreneurial discovery that fuels the market process in and of itself entails any ethical convictions whatsoever. One may certainly be thoroughly convinced, on independent ethical grounds, that the finders should not necessarily be keepers, that discovery confers title upon the discoverer to no claims against others or against society in general. Recognizing the key role played by discovery in driving the market process need not cause any modification of these ethical convictions. Understanding that the competitive market is a process of discovery is a matter of positive economics—something to be recognized regardless of how one appraises the ethical aspects and implications of discovery. Lessons learned in positive economics need entail no modification in one's standards for normative-ethical appraisal. My position will be, however, that *given* fairly generally shared ethical intuitions concerning discovery and its consequences, it should follow, in practice, that arriving at an understanding of the capitalist process as constituting one of discovery *will* generally entail appreciation for ethical features of the capitalist system that might otherwise easily be overlooked. My task in this chapter will therefore not be to teach a new ethics, or, for that matter, any ethics at all. It is to show how the ethical foundation needed to provide grounding for a finders-keepers rule is *already* widely accepted. I believe that, given this foundation, the demonstrations in this book concerning the discovery character of market processes should indeed entail, for many critical observers of capitalism, ethical conclusions about capitalism that they may otherwise very easily have missed.

I set out in this chapter certainly not to persuade anyone of the compelling ethical character of a finders-keepers rule. I have no wish *to establish* that ethical foundation to which I have referred as being already widely accepted. It is quite enough for me simply to point out that this foundation *is* widely accepted—without even seriously asking myself whether I wish to share in that acceptance. This chapter should not, therefore, be seen as an essay in moral philosophy, but as an exercise in the application of what I believe to be a widely-shared point of view within everyman's moral philosophy. We shall return to this point very soon.

My second responsibility is to repeat that, in calling for recognition of the ethical implications of discovery for appraisals of capitalist justice, I am emphatically not treating justice as coextensive with morality. If my discovery perspective leads me to defend capitalist assignment of incomes against charges of injustice, this certainly does not provide a complete defense of the morality of such income assignments, let alone of the capitalist system as a whole. To be sure, some discussions of justice treat this theme differently.[1] For them, to pronounce an inequality as just is to declare it free of all moral taint. To detect any morally undesirable implication of inequality may be enough to pronounce it unjust. There may not be much point to definitional disputes on this matter. But for me, it seems better to deal with moral issues one at a time, disentangling lines of argument from one another insofar as they appeal to different (but not necessarily incompatible) moral criteria. In appealing to the reader's intuitions in support of a finders-keepers rule, I shall therefore not be appealing to his intuitions concerning the overall morality of such a rule. I shall merely be asking the reader to acknowledge that such a rule provides, for a possibly long and arduous journey in applied moral analysis, a convenient and acceptable first stopping point, a reasonably secure transit point from which to consider what the next step in the analysis should be, and where it is likely to lead. To declare a finders-keepers rule just is to recognize that such a rule gets us, morally speaking, to a stage whence we can hope, possibly, to proceed further. So long as we do not delude ourselves that this first stopping

1. This seems particularly to be the case for Kai Nielsen, *Equality and Liberty, a Defense of Radical Egalitarianism* (Totowa, N.J.: Rowman and Allanheld, 1985).

point represents, necessarily, our final destination, we can benefit greatly by treating this first step as distinct from subsequent steps in the journey.

My third and final prefatory disclaimer best takes the form of an acknowledgment. The moral insights I claim to achieve on the basis of understanding the market as a discovery procedure, take for granted the basic acceptability of key features of the entitlement theory of justice developed by Robert Nozick. My insights are to be seen as, so to speak, riding piggyback upon Nozick's entitlement theory. Despite the large critical literature that has grown up around Nozick's work, it seems to us that the basic features of that theory are still capable of commanding widespread assent. While I hope to show that at least some features of a finders-keepers ethic are consistent also with certain crucially *non-*Nozickian intuitions, it remains the case that a finders-keepers ethic must, ultimately, appeal to the same basic notions of rights and the role of just property rights in a theory of justice, that nourish Nozick's own theory. This acknowledgment carries with it benefits and costs. Acknowledging the fundamental character of Nozick's theory means that I can, on many matters, refer to Nozick's argumentation. I can focus on the marginal contribution I wish to make to the moral appraisal of capitalism, without myself having to set forth the full philosophical foundations of the results I propose to attain. But, at the same time, my dependency upon Nozick might seem to imply that those who have *not* accepted the Nozickian theory will have little to gain from this chapter. It might appear that my standing on the shoulders of Nozick renders my results of no interest for those who have convinced themselves that Nozick's theory is a morally empty one. This would be, in my view, unfortunate, since at least part of my conclusions may be held to reinforce, to shield from apparently damaging criticism, the very Nozickian foundations to which I will be referring as settled authority. It is just possible that those skeptical of certain conclusions of Nozick, may find these conclusions more plausible once they are viewed from the perspective I introduce in this chapter.

ON THE ROLE OF MORAL INTUITIONS

As indicated I shall be appealing, throughout this chapter, to the moral intuitions of the reader. I shall be claiming that a finders-keepers rule can be shown to be consistent with widely shared moral intuitions. The possibility of employing such moral intuitions in constructing a theory of justice has been debated in recent years. Whether termed "moral intu-itions," "considered judgments," or "convictions," these "ordinary, unre-flective moral beliefs"[2] have, by Rawls[3] and others,[4] been held to play an important role in arriving at a "reflective equilibrium." This reflective equilibrium will consist of acceptance both of specific, substantive con-victions, and of a set of principles which render these convictions coher-ent. The reflective equilibrium method in moral philosophy has been described as: "starting with our initial considered convictions, we go back and forth between considered conviction, moral principles, . . . modifying a theoretical claim here, pruning a considered judgment there, abandon-ing a putative principle or background belief here, until we achieve a state of affairs in which our considered judgments, duly pruned and adjusted, match with our principles and theories."[5] Other philosophers have, how-ever, been skeptical of placing such reliance on our untutored convictions and intuitions. In their view, moral principles ought to be hammered out independently of our unprincipled beliefs. In their view placing reliance on moral intuitions represents "politics masquerading as philosophy."[6]

But my procedure, in this chapter, of appealing to widely shared moral intuitions is perhaps less vulnerable to such criticism. As stated, I am not, in this chapter, engaged in moral philosophy; I am probing the moral philosophy of my readers. I am not so much seeking to show the ethical superiority of a finders-keepers rule, as to show that, given widely shared ethical positions, a finders-keepers rule should be acknowledged as con-sistent with those positions. I am not, in fact, engaged in the method of reaching a reflective equilibrium (in which beliefs and intuitions may be pruned here and there), I am simply engaged in exploring the moral implications of widely shared beliefs—pruned or unpruned as they may already be.

2. Ronald Dworkin, *Taking Rights Seriously* (Cambridge: Harvard University Press, 1977), p. 155.

3. John Rawls, *A Theory of Justice* (Cambridge: Harvard University Press, 1971), pp. 47ff.

4. See K. Nielsen, op. cit., pp. 24–38.

5. Ibid., p. 26.

6. R. M. Hare, "Liberty and equality: how politics masquerades as philosophy," in E. F. Paul, F. D. Miller Jr., and J. Paul (eds.), *Liberty and Equality* (Oxford: Basil Black-well, 1985), p. 5.

THE NOZICKIAN FOUNDATIONS

Rightly or wrongly, most people, it seems to me, have a strong sense of property, and their sense of justice is firmly rooted in the conviction that justly held title to property is possible, and may not, under ordinary circumstances, be violated without injustice. Now it could be that this sense of property and its link to widely shared conceptions of justice, represents not a moral stance founded upon sound philosophical reflection, but one that stems entirely from custom-thought, or from bourgeois class interests, psychological aberration induced by the moral debilitation of capitalism, faulty reasoning, or whatever. For us it does not really matter. It is enough that this moral stance is a widely shared one. It is surely to this view of things that Nozick's articulation of his entitlement theory of justice appeals so strongly.[7] For this view the possibility and moral propriety of just title is so primordial and so important for the integrity of the individual that its protection from attack is seen to call for a distinct moral sense—the sense of justice. It is for this reason that a society in which the norms for just acquisition and for just transfer have been scrupulously respected, must be seen as a just society—regardless of the other moral failings from which it may indeed suffer.

The moral sense that just title to holdings, whether held privately or in common, may not be invaded without injustice, is indeed so widespread

7. And it is to this view that the so-called "economic analysis of rights," associated with the work of Ronald Coase and Harold Demsetz, appears, despite its elegance and explanatory power, so counter-intuitive. The economic analysis of rights (EAR) "seeks to discern which assignment of rights in the real world of costly and impacted bargaining best approximates the attainment of efficiency, that Pareto-optimal situation which would obtain in the frictionless world of costless bargaining" (Charles Fried, *Right and Wrong* [Cambridge: Harvard University Press, 1978], p. 92). In this utilitarian approach to rights, "rights are assigned *instrumentally*, in order to procure the efficiency as a consequence" (ibid., p. 97). As Fried points out, "What is striking about this approach is the sundering of ethical decisions from decisions about rights" (ibid., p. 96). The economic analysis of rights offers a rich source for explaining remarkably well historical events in regard to property institutions. But the widespread ethical approach to property is simply not prepared to surrender its convictions regarding the moral basis to the history of property. "EAR offers plenty of good reasons for those assignments of rights which seem intuitively clear to us, but the reasons have nothing to do with the inherent 'rightness' . . . or the 'wickedness' [of the positions of victims of civil wrongs and of those of the wrongdoers]" (ibid., p. 98).

that even those who seek to abolish private property (on the basis of arguments concerning justice) sometimes rest their case on this very sense. John Roemer, in developing his carefully reasoned Marxist opposition to the institution of private property, traces a good deal of alleged capitalist exploitation to "robbery and plunder," exemplified by the enclosure movement which disenfranchised the yeoman peasant who had "had access to the commons and a small herd, and perhaps a small plot of land of his own."[8]

From the perspective of this moral sense a great deal of weight comes, indeed, to be placed precisely on that moral imperative that excludes robbery and plunder, in other words on strictly just dealing. What Nozick's theory has done is to focus with exclusive intensity upon the possibility of a society in which individual holdings have, from the very beginning, at every step, eschewed robbery and plunder. Where this has been achieved, Nozick argues, injustice is necessarily absent. If no one has acquired holdings unjustly, the results can hardly be pronounced unjust. It is upon this "historical" notion of justice, a notion built on the conception of a past without unjust acquisition of holdings, that I shall be depending for most of what follows in this chapter.

To be sure, accepting the importance of avoidance of robbery and plunder does not, in logic, commit one to the Nozickian lingustic usage which confines the meaning of "injustice" exclusively to robbery and plunder (and their equivalents). Robbery may be one form of injustice; perhaps there are others. Perhaps failing to share one's wealth equally with others is injustice, too. But it seems to be the case that for most of us, there is a profound difference between the moral revulsion one feels in regard to robbery and plunder of that which is rightfully another's, and whatever moral outrage one may feel about a refusal to share one's wealth equally with others (or to see to it that others so share their wealth), or about other possible ethical failings. Antony Flew was surely not totally off the mark, linguistically speaking, when he forcefully challenged use

---

8. J. Roemer, *Free to Lose: An Introduction to Marxist Economic Philosophy* (Cambridge: Harvard University Press, 1988), p. 58. As Roemer makes clear, this point was, of course, made most forcefully by Marx. Marx had poured scorn on "idyllic" accounts of primitive accumulation of capital. "In actual history it is notorious that conquest, enslavement, robbery . . . play the great part." K. Marx, *Capital, A Critique of Political Economy* (New York: International Publishers, 1967), p. 714.

of the term "justice" to describe "the business of enforcing equality of outcome."[9] For perhaps most of us, Rawls's use of the term justice to describe the set of moral imperatives to which his theory points, is indeed a rather forced terminology. Kai Nielsen may be on solid lexicographical ground affirming (*contra* Flew) that the term "justice" *may* legitimately be applied to additional moral concerns besides that of eschewing violations of just entitlements.[10] But the truth remains that there does seem to be a widespread sense that it is important to distinguish sharply between the desirability of protesting against robbery and plunder, and the desirability of other moral and ethical achievements.[11] Use of the term "justice" in Nozick's sense, respects and reflects this widespread sense. I shall, without further apology, be concerned to explore the implications of this widespread use of language, and this widespread sense of moral distinction. What I hope to show is that, in the light of the discovery insights developed in earlier chapters, this sense of moral distinctions implies substantive conclusions defending capitalist justice, that go significantly beyond Nozick's own account. The issues involved go to the heart of the justice of the institution of private property.

THE BASIS FOR JUST INDIVIDUAL HOLDINGS

I shall be arguing that, within a Nozickian entitlement theory of justice, discovery does tend, in the eyes of many, to confer just title to holdings. My argument will rely upon certain intuitions concerning just title which are certainly not confined to those recognizing the validity of the entitlement theory. In fact, these intuitions appear to be crucially important for a variety of quite different theories of justice, non-Nozickian as well as Nozickian.

What appears to be accepted in common by all these different theories of justice is that, in order for an individual to have a just claim to a certain holding, he must be able, in principle, to establish some differential link to that holding that sets him significantly apart from others. He must, for example, have produced it, or have mixed his labor with it, or have

---

9. Antony Flew, *The Politics of Procrustes* (Buffalo: Prometheus Books, 1981), p. 83.

10. K. Nielsen, op. cit., p. 11.

11. No doubt the term "robbery and plunder" can be stretched to cover any refusal to adjust one's holdings to *any* specified morally suggested pattern of distribution. But, once again, this is not the ordinary way in which such terms are used.

invented or authored it, or have worked so hard in regard to it that he is deemed to have deserved it. A fundamental objection to the institution of private property in fact stems from the claim that such special links differentiating one individual's relationship with nature-given endowments significantly enough from that of others can*not* be shown to be plausible. The demand always to be made concerning John Doe's claim to a piece of private property is that he shall demonstrate the morally significant way in which that piece of property should be *his* (rather than someone else's, or no one's, or everyone's).

Arguments for egalitarianism—except for those varieties of egalitarianism for which the imperative of equality of outcome is the "bedrock" of moral intuition[12]—are typically based in one way or another on the presumption that such morally significant linkage cannot be established. Those rebutting this egalitarian presumption argue for a variety of such possible linkages. In presenting the entitlement rebuttal to egalitarianism, one (egalitarian) philosopher put this rebuttal as follows:

> Goods to be distributed do not come down, like manna from heaven; they come with entitlements. Certain people have produced them, bought them, been given them, inherited them, found them, struggled to make them and to preserve them. To think that we can override their entitlements in setting out ideal distributive patterns is to fail to respect the people.[13]

An entitlement theory must, first of all, establish the persuasiveness of the entitlement claims upon which its theory rests. I wish, in this chapter, to focus on one phrase in the above list ("Certain people have . . . found them . . ."); I believe that the entitlement claim based on this phrase has been grossly understated. I shall argue that, when John Doe has found something—a seashell, a profit opportunity, or whatever—this establishes, if widespread moral intuitions are to be consistently applied, a morally significant linkage upon which a valid entitlement claim can rely. But we must first consider some more explicitly understood linkages, in particular the very first in the above list ("Certain people have produced them . . .").

---

12. See, e.g., Nielsen, op. cit., pp. 7–8.
13. Ibid., p. 63.

PRODUCTION AS A SOURCE OF JUST ENTITLEMENT

There is no doubt, indeed, that for many people the person who has produced an item is its rightful owner. It is surely because of this that one virtually unchallenged principle of distributive justice is held to call for distribution according to productive contribution. As Milton Friedman has pointed out, "Even the severest internal critics of capitalism have implicitly accepted payment in accordance with product as ethically fair."[14] Capitalism, in the eyes of Marxist critics, is exploitative and unfair precisely because in their view "labor produced the whole of the product but got only part of it . . ."[15] If one views output as having been produced, morally speaking, by that labor alone, this means that one sees that output as having been originated entirely by that labor. The laborer has, therefore, established an absolute claim to just title over what owes its existence entirely to his efforts. If one sees output as having been produced, morally speaking, not by labor alone, but by labor in combination with other productive resources and tools of production, then this leads directly to Milton Friedman's capitalist ethic: "To each according to what he and the instruments he owns produces."[16] To be sure the circumstance that production requires the cooperative contributions of many persons, as laborers, landowners, capitalists, and entrepreneurs, is responsible for the problem of distributing the product among those who have jointly produced it. This is the problem of disentangling the separate contributions made by the various components of the productive team. This has indeed been responsible for much controversy and doubt; but all of the controversy and doubt stem precisely from this commonly accepted moral premise, that the output rightfully belongs to those who have produced it.

But the very nature of production has contributed to a certain apparent weakness, something of an Achilles' heel, in the moral case for production as the root of ownership. Production consists in the transformation of inputs into output. Whether one identifies "the producer" as the owner of the inputs which eventually constitute the output, or as the pure

14. Milton Friedman, *Capitalism and Freedom* (Chicago: University of Chicago Press, 1962), p. 167.

15. Ibid., p. 167.

16. Ibid., pp. 161f.

entrepreneur who, himself owning no inputs, assembles them to generate the product[17]—the justice of the producer's claim to ownership of the product is hostage to the legitimacy of his control over those inputs. Production achieved through the deployment of stolen resources cannot confer just title to the product. The moral case for ownership rooted in production is necessarily an incomplete one; it requires supplementation by a theory of just entitlement to productive resources.

Entitlement theorists have, of course, well understood this challenge; they have vigorously asserted the possibility of just entitlement to productive resources. In fact they have almost reversed the sequence of reasoning. It is not so much that a production ethic requires to be supplemented by a theory of resource entitlement, but that just ownership of resources (taken as the initially unquestioned point of departure) carries with it the moral case for producer-title. The producer's title to the product is derived from his title to the inputs.

But the matter of establishing just private title in resources is not a simple one. Consideration of this matter carries us very swiftly to the root of the problem of establishing just private title to "original" factors of production—to non-produced resources provided directly by nature. The moral case for ownership rooted in production must depend crucially upon a *non*-production theory of just title in nature-given resources.

As we shall see, my argument will be that a discovery (as against a production) theory of entitlement may be able to serve as the moral basis for an entitlement approach that encompasses not only produced goods, but, at the same time, the original, nature-given resources without which production cannot, ultimately, be imagined. Let us briefly survey the problems which moral philosophy has confronted in searching for a morally compelling basis for just title to nature-given productive resources. I shall discuss the two great classes of such resources, labor and land—labor representing the inborn talents and abilities of human agents of production, land representing the nature-given raw materials, implements, and energy sources, to which all output must ultimately be traced back. Our brief survey will prepare us for the sharp contrast I wish to draw between the discovery basis for entitlements on the one hand, and more conventional foundations for entitlements on the other.

17. Frank H. Knight, *Risk, Uncertainty and Profit* (New York: Houghton Mifflin, 1921), p. 271.

SELF-OWNERSHIP AND JUST ENTITLEMENT

There can be little doubt that most people feel an innate moral certainty concerning their right to the free exercise of their inborn talents and to the enjoyment of what they can attribute purely to their talents and their efforts. For most, indeed, these rights are likely to seem inseparable from their right to be respected as free individuals.[18] Such self-ownership rights, if recognized, must go far to support the entitlement view in recognizing produced output as being the justly owned property of its producer. Not only does the concept of self-ownership directly validate such title insofar as the product is to be attributed to the producer's own efforts (or the efforts of employees whose labor services he has hired in freely negotiated voluntary employment agreements), it is also crucial for the commonly cited theories of title to naturally endowed, original, physical resources. Thus, as we shall note, Lockean justifications for private land ownership, for example, depend on the legitimacy of the homesteader's title to the labor which he mixes with the nature-given resource.[19]

Egalitarians and, more generally, critics of the institution of private property, have indeed found it necessary to challenge most sharply this widely held notion of self-ownership. Quite apart from a certain philosophical propensity to believe that, absent all differences in nurture, acculturation, and opportunity, human characters and abilities would not in fact differ significantly (so that self-ownership could hardly by itself lead systematically to justified differences in holdings),[20] egalitarians have particularly emphasized the "moral arbitrariness" of genetically-based differences in human abilities and character. They have concluded, on the basis of such moral arbitrariness,[21] that self-ownership—conferring legitimate title to one's unique talents, abilities, and character traits—cannot itself be just. Thus for Rawls it is held to be "one of the fixed points of our considered judgments that no one deserves his place in the

18. See Murray N. Rothbard, *For a New Liberty: The Libertarian Manifesto* (rev. ed.; New York: Collier Books, 1978), pp. 28f.

19. See Richard A. Epstein, "Possession as the root of title," *Georgia Law Review*, 13, 1221 (1979), p. 1227.

20. See the carefully crafted arguments against meritocracy in K. Nielsen, op. cit., chs. 7, 8.

21. Ibid., p. 181; see also Roemer, op. cit., p. 154.

distribution of native endowment. . . ."[22] Because of this undeservedness of talent, Rawls argues, a system which permits human talents to determine distributive shares, cannot be a just one.

> The existing distribution of income and wealth . . . is the cumulative effect of prior distributions of natural assets—that is, natural talents and abilities—as these have been developed or left unrealized, and their use favored or disfavored over time by social circumstances and such chance contingencies as accident and good fortune. Intuitively the most obvious injustice of the system of natural liberty is that it permits distributive shares to be improperly influenced by these factors so arbitrary from a moral point of view.[23]

Nozick has carefully dissected the reasoning which links the moral arbitrariness of genetic endowments with the claimed injustice of a system which permits reward to talent and character. He concludes that Rawls reaches his conclusion by having rather narrow and rigid views concerning (1) the source for a person's autonomous choices, and (2) the legitimacy of self-ownership. Rawls attributes *all* human choices, it appears, to an undeserved genetic heritage and undeserved family and social circumstances. This leaves very little to be chalked up to the credit of a person's own autonomy and responsibility. As Nozick remarks: "So denigrating a person's autonomy and prime responsibility for his actions is a risky line to take for a theory that otherwise wishes to buttress the dignity and self-respect of autonomous beings."[24] More importantly, Nozick concludes that Rawls views the distribution or natural abilities as a "collective asset": "everyone has some entitlement or claim on the totality of natural assets (viewed as a pool), with no one having differential claims."[25] In other words, self-ownership is, fundamentally, inconsistent with Rawlsian justice.

So that the dispute around self-ownership comes down to the question of whether the moral arbitrariness surrounding a person's natural endowments and innate qualities justifies our treating those qualities as part of a resource pool belonging to the entire human race. If all human resources

22. Rawls, op. cit., p. 104.
23. Ibid., p. 72.
24. Nozick, op. cit., p. 124.
25. Ibid., p. 228.

are treated as a collective asset of the human race, one's notion of the individual becomes, of course, severely attenuated: the individual must be thought of as abstracted from all his socially valuable personal qualities. As Nozick comments, the Rawlsian position "presses *very* hard on the distinction between men and their talents, assets, abilities, and special traits. Whether any coherent conception of a person remains when the distinction is so pressed is an open question."[26] But, on the other hand, Nozick has very little to offer in direct contradiction of the charge that the moral arbitrariness of natural endowments does in fact erode the legitimacy of self-ownership. By *not* pressing the distinction between men and their talents, Nozick is led towards a self-ownership position. And this does (*contra* Rawls's considered judgment) certainly cohere with widely shared moral convictions concerning the integrity of the individual. Yet we have not been given any *reason* to accept this (bedrock?) position, that the natural assets associated, however loosely, with a person's body, are exclusively his own. Why *should* these natural assets be treated differently from other, non-human, nature-given resources? Let us take note of the problem of establishing private ownership in nature-given physical resources.

ESTABLISHING TITLE TO NATURE-GIVEN PHYSICAL RESOURCES

The major problem facing entitlement theories is undoubtedly that of accounting for the initial private acquisition from nature of original resources. How does a piece of land, or even an acorn, which was initially not mine (even if it was not anyone else's either) become my private property? What action of mine can suddenly impose upon others the moral imperative to respect my ownership rights in what had hitherto not been mine? The traditional justifications have relied heavily on Locke's labor theory of initial acquisition. Locke relied, in turn, on the assumption of self-ownership. The only problem for Locke was that of explaining how unowned physical resources held in common by all mankind[27] can be

---

26. Ibid. (Italics in original.)

27. On the question of whether Locke assumed that, in the state of nature, resources were unowned, or owned in common by all, or simply "held in common," see Epstein, op. cit., pp. 1229f.; Onora O'Neill, "Nozick's Entitlements," *Inquiry* (Winter 1976), reprinted in J. Paul (ed.), *Reading Nozick* (Totowa: Rowman and Littlefield, 1981), p. 316.

annexed by the individual. Self-ownership in one's labor power provides the Lockean solution.

Though the earth and all inferior creatures be common to all men, runs the famous passage,

> yet every man has a property in his own person; this nobody has any right to but himself. The labour of his body and the work of his hands we may say are properly his. Whatsoever, then, he removes out of the state that nature hath provided and left it in, he hath mixed his labour with, and joined to it something that is his own, and thereby makes it his property.[28]

Much ink has been poured in efforts to explicate the moral philosophy underlying Locke's theory. These efforts were made all the more complicated (especially for its relevance as a defense for capitalist property institutions) by the famous Lockean proviso, with which Locke circumscribed his thesis. Mixing one's labor with an unowned natural object does not ensure just title under *all* circumstances, the Lockean fine print spells out—only "where there is enough, and as good left in common for others."[29]

It is fair to say that contemporary discussion has, at the least, been skeptical concerning the Lockean theory. Quite apart from challenges to the self-ownership premise, critics have severely questioned the simple assumption that joining one's labor to an unowned object constitutes a morally acceptable final annexation of it, even under circumstances in which the Lockean proviso has been satisfied. Even stout defenders of capitalist private property have conceded severe doubts concerning the Lockean foundations. Thus Epstein found it difficult to see how my laboring upon a natural asset can bind the rest of the world. Who says that without the consent of the rest of the world I have the *right* to perform labor upon that which is not mine?[30] Nozick wonders "why isn't mixing what I own with what I don't own a way of losing what I own rather than a way of gaining what I don't? If I own a can of tomato juice and spill it in the sea . . . do I thereby come to own the sea, or have I foolishly dissipated my tomato juice?"[31]

---

28. John Locke, *An Essay concerning the True Original Extent and End of Civil Government*, section 27.

29. Ibid.

30. Epstein, op. cit., pp. 1227f.

31. Nozick, op. cit., pp. 174f.

We have reached something of an impasse. I have claimed that an entitlement approach conforms most closely to commonly held moral intuitions concerning property rights. Yet these intuitions appear to face fundamental difficulties. To the extent that a theory of property depends upon some notion of morally acceptable annexation from the state of nature, it appears to rest, somewhat uncritically and unsatisfactorily, on the premise of self-ownership. Moreover, even when we accept the self-ownership premise, the way to understanding the institution of private property under capitalism seems to be blocked not only by challenges based on the Lockean proviso, but also by a certain arbitrariness in the thesis of Lockean annexation-through-labor-mixing. I shall argue that these difficulties for the commonly held intuitions can be dispelled by giving attention to the role of discovery in the establishment of just title. Giving such attention will, I shall claim, point to the moral legitimacy of the finders-keepers rules, and go far to support the commonly held convictions concerning property rights. It will be helpful to take note of the sense in which contemporary discussion in moral philosophy concerning property rights implicitly denies scope for a discovery role.

ON GIVEN RESOURCES AND GIVEN PIES

Careful consideration of discussions concerning just acquisition from nature reveals rather clearly that almost invariably the unquestioned implicit assumption of the discussion has been that the item to be acquired is *already there*. The seashell is on the beach waiting to be picked; the forest land is there waiting to be homesteaded into arable farmland. The human talents and traits over which the self-ownership thesis asserts dominion are, from the moment of birth, neatly packaged somewhere in the personality of the individual with whom they are associated. It is here that I wish to take issue with entitlement theories. For entitlement theories, the discussions in the literature treat the world as initially existing on a platter, waiting to be appropriated. This has had profoundly important, although in my view unfortunate, implications for the ethical appraisal of the institution of private property. Entitlement theory sees, in the possibility of just original acquisition from nature, the basis for a just capitalism. This means that, in an ideal capitalist system based on just original acquisition and exclusively just subsequent transfer of titles, the subsequent outcomes, at all times, must be pronounced just—whatever the instantaneous patterns of wealth and/or income distribution may be, whatever may be the intergenerational pattern. What this means for an entitlement view of the world is surely the following. Not only the resources originally acquired from the state of nature in the early history of the system are seen as having been at that early date "already there," waiting to be appropriated. Also the streams of output that will flow from capitalist firms, households, and factories over all the subsequent centuries are to be seen as having already "been there"—admittedly only in inchoate, embryonic form. This claim may seem a strange one; let me elaborate.

In discussing the ethics of capitalist distribution of output, Nozick argued that the "situation is *not* one of something's getting made, and there being an open question of who is to get it. Things come into the world already attached to people having entitlements over them."[32] In other words, the entitlements which people have over productive resources entail corresponding entitlements to the products produced with these resources. In acquiring the original resources from the state of nature the primitive property owner is, ipso facto, acquiring title to all the outputs that, throughout future generations, can be exclusively attributed, directly or indirectly, to these presently acquired resources. In the totality of all original acquisitions from nature, then, there lie implicitly and embryonically the complete subsequent patterns of income and wealth distributions over all future time.

Of course it is recognized that in originally acquiring an acre of farmland by carving it out of primeval jungle, the primitive Lockean homesteader is not exactly committing himself, as yet, to production plans covering the distant future. He may not yet have decided whether or when his farmland will grow wheat or barley, or some other crop; whether this farmland will remain farmland for ever, or whether it will, succumbing to encroaching urbanization perhaps, at some future time become the site for an office skyscraper or apartment house. These decisions will only come to be made during the course of subsequent centuries of economic history. So that it might be argued, in defense of the entitlement literature, that while it may perhaps be charged with treating *resources* as being *there*, it should not be held guilty of treating subsequent *output* as being *there*, at the moment of original resource acquisition. Output

32. Ibid., p. 160.

emerges only after production decisions are made, possibly centuries after resources have been acquired from the state of nature. Yet, surely, for the entitlement view I have described, once these subsequent production decisions *are* made, they clarify and identify retrospectively the purposes which, explicitly or not, actuated the original pattern of acquisitions. The distributions of product which subsequently occur do turn out, once the production decisions are made over the subsequent centuries, to have been, in a sense, implied in the original acquisition.

Let us remember that the entitlement view seems to ascribe output entirely to the inputs from which it is fabricated. (It was for this reason that the entitlement view saw each unit of output as coming into the world bearing an ownership tag—that identifying the owners of the inputs used in production.) This, it will be recalled from chapter 2, is the view which sees production as being *pure* production. In pure production, it will be recalled, command over inputs ensures command over output; output is already inherent in the inputs. Once one has command over inputs, the emergence of output is, given the decision to produce, inevitable. While a given mix of inputs might, under alternative decision-making scenarios, have yielded different output, *each* of these alternatives was, in a sense, implicit in the input mix. The subsequent decision rejecting all these alternative production plans necessarily brought to a sharp focus the only remaining production possibility. Once this decision has been taken, then, we can recognize, in retrospect, that the output that subsequently rolls off the assembly lines was indeed *already there,* in the originally acquired input mix. What is true of any one subsequent decision, with respect to one bundle of inputs, is true of all the myriads of decisions over subsequent history, with respect to all the resources originally acquired from nature over that history. Not only were the resources there, the flow of society's outputs over the centuries, too, were there. If the history of production is the unrolling of a tapestry that, at least from the *ex post* perspective, is seen as having been waiting to be extracted from owned inputs, then the distribution pattern depicted in that tapestry was a pattern in which a given output pie was being sliced up, at the moment of original input acquisition.[33]

---

33. Loren Lomasky recently took Bruce Ackerman to task for implicitly taking a similarly restrictive perspective. Ackerman (*Social Justice in the Liberal State* [New

That all this is implied in the entitlement theory underscores our claim that this theory, like the other theories in the literature of property rights,[34] has ignored the possibility of discovery in production and in original acquisition. It will be recalled from chapter 2 that the discovery element in real world production sets such a real world entirely apart from the model of pure production. Once we admit the discovery element into production we recognize that command over inputs by no means ensures command over output. Each decision is a creative act, a leap of faith expressing the decision maker's vision of an essentially uncertain future. Inputs by themselves do not ensure the production of anything—certainly not of anything valuable. What finally does emerge from the decision to deploy inputs cannot, even *ex post*, be attributed entirely to those inputs. It must be seen as the fruit of the purely entrepreneurial decision to permit those inputs to be combined and be put to work in the way they were. Yet that purely entrepreneurial decision to which realized output is to be attributed cannot itself be seen as an input. Entrepreneurship is not

---

Haven: Yale University Press, 1980], pp. 31f.) offered a "spaceship" story in which the voyagers come upon a new world containing one single scarce productive resource, manna. Recognizing that the scarce manna can set off power struggles, the voyagers proceed to discuss the question of initial distribution. They conclude that the morally indicated pattern of initial distribution is one of simple equality. Lomasky criticizes Ackerman ("Has Ackerman rigged the story? Yes . . ."), and proceeds to list features of the story which render it less than useful in appraising private appropriation of unowned natural resources. One of Lomasky's points is "The manna is just *there*. It has not been grown by anyone from manna seeds, dug by anyone from manna mines, caught in manna nets, or raised from manna pups. Manna is, after all, manna" (Loren Lomasky, *Persons, Rights, and the Moral Community* [New York and Oxford: University of Oxford Press, 1987, pp. 132f.]). Our point is that even that which is produced from manna, too, is in the relevant sense, already present, from the very start, in the manna, waiting to be distributed. Slicing up the given manna pie is, ipso facto, slicing up the output-from-manna pie.

34. Although our discussion in this section has focused critically on the entitlement theory, its main critical thrust applies equally to a Rawlsian approach. For Rawls the resources (and their eventual products) are treated precisely as if they were Bruce Ackerman's manna (see above, fn. 33). From behind the veil of ignorance (a metaphor synonymous with Ackerman's spaceship) the good things of the world that are to be distributed are viewed exactly as Ackerman's voyagers view the manna that awaits them.

an instrument within the decision maker's grasp, an instrument that he consciously and deliberately deploys in order to achieve an-already-perceived-and-desired objective;[35] entrepreneurship *is* the perception of the worthwhile possibility and desirability of that objective. The purely entrepreneurial perception of the worthwhile production opportunity cannot be boxed into the pure production model in terms of which entitlement theory has been cast. Entrepreneurial decision making[36]—that which I identify in this book as pure discovery—is not the conversion of inputs into outputs; it is the determination (in the teeth of the ineradicable and inscrutable uncertainties of the future) that an attempt to convert inputs into outputs is worthwhile and desirable.

My claim is, therefore, that the entitlement theory (like the other theories of property rights) treats both outputs and inputs as already there, as waiting to be assigned. The morally significant implication of the view that sees resources and output as already "being there," is that *this view then commits us to treating the existence of these resources and outputs as being essentially independent of all human decisions,* whether decisions to appropriate resources from nature, or decisions to transform resources into output. Such a treatment can never permit us to see an individual as having *originated* anything of value—since these valuable things do not owe their existence to any decision of his. Even where a decision to produce is surely to be credited with the emergence of outputs from inputs, this view deters us from attributing the existence of output to the producer's decision. This is so because, on this view, the output really existed, even before the decision to produce, in the form of the resource mix from which the output is transformed. I shall argue that it is this narrow view of production which is responsible for the impasse described in the preceding section. If the producer did not *originate* the output, then his title to it must be derived from his title to the inputs out of which the

35. See my *Perception, Opportunity, and Profit* (Chicago: University of Chicago Press, 1979), pp. 180f., and my *Discovery and the Capitalist Process* (Chicago: University of Chicago Press, 1985), pp. 21f., for references and discussion on the case for following Schumpeter in choosing *not* to view entrepreneurship as a factor of production.

36. For more extensive discussions of the nature of entrepreneurship, see my earlier works, *Competition and Entrepreneurship* (Chicago: University of Chicago Press, 1973); *Perception, Opportunity, and Profit* (op. cit.); and *Discovery and the Capitalist Process* (op. cit.).

output has been transformed. But sooner or later this procedure brings us face to face with the problem of how he acquired just title to "original" inputs—which did *not* emerge from owned inputs, and which he did not himself originate either.

If we are to introduce moral insights based upon discovery, into the property rights discussion, this will be as a result of our perceiving the world of resources and of production as displaying, at every turn, scope for pure discovery. We will, in consequence, refuse to treat resources acquired from nature as having already been there; we will, *a fortiori*, refuse to treat the social output as a pie waiting, as it were on a platter, to be distributed.

PROPERTY IN A WORLD OF DISCOVERIES

In a world rich in opportunities for discovery, it seems a fundamental error, morally speaking, to treat resources and outputs as if they never need to be discovered, as if they have already been there from the beginning of time. If, as I shall argue, an undiscovered resource is, in the moral sense, a non-existent resource, then it will turn out to be crucially important in the moral appraisal of the institution of property, to recognize that resources (and, *a fortiori*, products) come into existence as a result of discoveries, of purely entrepreneurial hunches and vision. Once the element of possible discovery has been introduced, our discussions in chapter 2 teach us that the products never do come into existence—in the relevant sense—merely as a result of the transformation of inputs; that cannot be the case because if output *could* come into being merely by transforming inputs, then we would say that the output *already* existed, in inchoate form, in those very inputs which assure the availability of the product when we give the command. Both resources and products are brought into existence only through acts of pure discovery. Discovered natural resources have been brought into relevant existence by their discovery, since an undiscovered resource is, for all relevant human and moral purposes, non-existent. The entrepreneurial decision to deploy inputs to achieve output objectives is what brings those output objectives into existence; before that decision was taken, the inputs did not, in the morally relevant sense, provide command over anything. The outputs were not merely not present in their final physical form, they were as totally non-existent as undiscovered resources are. As argued in preceding chapters, capitalist production and capitalist market exchange occur under conditions which call for discovery at every turn. The human condition, we saw, is one in which alert individuals can continually notice hitherto unseen opportunities for improving their situations, or hitherto unsuspected dangers to be avoided. The flow of events is never that of an unfolding tapestry already woven in the fabric of the past: it is always replete with genuine novelties and surprises; the decisions which punctuate and propel this flow are always genuinely *originating* decisions, as Shackle has taught us.[37] Once we recognize this true character of human history, including especially economic and business history, we can no longer be satisfied with a moral philosophy which, in its consideration of property rights and property institutions, treats the world as if the future is an unending series of fully perceived manna-deposits waiting to be assigned and distributed.

We must, then, ask ourselves in what ways the circumstance of pure discovery enters into or is relevant for those commonly held intuitions concerning property which we found, in so many important respects, to be consistent with the entitlement approach to understanding the institution of property. My thesis will be a simple one: that the moral intuition that commonly sees production as a source of just title to output is not based on a pie-ingredients ethic, in which title to the pie-ingredients confers natural title to the resulting pie. The producer is not, that is, seen as entitled to the product because he produced it by transforming and combining inputs over which he had just title. Rather, the producer is seen as entitled to the product because he genuinely originated the product *ex nihilo;* he originated it by "discovering," in entrepreneurial fashion, an opportunity to fashion a product out of items (which themselves, up until this discovery, did not at all constitute that product, even in inchoate form). Jones, the producer of a ladder out of lumber found at the bottom of his deep hole, originated that ladder out of nothing but a gleam in his eye. Before he had the idea that it might be possible and worthwhile to fashion his ladder, all that Jones had at his disposal was worthless junk which he in fact considered a positive nuisance. My thesis is, then, that the entrepreneurial origination of product is what, at bottom, nourishes

37. See, e.g., G. L. S. Shackle, *Epistemics and Economics: A Critique of Economic Doctrines* (Cambridge: Cambridge University Press, 1972), pp. 351f. See also Shackle, *Decision, Order and Time,* 2nd ed. (Cambridge: Cambridge University Press, 1970).

the intuition which sees the act of production as a source of just title. Acceptance of this thesis, I believe, will transform our perspective on the moral foundations of the institution of private property in virtually all its aspects.

FINDERS, KEEPERS

1. A coin falls out of a hole in my pocket while I am walking from one room in my home to another. When I discover my loss I turn back to pick up the coin. If I do not find it immediately, I proceed to look for it, perhaps, at the sides of the room. Even though I have not yet found the coin, I regard it still as my own. If a visitor spies it, I will not say that he should, for that reason alone, be entitled to keep it. But if the loss occurs while I am walking through a crowded public thoroughfare, matters are quite different. When I discover my loss I now realize full well that *this* loss is final. I no longer treat the coin as one of my owned holdings. If I do happen to find it in the street it is as if I found a coin that someone else has lost. If I see someone else picking up and pocketing the coin which I have lost, I feel no sense of having been robbed; someone else has been luckier than I was, that is all. The coin "lost" in my home is "bound to turn up"; its temporary loss does not mean that I no longer own it. But the coin lost in Times Square has passed out of my life; as far as I am concerned it no longer exists. When I, or someone else, finds my lost coin, he is, as far as I am concerned, finding a different coin than mine.
2. I am hiking over some wild, mountainous terrain, over which no human dominion has ever been established. My eye is caught by the glint of something that turns out to be a raw diamond, in a place where no one has suspected that diamonds were to be found.
3. I am lying awake, or strolling at the shore, or waiting for a train, when I am struck by a new idea. The idea turns out to be a useful one, perhaps for me alone, perhaps for many persons (in which case careful exploitation of this idea can make me wealthy).

In each of these cases what is found is, as it were, introduced into the scope of human concern, from a state of virtual non-existence. The valuable idea was certainly not fabricated out of prior inputs, it was not the result of a deliberately undertaken research program; whatever the possible psychological causes may have been, the truth is that, as far as I knew, the idea simply popped up in my mind, out of nowhere. Similarly, my finding the raw diamond is the finding of something for which nobody was searching. No one suspected its possible presence. For all human purposes it was simply not in existence; my discovery of it can, in a straightforward, morally-relevant sense, be regarded as its origination. Even the coin lost in Times Square should, surely, despite its physical presence, be regarded as being no longer in existence. When I, or someone else, find it, this brings it back into existence. Neither I nor anyone else suspected that it was worthwhile to search Times Square for this coin. The coin had, for all intents and purposes, ceased to exist. For the physical scientist *qua* physical scientist, certainly, the indestructibility of matter matters; no one is denying the physical existence of the coin. But insofar as concerns human obligations, entitlements, dreams, and anxieties, the loss of the coin writes the final page to the coin's story. Its discovery, whether by me or by another, begins an entirely new story.

I submit that it is in line with these insights that for so many of us, the one who finds the coin in Times Square, the one who finds the raw diamond, the one to whom the new idea occurs, is the just owner of what he found. The finder of the coin should be its keeper, I believe, not because he produced it out of his resources, but because the coin came into existence for its finder, as it were, while still non-existent for everyone else. As far as others are concerned, its finder originated it; he is entitled to keep it. For others to take this coin or this diamond from its finder, we feel very strongly, is for them to act unjustly, to engage in robbery and plunder.

Admittedly, to say that the finder of a coin (or of a raw diamond, or of an oil deposit, or of a hitherto undiscovered continent or planet) originated or created what he found, is, at one level, to indulge in obvious metaphor. Columbus did not really create America; America existed before Columbus. The raw diamond was, after all, waiting to be discovered; its discoverer did not literally create it. Our point is that this metaphor, if it be such, is expressive of what we believe to be an obvious moral truth: the prior physical existence of the discovered diamond or of the found coin is utterly irrelevant. The inspired sculptor who takes a lump of cast-off raw marble, and converts it into a soaring masterpiece, has *created* something. The prior existence of the marble can only in the most minor sense be credited with what emerges from under the sculptor's chisel.

Moral credit for, and economic ownership of the masterpiece belong to its creator, not because the marble was his, not because he used his own labor and his own chisel (instead of the labor of an unjustly exploited laborer, or a chisel stolen from a carpenter), but because he created it. He is its author, therefore it is his. Where an entity owes its existence, in every morally relevant sense, to the creative act of an individual, we feel very strongly that no one else has any right to deprive that individual of the enjoyment of that which he has created.[38]

DISCOVERY AND PROPERTY RIGHTS

If I am correct in my interpretation of the finders, keepers intuition, we have within our grasp, surely, a powerful tool for moral understanding. We are now in a position to appreciate the widespread moral convictions concerning the sanctity of property rights, from a fresh angle. Goods come into existence as a result of entrepreneurial decisions to buy input services and combine and transform them into products. These entrepreneurial decisions are, as we have seen throughout this book, acts of discovery. They are truly originative acts; they create the outputs which roll off the assembly lines. The prior existence of the inputs, I have pointed out, does not contradict our perception of the creativity of the entrepreneurial decision to produce. Inputs do not ensure output in a world of open-ended uncertainty. More to the point, inputs do not ensure the worthwhileness of the outputs they may generate. In deciding to produce, the entrepreneur sees an opportunity which others have not seen. (They cannot possibly have seen, or else the inputs would no longer have been available, nor could the value of the output have failed to have already been lowered competitively to render its production unprofitable.) So that, in deciding to buy inputs and sell output at a profit, the entrepreneur has discovered, created, a value in the inputs which no one else has yet perceived.

To be sure, the entrepreneurial producer's creativity entitles him to what he has created only insofar as he was entitled to deploy the inputs. If the sculptor stole the marble from its rightful owners, or acquired it from them in fraudulent fashion, what he has himself created is inextricably

---

38. This section has by no means exhausted the intuitions regarding discovery. For a discussion raising serious doubts about the morality of finders-keepers, see ch. 7.

entangled with that which he has stolen from others. The discovery by the entrepreneur-producer of a productive opportunity, while it may be seen as the discovery of the true high value of the relevant inputs (as compared with the "mistakenly" low value assigned to them by the market), does not constitute a creation of those inputs *ex nihilo*. These inputs were owned and valued by their owners (even if not at their full true value); they certainly existed before our entrepreneur stole them and transformed them into something no one had suspected could be forthcoming. So that we must certainly make the producer's discovery-title to what he has produced depend on his having acquired just title to the necessary ingredients of production. Ultimately, pressing the logic of this story to its conclusion, we ask how the owners of the unproductive resources acquired originally from the state of nature, became the exclusive just owners of those resources. This question, for the finders-keepers theorist as for entitlement theorists, is of primordial ethical importance. All the pure discoveries made during the course of centuries cannot in themselves launder out any original injustice that may have occurred at the moment of original acquisition from nature. If initially acquired original inputs were unjustly plundered from others, or from the human race in general, all the subsequently discovered valuable uses that can be made out of these inputs (or out of products made out of those inputs, and so on, and so on) are sculptures created out of stolen marble.

But a finders-keepers ethic, a discovery ethic, proceeds to discern justice in original acquisition from nature, differently than entitlement theorists have done until now. Until now, entitlement theorists have relied (as indeed Locke himself suggests we do) on what is a modified pie-ingredient ethic for justifying Lockean acquisition from nature. Because my labor is mine, therefore the unowned natural object with which I mix my labor becomes mine. We have seen how this approach raises serious difficulties. A finders-keepers ethic makes it possible for us to see things differently. When I find an unowned natural object and, considering its annexation worthwhile, proceed to take physical possession of it, I have discovered it—or, at any rate, I have discovered the worthwhileness of taking possession of it. What no one thought worthy of taking, was something valueless; economically—and morally—speaking, it did not exist. My discovery of the natural resource, my realizing its potential value, has meant that I have brought it into existence. I have assigned value to it; therefore it has become mine.

So discovery turns out to be the key to understanding our convictions regarding property, from its very beginnings and until our own time. Resources acquired justly from nature were discovered resources. Subsequent conversions and transformations of these resources represented discovered increments of value. The income assignments that occur during any given time slice of the just capitalist process can, each and every one of them, be recognized as proceeding simply and directly from the just results of current and earlier acts of creative discovery, acts of origination. Our finders-keepers ethic can perhaps be more completely understood by examining the quite drastically novel perspective this ethic opens up for us in regard to the famous Lockean Proviso.

DISCOVERY AND THE LOCKEAN PROVISO:
SOME REVOLUTIONARY IMPLICATIONS

Locke's famous qualification (of his labor mixing theory of original acquisition from nature) stipulates that original acquisition of any resource from nature occur only where there is "enough and as good left in common for others."[39] Both defenders and critics of private property institutions have emphasized the potentially far-reaching implications of this proviso. Critics have seen it as being difficult, if not impossible, to satisfy. "Locke's account . . . seems tolerably plausible where populations are thinly spread and the environment reasonably bountiful. It is in such situations that the 'enough and as good' condition will perhaps not be violated. But that, to put it mildly, is hardly our world."[40]

The point is that in a world of scarcity Locke's proviso simply cannot be satisfied. But this raises serious and puzzling questions. Surely it is *only* in a world of scarcity that private property matters. If Locke's proviso is logically applied, it "makes it impossible for anyone *ever* to acquire ownership of anything so long as there are conditions of scarcity. Thus even if the first possessor leaves enough for others to take, it will necessarily be the case that the second, third, or some remote possessor will not be able to take because by doing so he will deprive others of as much again and as good. Since, therefore, it was only the prior appropriation by the first taker that limited the rights of any given subsequent taker, it

---

39. Locke, op. cit.
40. Nielsen, op. cit., p. 254. See also Roemer, op. cit., p. 157.

follows that the first taker cannot act at all because of the way in which his conduct impinges upon the rights of acquisition of others."[41]

Nozick attempts to salvage a Lockean basis for original acquisition that should have relevance for the real world by extending the proviso to permit any acquisition that does not worsen the condition of others. Even if there is not enough and as good left over (of all the scarce resources that are appropriated from nature) for others, these others are, nonetheless, made better off by the many advantages flowing from capitalist production and exchange.[42] Some critics have accepted Nozick's extension;[43] others have found it forced and implausible.[44] Certainly it goes beyond Locke's own formulation of his proviso. And, moreover, it is not entirely clear that a capitalist system will always meet even this broadened Lockean qualification. Nozick concludes, a little unconvincingly, perhaps, "I believe that the free operation of a market system will not actually run afoul of the Lockean proviso."[45] All this, as Nozick's critics have not been slow to point out, hardly makes for a firm moral philosophical foundation for capitalist property rights and for the far-reaching implications of the entitlement theory of income distribution (which Nozick seeks to build on the basis of those rights).

But it should be noticed that the premise supporting this apparently unanimous acceptance of the need for the Lockean proviso (or for some similar qualification circumscribing original acquisition from the state of nature) presupposes something which we should not at all be prepared to take for granted. The premise supporting the Lockean proviso, it is widely agreed, is that, absent such a qualification, the private annexation of an unowned resource from nature may be harmful to the interests of others. Unless there is "enough and as good" left for others, these others are harmed by private annexation of that which had been held in common by all. If others are harmed by my annexing something from nature, even if that something is as yet unowned, the premise declares, my acquisition cannot be pronounced just. This premise, stated in this

41. Epstein, op. cit., p. 1228, drawing upon the reasoning presented earlier by Nozick (op. cit., pp. 174–78).

42. Nozick, op. cit., p. 177.

43. O. O'Neill, op. cit, pp. 312ff.

44. Roemer, op. cit., pp. 156f.

45. Nozick, op. cit., p. 182.

fashion, is certainly plausible. Yet its application to original acquisition from nature presupposes something by no means so obvious. To believe that your acquisition of a scarce, unowned resource (of which there is not enough left over for me) is actually harmful to me, one must presuppose that prior to your act of acquisition I had some claim to the scarce resource—certainly that the resource existed (or was at least *going to exist*) prior to the appropriation. My discussions in the preceding sections will have suggested how careful we have to be not to accept these presuppositions without question.

If the entire human race is seen as holding in common a pool of some known scarce resource, then your appropriation of some part of the pool worsens my position (and that of everyone else), since it reduces the size of the pool in which I have—in some sense—a share. Your taking for yourself occurs at the expense of there not being enough left for me.

And even if that which your act removes from the common pool is not now actually in existence, but is clearly expected to come into existence, we can appreciate that your acquisitive act may be harmful to the rest of us, insofar as it erases from our confident expectations something upon which we felt we could rely. But, and here is the crucial point, *if your acquisitive act consists in originating something that had not been in prior existence—and the specific possibility of which had not been anticipated—it is hard to see how your act can be described as being harmful to everyone else.* You have not stopped me from enjoying anything I could have otherwise enjoyed—since as far as I knew there was nothing here, either now or in the future, which I could have enjoyed (or expected to enjoy). Here, surely, we observe the far-reaching and perverse moral implications of treating all existing physical objects as if they are already part of our moral calculus, even under circumstances in which these objects enter into no one's hopes, dreams, and anxieties. To treat an unsuspected oil deposit as being *here* (so that the pioneering prospector who appropriates it upon realizing what he has found, is seen as taking away something from the rest of mankind) is seriously to misread the morally relevant facts of the situation. Surely the premise underlying the Lockean proviso has no relevance to such situations.

These observations seem to be consistent with widely shared moral convictions. Even Nozick who, as we have seen, has endorsed the wide relevance of a suitably reformulated Lockean proviso, appears to have appreciated, at least to a limited extent, the force of our intuitions in raising these considerations. Nozick deals with the case where someone "appropriates the total supply of something in a way that does not deprive the others of it. For example, someone finds a new substance in an out-of-the-way place. He discovers that it effectively treats a certain disease and appropriates the total supply. He does not worsen the situation of others; if he did not stumble upon the substance no one else would have, and the others would remain without it."[46] Exactly. The moral logic that generates the Lockean proviso simply does not apply here, since no one knew of this substance at all, and moreover, no one dreamed of its curative properties. What we wish to insist upon, *contra* Nozick (and the other property rights theorists), is that matters are not relevantly different even in cases where the "new" substance was known by all to exist, but its curative properties were not recognized. If everyone believed the substance to be worthless dirt, and a discoverer somehow came to realize its extraordinarily valuable properties he, too, has not deprived the other of anything valuable. If he did not stumble upon the curative powers of the "dirt," there is no assurance at all that anyone else would have; there is every reason to believe that others would have remained without the cure.

I may press my point further, and point out that matters would not be relevantly different in cases where the substance was known by all to exist, and the curative properties of the substance, too, were widely recognized—but the substance has somehow not been appropriated (perhaps because people had underestimated its commercial potential, thinking that costs of processing the dirt into life-giving drugs made such a venture not worthwhile; or perhaps because people mistakenly believed that the curative dirt was so widely available as to render appropriation of any of it unnecessary; or whatever). The entrepreneur who takes possession of this dirt (because he believes such appropriation to be commercially profitable) has discovered the value of that which others had believed to be without value. He too, has not deprived others of anything they saw as valuable. If he had not stumbled upon the true high commercial value of the dirt, there is no assurance at all that anyone else would have; there is every reason to believe that patients would have remained without the cure.

46. Ibid., p. 181.

But despite Nozick's recognition, in regard to the unknown new substance, of something like a finders-keepers ethic, he immediately adds qualifications to his defense of the discoverer's appropriation. He points out in regard to this new substance, that "as time passes, the likelihood increases that others would have come across the substance."[47] This suggests, Nozick believes, that the Lockean proviso has relevance here after all, and might indicate that while appropriation of the substance might be in order, its bequest might be limited. All this raises some fairly subtle issues for a finders-keepers ethic.

To maintain that a natural object discovered by you today *would* have been discovered by me, or by someone else, tomorrow (so that your taking it today deprives others of something which they would have had available to them at some future date), is, in effect, to rewrite history in the light of subsequent events. Up to the moment you made your discovery no one could have predicted that others *would* have made the discovery in the future (since no one had, until then, any inkling that anything existed to be discovered). To declare your appropriation to have been harmful to others is, indirectly, to treat undiscovered natural resources as if they were, in a morally relevant sense, already there (or already going to be there). Nozick has given us no philosophical grounds for such a treatment. *Ex ante,* it is not clear how the discoverer acts unjustly in originating for himself something which, at this moment, does not exist (and, *from the perspective of this moment,* will never exist) for anyone else.

But the finders-keepers ethic demands yet further consideration of the argument (that the likelihood that the new substance would have been found by others later on, requires us to apply the Lockean proviso). Let us grant, for the sake of argument, that your taking of a new substance that I would have later discovered does, in some morally relevant sense, constitute a harm for me. The property theorists (including Nozick) have seen such harm as irreparably damaging the justice of your appropriation. Let us ask ourselves, why? Ordinarily, of course, any act of yours which harms another is deemed unjust, if the harm involves an unjustified invasion of the other's rights. But in the case of the discovery, the harm done to others (conceding, for the sake of argument that harm *is* being done) is not obviously unjust at all. One writer writes a novel with an inspired

47. Ibid.

theme, the novelty of which both the critics and the reading public find excitingly pathbreaking. In publishing this novel he is (on our presently adopted premise) harming others who feel they too might well have hit on this exciting new theme. Shall we really say that in publishing his book the first writer is acting unjustly? Or should we not rather say that in publishing his book he is simply exercising his rights to disseminate what he, and he alone, originated? Others *might* have originated similar books; in no way, surely, does this mean that the book the first writer created, from nothing but typewriter and white paper, was not his to publish as he chose.[48] Certainly an entitlement approach should recognize that any harm you do to others by the free exercise of your rights, cannot be pronounced unjust if no rights of others are being violated. Others have no rights in your book (*they* did not write it!); they may indeed be being harmed by your exercise of your rights, but they are not being unjustly deprived of any rights of their own. Once again, it seems, the plausibility of the Lockean proviso stems from the error of treating natural, unowned resources as already here (so that it makes sense to speak of the rights which others may possibly have in those resources, and therefore to treat acts of acquisition which frustrate those rights as being unjust). The discovery insights I have been emphasizing seem to hold highly destructive implications indeed for the strict justice of the Lockean proviso.

DISCOVERY, MORALITY, AND GOOD LUCK

My contention that the discovery element in the capitalist process should be seen as the source of much of our moral convictions concerning property rights, may be questioned on the following grounds. Surely, to the extent that discovery differs from the deliberate pursuit of a perceived objective, it cannot be credited to the determined effort, the single-minded dedication, the painstaking concentration, of the successful discoverer. No effort, no dedication, no concentration, could have possibly entered into the discovery (or else it would not be a discovery at all, but the achievement of a planned objective). But if this is so, does this then not mean that we wish to confer just title to property upon those who have no other moral claim to it than their being the fortunate

---

48. On the points made in this section see also my *Perception, Opportunity, and Profit*, op. cit., pp. 219–23.

beneficiaries of sheer good luck? Good luck seems an exceedingly weak moral reed upon which to lean so important an institution as private property. (It will be recalled, from an earlier section of this chapter, that the "moral arbitrariness" of genetically based differences in human ability and character has frequently been cited in challenging the justice of self-ownership. As Roemer put it, "if one views the distribution of these internal talents as morally arbitrary and itself an instance of luck, one may oppose a method of economic organization that enables people to benefit by virtue of their draw in the birth lottery."[49] Even those who view the individual as inseparable from qualities with which he has been naturally endowed, may share Roemer's reservations regarding the justice of a method of economic organization that enables people to benefit by virtue of their draw in other situations entirely governed by luck.)

In response to this objection I must remind the reader of our discussion in chapter 2, in which I denied the thesis that every desirable event must, unless it be the result of the calculated implementation of deliberate plans, be chalked up entirely to the moral arbitrariness of sheer good luck. I argued, it will be recalled, that many good things enter our lives only through our alertly grasping opportunities that present themselves to us. Good fortune alone is not sufficient to yield us these good things. The motivated alertness of the beneficiary is a necessary condition for their attainment. It is, I have argued, this motivated alertness on the part of the discoverer which transforms a nonexistent (i.e., wholly unknown) item into a perceived, fully existing, resource; in other words it is this motivated alertness which permits us to see the discoverer as the author and creator of what he has discovered.

For others to look askance at the good fortune of the discoverer, and to grumble about the moral arbitrariness of Lady Luck in favoring the discoverer rather than them, is no different than for those who did not write exciting, pathbreaking books (in the preceding section) to complain that (had its author *not* written it) they *might* have been the pioneers of this genre. The fact was that another authored the book, not they; they have no claim over the book that was written by another; he originated it, not they. Quite similarly, I argue, the simple fact is that those complaining over the moral arbitrariness of luck *did not* grasp (even if we concede that,

49. Roemer, op. cit., p. 154.

had luck favored them, they might have grasped) the fortunate opportunity. Notice that I am not saying that others might in fact have alertly benefited themselves by the same good luck that has benefited the successful
discoverer. I readily concede that in many cases the discoverer has indeed
been placed by luck in an especially favored position from which to notice
what is available. I argue only that, after all the benefits of luck are taken
into account, the successful discoverer is indeed the effective origin of
his own success. Without his alertness, good fortune would have swiftly
moved beyond reach. The discoverer need not apologize for any moral arbitrariness in his discovery; he, and he alone, originated his success, in
the final analysis. (Of course these considerations are only reinforced for
cases in which others, too, might equally have benefited from good luck,
but somehow missed the opportunity.)

These considerations are, surely, not wholly irrelevant for discussions
that raise the issue of the moral arbitrariness of the genetic lottery which
grants superior human talents to luckier-born individuals than to others.
It will be recalled that this issue was left, in our review of the entitlement
theory of justice, somewhat in the air. It was not entirely clear how an
entitlement theorist would be able to pronounce the genetic lottery a just
one (other than by appealing to our bedrock intuitions concerning self-
ownership—no matter what moral arbitrariness it may seem to entail).
What we should now recognize is that good luck, in the way of genetic
or social-cultural endowment, never is by itself sufficient to ensure that
its beneficiary indeed grasps what good fortune has placed before him.
It requires entrepreneurial insight to appreciate talent, ability, character, and even beauty and physical strength. Certainly, under normal circumstances, it is to be expected that the direct beneficiary of superior
endowment is the first to appreciate what has been presented to him. But
again and again we encounter cases where only some inspired educator,
employer, coach, or spouse has sufficient faith in an individual's potential
to ensure that no part of the full social value of that potential was wasted.
Personal endowment may be a matter of moral arbitrariness; taking
advantage of these endowments and turning them to their full market
potential calls for that motivated alertness on the part of the individual
which we have identified as the discoverer's creation of what he finds.

So that a discovery-based finders-keepers ethic reinforces the justice of original acquisition from nature along two distinct dimensions.
First, it offers a fresh approach to original acquisition which sees it as the

discovery and origination of (rather than a matter of mixing one's labor with) the unowned natural resource. Second, it offers a reinforcement for the Lockean mixing-of-labor theory of original acquisition, by buttressing its premise of self-ownership. This brings me back, in concluding this chapter, to reviewing the relation between a discovery ethic and an entitlement theoretic approach to distributive justice.

DISCOVERY AND ENTITLEMENT

Much of this chapter has consisted of criticism of the entitlement theory of justice (particularly in its treatment of original acquisition, and of its acceptance of the moral logic supporting the Lockean proviso). Yet I opened this chapter by acknowledging our fundamental debt to Robert Nozick's entitlement theory, and by describing the discovery theory as "riding piggyback upon Nozick's entitlement theory." It will be useful, in concluding this chapter, to review, briefly, the sense in which a finders-keepers based theory of capitalist justice rests on an entitlement-theoretic basis.

For an entitlement theory a "distribution is just if it arises from another just distribution by legitimate means. The legitimate means of moving from one distribution to another are specified by the principle of justice transfer. The legitimate first 'moves' are specified by the principle of justice in acquisition. Whatever arises from a just situation by just steps is itself just."[50] The sketch I have given of a finders-keepers approach to distributive justice, a discovery theory of justice, fully accepts and depends upon this framework of the entitlement theory. It differs from the entitlement theory provided by Nozick in the details concerning the principles of just acquisition and just transfer. Nozick relies on a Lockean basis for original acquisition; I wish to draw attention to the insights of the finders-keepers ethic in regard to original acquisition. Nozick's notion of just transfer depends entirely on the justice of voluntary transfer; the discovery theory draws attention to the pervasive elements of discovery that characterize market transactions in the disequilibrium market. The important sense in which the discovery theory rides piggyback upon Nozick's theory is in its rejection of end-state principles of justice, as well as of patterned (historical) principles of justice.

50. Nozick, op. cit., p. 151.

The widely shared moral intuitions to which I referred at the outset of this chapter, relate to this basic appreciation for Nozick's unpatterned historical theory (a theory which relies entirely on the justice of earlier steps leading to today's distribution, but which does not, in any simple sense, invoke a limited number of specific principles according to which just distribution might be patterned).[51]

Once the Nozickian framework is accepted, the discovery elements I have argued for fit in naturally and easily. They transform the entitlement theory, I believe, into a theory of justice that conforms with considerable precision to widely shared judgments concerning property and justice.[52] Introduction of these insights concerning discovery has, moreover, potential for persuading critics of capitalist justice who have found the entitlement theory as enunciated earlier, less than fully convincing on certain fundamental problematic issues.

51. See Nozick, ibid., pp. 153–60.

52. See ch. 7 for additional discussion of the way in which the discovery view and Nozick's entitlement view complement each other.

7. DISCOVERY AND THE JUSTICE OF CAPITALISM

The time has come to draw together the various strands of our discussions, and to sum up what, taken altogether, they teach us about the justice of capitalism. I have argued (1) that the capitalist process consists, very significantly, of innumerable acts (on the part of *all* market participants) of entrepreneurial discovery; (2) that acts of discovery are to be sharply distinguished, in terms of positive economics, from acts of deliberate production; (3) that the notion of discovery carries with it, at the level of ethics, specific insights which, in the view of many, invest the finders-keepers rule with moral weight; so that (4) standard treatments of economic justice under capitalism need to be sharply revised in order to incorporate the full moral reach of the finders-keepers rule.

All this adds up to a highly significant perspective which has, unfortunately, been missing in the existing philosophical and economic discussions of capitalist justice. It is by no means my purpose to minimize the significance of this new perspective. Yet, on the other hand, I do not wish to overstate the case for emphasizing discovery in regard to the justice (let alone the overall morality) of capitalism. It has not been my objective to show that discovery, and the moral implications of discovery, are the *only* moral considerations to be taken into account in regard to the justice of capitalist income assignments. This concluding chapter will draw attention to some qualifications which must be borne in mind in regard to the moral principles rooted in the phenomenon of discovery, and in regard to their specific applications. It will also suggest how the fresh perspectives arising out of the phenomenon of discovery may be fruitfully integrated with more conventional criteria for economic justice. Such an integration, it is to be hoped, will provide a balanced perspective from which to assess the economic justice of capitalist income distribution.

FINDERS, KEEPERS RECONSIDERED

It was argued in the preceding chapters that a finders-keepers rule is consistent with widespread ethical judgments. I traced this shared intuition back to the insight that the discoverer can be seen as the originator and creator of what he discovers. We must also consider, however, a serious counter-argument that might be raised *against* the finders-keepers ethic: that what a discoverer gains must necessarily come as a result of exploiting the ignorance of others, and thus comes dangerously close to having been gained by consciously defrauding those others. This argument is one which we have not yet confronted, although certain elements in it were indirectly addressed in our earlier discussions. Let us examine the matter.

In chapter 5 I considered the case of an entrepreneur who buys at a low price and resells what he buys at a higher price. I discussed the possible problem this raises for justice in transfer (since the original seller might claim that his consent to the original sale at the low price was made without awareness of the "true" higher value of what he sold, so that his consent to the sale was not a fully informed consent and the transfer was thus not completely a voluntary one). I pointed out that the very circumstance that the true higher value was totally unexpected (so that invalidation of the sale on the grounds of mistake might reasonably be proposed) assures us that the pure profit made by the entrepreneur (through resale at the higher price) was in fact discovered entirely by the entrepreneur. This convinced us that, given a finders-keepers rule, a revocation of the original sale on the grounds of mistake cannot be countenanced, since such a revocation would assign to the original seller a gain which someone else, not he, discovered. Now we are challenged by the argument that the entrepreneur's discovery constitutes an exploitation by him of the seller's utter ignorance of the true high value of what he sold. We are asked not to invalidate the original sale on the grounds of mistake, but to condemn the entrepreneur for benefiting from his discovery. We are asked, in effect, to concede that even if discovery *is* a kind of origination and creation, it cannot confer just title where it occurs at the expense of another's sheer ignorance. To declare the exploitation of another's ignorance just, the argument would run, would be not much different from countenancing a gain won by deliberately misleading one's trading partners. (Presumably we would condemn fraudulent behavior even if the victim has voluntarily signed an agreement in which he agrees to forgo all attempts to invalidate the deal on grounds of mistake.) It is true that our entrepreneur (who gained by buying low and selling high) did not offer any assurances to the original sellers misleadingly suggesting that his price was the highest they could obtain anywhere. But his gain arises, surely, from his failing to divulge to them an item of information which they would very much have wished to have (and which, had they had it, would certainly have deterred them from selling to our entrepreneur).

Is there really much moral difference, the critic may ask, between cheating one's trading partner by deliberately feeding him misleading information, on the one hand, and, on the other hand, winning profits in the market by buying from him knowing that he operates under a mistaken assessment of the true market value of what he sells?

This way of presenting the argument against the finders-keepers ethic points to a possible inconsistency between two widely shared common moral judgments. The first judgment declares the discoverer of an unowned beautiful seashell at the shore to be its rightful owner. The second judgment declares it unfair to gain as a result of a deal which one was able to conclude only by deliberately concealing from one's trading partner crucially relevant information (which, had one's trading partner known it, would have led him to refrain from trading). Was there any logical mistake in our conclusion on the basis of a finders-keepers ethic (similar to that which endorses seashell discovery) that pure entrepreneurial profit is just? Let us further explore this dilemma.

A visitor to the seashore stands rapt as he watches an extraordinarily fine sunset. So entranced is he by the sublime view that he fails to notice the seashell lying on the sand just at his feet—a seashell of such surpassing beauty that, were he to notice it, he would immediately pick it up and add it to his collection of seashells. A second visitor does notice the seashell; and formulates a plan of action. Stealthily (so as not to alert the sunset watcher) he approaches, and with a swift, near-silent motion, triumphantly grabs the prize seashell from beneath the nose of the sunset watcher. Has the discoverer of the seashell exploited the sheer ignorance of the sunset viewer? Did he have a moral obligation, in strict justice, to have alerted him to what he could have discovered? By deliberately failing to alert him, was he "cheating" him (in the same way he might have cheated an owner of a resource into selling it at a low price by falsely convincing him that the resource has little industrial value)? When the sunset viewer comes down to earth and realizes what he has forfeited (as the result of his preoccupation with the sunset), does he view the second visitor to the seashore (who appropriated the seashell) as having unfairly "stolen" something away from him? Will he accept the argument that the second visitor may put forward, to the effect that he merely picked up an unowned seashell (which indeed happened to be located near the sunset watcher, but which was completely unowned, nonetheless)?

And if an observer (or at least the sunset watcher) does view the appropriation with a certain moral censure (because the appropriation was effected only by stealth, deliberately forestalling a discovery which the sunset enthusiast would inevitably have made for himself very soon), should not the same censure attach to *anyone* picking up an unowned seashell, anywhere? Even if a seashell is not lying at the feet of any sunset watcher, is it not the case that *someone* would have noticed the shell, sooner or later? (And while, of course, that hypothetical someone would have no stronger claim to the shell than any other present appropriator of it, does this line of reasoning not lead to a kind of frustrating paradox? Once appropriation-by-discovery is permitted, no such appropriation can be made without taking advantage of the lack of alertness on the part of other potential discoverers.)

These difficulties seem to stem from a tendency we have to treat knowledge as costlessly available, and to treat costlessly available knowledge, morally speaking, as if it were already known. To pick up a seashell lying at the feet of a sunset watcher by exercising stealth may seem, therefore, to deprive the watcher of knowledge to which he is entitled. To benefit oneself by not divulging information which someone else might have costlessly learned for himself, may strike us as almost equivalent to defrauding him. To block a discovery which a person may have made (by forestalling costless learning of correct information) may then seem not greatly different from deceitfully feeding the victim with harmfully incorrect information.

Once it is understood, however, that available information, even costlessly available information, may easily be overlooked for no particular reason, there does not appear to be quite the same moral questionability attached to discovery. The successful discoverer has simply been more alert than others; he has not "blocked discovery" by others. There does not seem to be a clear moral imperative *based on considerations of justice*, to divulge what one knows to others, even if this information may be useful to those others, and even if the information can be costlessly provided. Of course there may be powerful moral considerations pointing to a duty so to divulge information to another, but failure to do so does not appear obviously to entitle that other to consider himself robbed of something that was (or should have been) his own. He was neither robbed nor cheated (even if the better informed individual deliberately gained by shirking the possible moral duty of costlessly informing others of what might have been useful to them). Failing to divulge information to others (without engaging in misrepresentation) may not be very noble; it may even, under certain circumstances, be deemed to be downright disgusting; but it constitutes neither robbery nor fraud. There may seem to be only a fine line separating the case of failing to share information, from the case of deliberately concealing information which would otherwise certainly have been discovered. But this line does seem morally significant. This latter case, in turn, seems significantly different, morally speaking, from the case in which an individual engages in misrepresentation, feeding false information to another for his own gain.

This discussion suggests rather strongly that common intuitions concerning finders being keepers need not be declared logically incoherent in the light of widely shared moral intuitions condemning fraud, and looking askance at the exploitation of the ignorance of others by deliberate concealment of truths that would otherwise have become apparent to all. The moral issues are, admittedly, not simple. There appear to be a number of moral gradations, in regard to the reprehensibility of gaining benefit by failure to disclose available information. The main point for our discussion seems to be that it is difficult to see how, in terms of justice, the exploitation of a discovery one has alertly made can ever be questioned (merely on the grounds that others are now precluded from making that discovery; or on the grounds that others might have made the discovery). Moreover, the residual moral qualms one may have (on grounds other than strict justice) regarding the decency of deriving benefit based on the removable ignorance of others, seem to recede the more impersonal the relationship is between the parties. Certainly these qualms must recede almost entirely as the task of informing others becomes more and more costly.

Finally, any qualms regarding *a system* based on entrepreneurial discovery must surely take note of the overall incentive structure depending on the admissibility of pure profit. As noted in earlier chapters, where discovery and the deriving of benefit from discovery is proscribed, the strong likelihood is that those others (the exploitation of whose ignorance causes such qualms) would be, systematically, less well informed and less well-off than under free-market capitalism, in which entrepreneurial profit provides the driving motivation and incentive.

A simple finders-keeper rule may be a rather crude moral rule of thumb, paying insufficient attention to the subtle moral nuances involved in benefiting through the ignorance of others.[1] On balance, however, the rule seems to provide a healthy basis in terms of the norm of justice, upon which to construct the capitalist framework. The widely held finders-keepers ethic indeed demands to be incorporated into theories of capitalist justice.

DISCOVERY AND FIRST POSSESSION

Our discussions have highlighted the sense in which conventional capitalist property institutions conform to widely shared judgments in regard to the justice of discovery. The finders-keepers rule, we found, can introduce illuminating clarity into capitalist presumptions concerning the justice of private property and the justice of pure entrepreneurial profit. But I do not wish to leave the impression that a finders-keepers rule provides clear-cut moral guidance, in respect of distributive justice, enabling us unerringly to resolve otherwise ambiguous situations. The finders-keepers rule provides a principle to be incorporated into moral appraisals of capitalist justice; but the principle may not itself always be sufficient to generate definitive rulings on controversial cases. The finders-keepers rule leaves unanswered a number of vexing questions surrounding its practical applications. Many of these questions are parallel to similar questions raised in applying alternative criteria for justice.

Take, for example, the term "discovery," or "finding." I do not really wish to say that the first discoverer of a resource should be declared its just owner even if he did not raise a finger to take possession of what he has found or discovered. (In fact I am inclined to say that where A discovers an unowned resource but does not take possession of it, this suggests he has *not* really discovered its true value. The first one taking possession should, I would argue, really be recognized as the first genuine discoverer of the economic value of the unowned resource.) Such dilemmas have plagued courts for thousands of years. Richard Epstein recently cited several classic cases in which such questions were the central issue. In *Pierson* v. *Post,* an early nineteenth-century case, the plaintiff, Post, "was pursuing a fox across an unowned stretch of beach with his hounds when Pierson, almost from nowhere, rode up to capture the fox, which

---

1. No doubt this is responsible for the passionate disagreements concerning the morality of insider trading on security markets.

he kept even after Post demanded it be handed over. Post then sued Pierson claiming that Pierson had "indirectly" injured Post by taking the fox into his possession."[2] Here the question is whether Post's being in hot pursuit of the fox, that he would (apart from the interference by Pierson) have captured, constitutes valid possession of it by Post. A finders-keepers rule is not of very much help in adjudicating this case; the issue is not who saw the fox first, but who successfully took possession of it first.

In a late nineteenth-century case, *Swift v. Gifford,* "a dispute occurred between two fishing crews over the ownership of a whale. The crew of the ship *Rainbow* threw a harpoon that, with its line still attached, remained fast in the side of the whale even though the whale itself escaped. The crew of the ship *Hercules* captured the whale while the *Rainbow* was still in pursuit." The case revolved around "a universal maritime custom" which "assigned the whale to the *Rainbow* because its harpoon first stuck in the whale, even though the *Hercules* first captured it."[3] This case (and an earlier English case cited by Epstein involving water rights) illustrates the role of tradition in determining what constitutes possession. Clearly the bare rule of finders, keepers, cannot guide the law in resolving such disputes. And if such ambiguities surround the taking of possession of foxes, whales, and water, we can understand the problems involved in defining the effective discovery of land. What actions constitute, not merely discovering the availability of unowned—and in fact unknown—land, but its annexation? How much work must be performed upon the land? How much of an acre of land must be improved, in order for all of it to become the property of the homesteader? These dilemmas will have to be dealt with in the law governing private property in land. A finders-keepers rule, while it may indeed serve as the foundation upon which the law is erected, cannot contribute very much to the formulation of specific guidelines for implementing the general principles underlying original acquisition.

PROBLEMS OF RECTIFICATION AND RESTITUTION

Another serious class of challenges to the justice of any capitalist system arises out of the likelihood that today's property titles may have derived, historically, from past unjust acts of robbery and pillage. As noted in

2. Richard A. Epstein, "Possession as the root of title," *Georgia Law Review,* 13, 1221 (1979), p. 1224.

3. Ibid., pp. 1230f.

the preceding chapter, Marx drew caustic attention to this possibility (or historical fact). A finders-keepers rule does not provide guidance on the question as to when, if ever, do past acts of injustice cease to negate the legitimacy of current title-holders. Entitlement theorists have debated this critically important issue. Various possible ways of reconciling respect for current title with moral revulsion against methods of title acquisition in ages past can be, and have been, proposed. It is not apparent how finders-keepers insights can provide any illumination in this regard.

DISCOVERED PIES AND GIVEN PIES

A good deal of my criticism of the literature of justice has consisted of the charge that it treats resources and products as if they have in effect been available for the taking, and have been waiting to be distributed, from the very beginning. I have argued, in contrast, that in reality resources and products have always had to be discovered. They have never "existed" up until the moment of their entrepreneurial discovery. It is upon this contention that I have based my case for the finders-keepers ethic and its relevance for the justice of capitalist income assignments.

Yet the standard (non-discovery) approach to the economics and the justice of the capitalist process cannot be pronounced entirely misconceived. It is certainly possible to perceive capitalism from a perspective in which discovery elements may be treated as subsidiary. Such a perspective yields insights concerning justice which ought not to be lost, even when one's grasp of capitalism is deepened to incorporate discovery. I should not, therefore, close this book without making clear the sense in which I believe discovery to be in fact intertwined with the "pure production" aspects of the market (which the standard literature has unfortunately so exclusively emphasized). A full appreciation of the appropriate criteria for assessing the justice of the capitalist process must be able to integrate both the discovery and non-discovery elements into a broadened and enriched understanding.

The sense in which capitalism can be grasped without attention to its discovery elements, is an *ex post* one. As noticed earlier in this book, an *ex post* view tends to subordinate the uncertainty that ineradicably suffuses the world. This uncertainty, unavoidably palpable as it is *ex ante*, seems to elude us when we look at history. The flow of events often seems *ex post* to have proceeded in ineluctable fashion; after the event we can see clearly how effect followed cause systematically and inescapably.

Looking back we can see clearly how we were blind not to have seen the way things were happening. It seems obvious *ex post* that inputs could and would yield definite quantities of specific products. It seems, from this *ex post* perspective, not illegitimate to reconstruct the analysis of decision making so as to conform with what turns out later to have been the case. It is this that has led economists (and hence the moral philosophers of economic justice) to treat the economic process as if no surprises can possibly occur; as if entrepreneurship consisted (not of determining for oneself what picture of the future shall be deemed most relevant for purposes of business planning, but) of selecting mathematically the best course of action out of already-fully-perceived alternative available programs for decision making. I have sharply taken exception to such an exclusive, narrow, view of decision making under capitalism. I have taken exception to it both at the level of positive theory (arguing that this view abstracts harmfully from critically significant causal links in the economic process), and at the level of moral appraisal (maintaining that this view blinds us to important relevant ethical insights). Yet a view which refused to take account of *some* valid features of the *ex post* perspective would itself be a flawed view. There are aspects of capitalism whose moral significance stems from considerations unrelated to discovery. I do not wish the discovery theory of justice to lose sight of these considerations. It is here that Nozick's entitlement theory of justice comes into its own, and turns out to be complementary to a discovery theory.[4]

As a person's life comes to be routinized, his regular schedule of activities, within a stable environment, makes up a repeated pattern of experiences from which major surprises are absent. Of course, no one's life is totally without surprises; no one is exempt from acting entrepreneurially. No environment is sufficiently stable for discovery and uncertainty to be totally absent. Yet one's life may be sufficiently even and serenely repetitive to warrant analysis in terms of a pure production approach. As a society adjusts to external shocks, as its economy gradually converges on the most effective ways of dealing with changed conditions, we can seek to understand its operation in terms of models of equilibrium. We may

---

4. This is in addition to the sense in which, as argued in ch. 6, a pure discovery theory is to be seen as riding piggyback on the entitlement theoretic rejection of patterned theories of justice.

criticize these models as harmfully deflecting our attention from centrally important cause-and-effect processes (which are necessarily absent from them). But we cannot deny a certain usefulness to these models. The simplifications of which we rightfully complain, do nonetheless capture features of reality which have significance.

Nozick's entitlement theory, as also J. B. Clark's marginal contribution theory, would have considerable relevance in a world without major surprises, in an economy which had attained a comfortable, even, "circular flow." The problem with these approaches is that it requires us to imagine capitalism as it never has been—without major surprises, without scope for major discoveries. But I would not, in drawing attention to the entrepreneurial opportunities which inspire the ceaseless inflow of new ideas and the continual impact of unexpected events, deny that, besides these discovery elements in capitalism, inextricably intertwined with them, are elements of fairly stable repetitive patterns. Entitlement insights concerning the possibility of just transfers in capitalist exchange, expressed in a framework from which discovery is absent, do capture moral intuitions worthy of our appreciation. The same is, of course, true with regard to Clarkian intuitions concerning the deservedness of capitalist factor incomes.

As an economy develops during any short period of time we may postulate a systematic approach towards fuller adjustment to the underlying data. We may argue that Nozickian and/or Clarkian moral considerations become increasingly relevant. On the other hand, as economies grow more affluent over longer periods of time and as opportunities for technological innovation become increasingly open, the innate uncertainties arising from the freedoms of the market-place render the equilibrium view less and less faithful a picture of the capitalist process. The extent to which discovery insights need to be introduced into both the economics and the moral philosophy of capitalism seems to be greater and greater as capitalism itself develops and becomes more intricate and more "open-ended."

If I have painted my picture of capitalism, in this book, with greater-than-warranted emphasis upon the pure discovery features of the system, this must be excused in the light of this historical circumstance. While capitalist output can legitimately be seen from the traditional equilibrium perspective, as a given pie to be distributed, I have drawn attention to the increasing relevance of quite different perspectives. From these increasingly relevant perspectives, capitalist output comes to be perceived less and less as a given pie waiting to be distributed, and more and more as a discovered pie, the discovered emergence of which generates moral imperatives of its own.

DISCOVERY AND THE DEFENSE OF CAPITALISM

Moral critics have denounced capitalism as unjust. Apart from all other moral failings which they have attributed to the market system, the critics have condemned it as treating its workers and its poor unfairly and unjustly, as being built upon foundations of injustice and exploitation. My thesis has not been to defend capitalism by declaring these criticisms to be based on morally flawed criteria. Rather I have attempted to present capitalism as a system which works differently than its critics (and most of its defenders) believe it to work. Once the capitalist process is understood in its full reality, I have maintained, its assignment of incomes (and the roots of its system of private property) can be appreciated in a different moral light. This different moral light, I have insisted, follows from an appreciation of the element of discovery which pervades the capitalist process. This new moral light need not entirely displace existing defenses of capitalist justice; but, as capitalist societies develop into increasing affluence, open-endedness, and freedom of opportunity, these defenses may find the support of the discovery perspective to be more and more significant. A defense of capitalist justice has not declared it innocent of all moral flaws. It certainly has not declared all behavior under historical capitalism to have been moral or even to have been just. A defense of capitalist justice suggests, however, that the system that has been so extraordinarily productive in raising the standards of human life need not be rejected out of hand on the grounds of innate unfairness. Moral improvement may be sought within the capitalist framework, without harboring a guilty sense of participation in a inevitably and fundamentally flawed form of social organization.

ARTICLES

PRODUCER, ENTREPRENEUR,
AND THE RIGHT TO PROPERTY

"The institution of property," John Stuart Mill remarked, "when limited to its essential elements, consists in the recognition, in each person, of a right to the exclusive disposal of what he or she have produced by their own exertions, or received either by gift or by fair agreement, without force or fraud, from those who produced it. The foundation of the whole is the right of producers to what they themselves have produced."[1] My purpose is to point out the ambiguity of the phrase "what a man has produced" and to draw attention, in particular, to one significant, economically valid meaning of the term, a meaning involving the concept of entrepreneurship, which seems to have been overlooked almost entirely.

Precision in applying the term "what a man has produced" seems to be of considerable importance. The ethical views associated with widely disparate ideologies, relating both to the justifiability of private rights to property and to the problem of justice in the distribution of incomes, appear to involve in some form the notion of "what a man has produced." Thus the Lockean theory of private property, which came to serve as the source of the moral case for capitalism,[2] has been understood as depending on the view that man has the right to the "fruits of his work."[3] As Milton Friedman has pointed out, the capitalist ethic (which he identifies as holding that "a man deserves what he produces"[4]) is shared by Marx, since Marx's view on the exploitation of labor, resting on the premise that labor produces the whole product, is valid "only if labor is entitled to what it produces."[5]

Without necessarily accepting, therefore, any one of these ethical positions, it seems worthwhile to achieve clarity by seeking to understand exactly what the notion "what a man has produced" is to mean. The

Presented at a Symposium on Property Rights, held at San Francisco, January 1973.

Reprinted from *Perception, Opportunity, and Profit: Studies in the Theory of Entrepreneurship* (Chicago and London: University of Chicago Press, 1979), 185–99 and 259–61, with permission of the Institute of Humane Studies; original source is *Property in a Humane Economy*, edited by Samuel Blumenfeld (LaSalle, Ill.: Open Court, 1974), 245–62.

literature seems to have perceived production *insofar as it flows from factors of production,* so that the statement "what a man has produced" has been intended to mean "what has been produced by those factors of production identified with the man with whom we are concerned." Briefly, a man is a producer insofar as he is himself considered a factor of production, or as he is the owner of factors viewed as responsible for output. Thus, Friedman seems to further identify the capitalist ethic with the view that "an individual deserves what is produced by the resources he owns."[6] J. B. Clark rested "the right of society to exist in its present form" on his marginal productivity theory of distribution, seeing it as satisfying the requirement that each man gets what he produces.[7] Locke's labor theory of property begins from the premise that "every man has a property in his own person. . . . The labor of his body and the work of his hands we may say are properly his."[8] Production is made possible only by the ownership of agents of production.

It follows that if we perceive production as flowing from factors of production, and if we correspondingly relate the ethical implication of "what a man has produced" strictly to that which derives from the factors of production that man owns including, of course, his own labor capacity, then the exercise of pure entrepreneurship in production (i.e., seen as involving no element of factor ownership) carries with it none of the favorable ethical connotations attached to "that which a man has produced." This conclusion requires some elaboration.

FACTOR OWNERSHIP AND ENTREPRENEURSHIP

It is well known that economic literature suffers from insufficient attention paid to the entrepreneurial role, so that we find few careful attempts to define precisely what this role consists of. In the more sophisticated discussions of entrepreneurship, a fairly sharp distinction has emerged between the factors of production, on the one hand, and entrepreneurship on the other. In Schumpeter's classic discussion, for example, the means of production include *all* agents required to produce the product in the state of circular flow (equilibrium). In equilibrium there is the tendency "for the entrepreneur to make neither profit nor loss . . . he has no function of a special kind there, he simply does not exist."[9] In disequilibrium, on the other hand, innovations in product quality and in methods of production are attributable to the initiative of pioneering Schumpeterian entrepreneurs. Although, that is to say, the new products or the new productive techniques require *no* resources beyond those consistent with the state of equilibrium, these new products and techniques would not have appeared at all in the first place had it not been for entrepreneurial daring and drive.

It follows that there is a built-in ambiguity, therefore, concerning the sense in which pure entrepreneurship can be considered a resource necessary for the emergence of the product. And this ambiguity is no doubt partly responsible for the disagreement among economists whether to treat entrepreneurship as a factor of production.[10]

However, until a product or technique has been introduced, possession of all necessary means of production (including relevant knowledge) guarantees nothing without the presence of entrepreneurial initiative. So even Schumpeter recognizes that entrepreneurship "may be conceived as a means of production."[11] On the other hand, if a would-be producer asks the question: "Supposing I decide to produce product X (or to utilize production technique Y), what means of production will it be necessary for me to obtain?" then it is clear that the answer will not include "the decision to produce product X (or to use technique Y)." And this is undoubtedly why Schumpeter stated that "ordinarily" he did *not* conceive of entrepreneurship as a factor of production.[12]

Clearly a sharp distinction must be drawn between means of production ordinarily conceived and entrepreneurship. The latter is *not* similar to factors of production insofar as concerns the theory of marginal productivity.[13] More fundamentally, entrepreneurship, even if considered a means of production, *cannot be purchased or hired by the entrepreneur;* that is, it is never perceived by the potential entrepreneur as either an available or a necessary productive factor. Either the entrepreneur is prepared to take the initiative or he is not.[14] If he is not prepared to take the initiative, the would-be entrepreneur simply sees the project as, on balance, not worth undertaking. He does not see it as a project for which a needed resource is unavailable. If he is determined to take the initiative again, then all he needs to obtain are the factors that would be required in the entrepreneurless state of equilibrium. Or, to put the matter in a slightly different form, the engineer asked to identify the productive agents to which a product is to be attributed, may indeed include intangibles such as "knowledge," but will *not* list "initiative," since the very notion of attribution presupposes the decision to produce. Accordingly, since the entire product can be attributed to the "other" means of production, it follows that entrepreneurship is not a means of production at all and cannot be credited with having contributed anything to the product.

To sum up, the literature revolving around the ethical implications of "what a man has produced," is concerned with what has been produced by the factors of production a man owns or even more narrowly, by the man himself seen as a factor of production. If one perceives pure entrepreneurship as not being a productive factor, it follows that it cannot share in the favorable ethical implications of being responsible for the product. On the other hand, if one views entrepreneurship as a productive factor, attributing some portion of the product's value to the initiative of the entrepreneur, parallel with the contributions made by the other factors, then that portion, however calculated or evaluated—*but no more than that portion*—may be considered as having been produced by the entrepreneur and as relevant, therefore, to the corresponding ethical implications.

In the following pages I will draw attention to the possibility of a position almost precisely opposite in all respects to that just presented. In this position, the favorable implications of the phrase "what a man has produced" *do not apply at all to factors of production.* Rather, pure entrepreneurship is responsible—in the sense relevant to the ethical connotations of "what a man has produced"—to the *entire* product. Moreover, this way of seeing matters is only helped by insight into the sense in which entrepreneurship is *not* to be considered a factor of production. In other words, paradoxically enough, the entrepreneur is to be considered the sole "producer" of the entire product—in the ethically relevant sense—precisely because he makes *no* contribution to production in the sense relevant to the theory of marginal productivity. A sentence from Knight presents, I believe, the essence of this argument. Much of it can be viewed as a commentary on the following: "Under the enterprise system, a special social class, the businessmen, direct economic activity: *they are in the strict sense the producers, while the great mass of the population merely furnish them with productive services, placing their persons and their property at the disposal of this class;* the entrepreneurs *also* guarantee to those who furnish productive services a fixed remuneration."[15]

SOME OBSERVATIONS ON THE LOCKEAN THEORY OF PROPERTY

A philosopher-critic of Locke's theory of property has summed up the theory as follows: (1) every man has a (moral) right to own his person; therefore (2) every man has a (moral) right to own the labor of his person; therefore (3) every man has a (moral) right to own that which he has mixed the labor of his person with.[16] This summary will serve us conveniently.

Apparently Locke took it for granted that, since a man has a moral right to his own labor in the sense of "working," he also has a moral right to that which his labor produces. This view, which we call proposition 3*a* (and which we have cited above as an example of the ethical values attached to the notion of "what a man has produced"), seems implicit in proposition 3.[17] However proposition 3 goes beyond the view that what a man has produced is morally his own. Proposition 3 asserts that when a man mixes his labor with unowned natural resources, in the natural state in which there is "still enough and as good left,"[18] he is to be considered as the natural private owner of what results from the mixing. Clearly, it is the ambitious proposition 3 that is of the greatest importance for Locke's own thesis. It is, however, with the more modest proposition 3*a* that I am concerned.

That in proposition 3*a* Locke has in mind labor-as-factor-of-production seems clear from his often cited extension of his proposition 3 to include hired labor. "Thus . . . the turfs my servant has cut, and the ore I have dug in any place where I have a right to them in common with others, become my property without the assignation or consent of anybody."[19] A man's own labor is his own in a sense no different from that in which the labor of his servant is an employer's. What has been produced by a man's own labor is his own in the same sense in which what has been produced by an employee's labor is the employer's.

It is true that Day is sharply critical of Locke, denying that one can talk significantly of owning labor in the sense of "working." Laboring, Day contends, is an activity, "and although activities can be engaged in, performed or done, they cannot be owned."[20] However, economists will find Locke's use of terms quite familiar and acceptable. Economists speak of agents of production (in the sense of *stocks*), and of the "services" of agents of production (in the flow sense). A man who "owns" an agent of production is considered by economists to own, by that token, also the services flowing from that agent. Again, by hiring the services of a productive agent, a producer is considered by economists to have acquired ownership of the service flow, by purchase from the previous owner of that flow (that is, the owner of the agent "itself"). In speaking of owning the services of an employee, therefore, the economist does not in fact have in mind the ownership of the *activity* of working, nor the ownership of that which the activity of working produces, nor even the ownership of the *capacity* for working.[21] Rather the economist is perceiving the employee as a stock of human capital, capable of generating a flow of services. So that, to the various different meanings Day discovers to be attached to the word labor should be added labor viewed as the flow of abstract productive service generated by a human being.

Viewed in this economist's sense, therefore, Locke's theory seems to say, quite understandably: (1°) Every man has a (moral) right to own the human capital represented by his person; therefore (2°) every man has a (moral) right to own the flow of labor services associated with his person; therefore (3a°) every man has a right to the product produced by these labor services—just as he has the right to the product produced by the labor services he has hired from an employee.

Clearly, therefore, proposition 3a°, with which we are ourselves concerned, relates to labor viewed as a physical factor of production. It appears, moreover, that even the notion of labor as *sacrifice*—a notion that might permit one to regard the product as being deserved by the laborer in the sense of reward for sacrifice—is foreign to Locke's theory. Thus, as Myrdal has pointed out, Locke's view "that labor is the source of property has nothing to do with pain and sacrifice but follows from the idea of labor as a natural property of the worker and as the cause and creator of value."[22] So Locke, at any rate, is not arguing his proposition (3a°) on the basis of any ethically merited *reward* for the pain or sacrifice of labor. Instead, it appears, Locke's proposition (3a°) rests on the ethical view that the product *physically derived from a man's property* should belong to him in the same sense that the natural growth from a man's property may be deemed to belong to him naturally.[23] This is entirely consistent with the usual interpretation of Lockean ethical arguments, as presented by modern economists, in terms of the language of the theory of marginal productivity.[24] We shall see that there are grounds for discovering, however, elements of an alternative perception of the ethical meaningfulness of production in Locke.

HUMAN WILL AND THE ACQUISITION OF PROPERTY

Contrasted with the notion of the product as *physically* produced by man, with or without the use of other productive resources, is the perception of the product as resulting from the *human will*. As discussed briefly above, I shall be arguing that for the purposes of ethically justifying property in products, it may be relevant to draw attention to the sense in which the product finds its source in entrepreneurial decision making rather than to the sense in which it is derived from factor ownership. While explicit recognition of this insight is almost entirely absent from the literature, it is possible to discover a number of remarks and views that suggest an "entrepreneurial" approach to a justification for property.

Thus, in Locke's own century, Pufendorf emphasized the distinction between an action that is forced and one that is performed freely. Only the latter is properly a *human* action, involving "an element of subjective spontaneity" and a "free project of the self."[25] A century later, Kant's theory of the acquisition of property through labor saw the labor itself as almost irrelevant to the act of acquisition. "When it is a question of the first acquisition of a thing, the cultivation or modification of it by labour forms nothing more than an external sign of the fact that it has been taken into possession."[26] It is not the mixing of labor with an object that makes it one's own, but "the transcendental operation of directing [one's] will upon [it]."[27] Hegel, too, saw in the human will the true source of property rights and moreover saw it as providing a justification for the acquisition of natural resources superior to that depending upon the mixing of labor.[28]

Moreover, it has seemed to some writers that Locke's labor theory of property, too, as well as the labor theory of value of the later classical economists,[29] cannot be properly understood unless one recognizes the special character of labor, the *human* factor, as compared with other factors of production. So, if one accepts their view, it turns out to be not quite correct to interpret Locke's theory of property as depending on the view that the product arises physically from an owned factor of production that happens to be labor. Thus Weisskopf, in his psychological analysis of classical economics, viewed as deriving from Locke, emphasizes labor as *an activity of the person.* Following on Myrdal,[30] Weisskopf points out that in the classical view nature is seen as dead, with only human labor seen as the *active* agent. Petty's dictum comparing labor to the father, the active principle of wealth, with land seen as the mother, is used by Weisskopf to explain the Locke-classical treatment of labor as the sole origin of wealth for purposes of justifying property rights and of explaining the determination of value.[31]

If Weisskopf's view of the matter is correct, then Locke's labor theory does not relate to that aspect of labor in which it is seen merely as a physical source of the product, but rather to the aspect of labor in which it is seen as inseparable from the active human will of the laborer. Plausible though Weisskopf's view may be for an understanding of the classical preoccupation with labor, it seems difficult to reconcile it with Locke's treatment of hired labor as being as complete a justification for property rights in the product as one's own labor. If Locke's treatment of hired labor envisages the employer as hiring not only the physical labor services of the employee, but also the active, spontaneous, human elements associated with these services, then of course he is not understanding these elements in their purely entrepreneurial sense in which, by definition, they cannot be hired at all.[32]

Finally, we notice that, more recently, Oliver, in drawing attention to the inadequacy of Marxian labor theory for a doctrine of "earned-income," in which a man is entitled to what he has produced, argues that Marx leaves no room for the role of the free will exercised by the laborer in his work, when such a role is essential for the very concept of "earning."[33] We thus have an example of the recognition of the role of the human will in ethical evaluation of "what a man has produced."

PRODUCTION: AUTOMATIC GROWTH OR HUMAN CREATION?

From the foregoing discussion, it will be apparent that we are confronted with two quite different views on the nature of production. I turn now to spell out explicitly what these two views are and to consider briefly their plausibility as foundations for the ethical view that what a man has produced ought to be his.

1. *Production as automatic growth from the factors of production.* The one view sees production as it would occur in the state of equilibrium. In such a state, each producing firm has already been fully adjusted to the conditions of the market. The services of necessary inputs (including the services of managers) flow smoothly into the firm in synchronized fashion, with the corresponding output flow emerging with equal smoothness. The market value of the input flow corresponds exactly to that of the output flow; alternative uses for input services offer no higher factor prices, alternative sources of input supply promise no saving. Certainly one can say that the output has been produced by the productive input services. But because there has, in such a state, been no room for

entrepreneurship, output must be seen as emerging *automatically,* as it were, from the combined input flow, exactly as fruit might grow from a tree without direction from the owner of the tree. To rest an ethical case for ownership in a product on the circumstance that a man's productive resources have produced it, in *this* sense, is to claim that the product is his not on the grounds that *he* has permitted the factors to create the product, but on the grounds that the product has grown—as it were automatically—from the factor services he owns.

2. *Production as a human creation.* The alternative view refuses to see the product as emerging automatically from a given combination of factor services. In this view, the product has come into being only because some human being has *decided* to bring together the necessary productive factors. In deciding to initiate the process of production, this human being has *created* the product. In his creation of the product this entrepreneur producer has *used* the factors of production his vision has brought together. He has not cooperated jointly with these factors, so that this view does not see the entrepreneur's contribution as consisting of a portion of the value of the product, with the remaining portion being the contributions of "other" productive agents. He has produced *the whole product entirely on his own,* being able to do so by his initiative, daring, and drive in identifying and taking advantage of the available productive factors. In this view, an ethical case for ownership in a product, based on one's having created it, depends strictly on one's *not* having been the owner of one of the cooperating input factors. To the extent that an entrepreneur was also a factor owner, he is credited with the creation of the product only in the sense that he purchases his factor services from himself, so to speak, rather than permitting them to serve alternative purposes.

If one uses the first of these two views on production as the basis for an ethical case for property in the product, or in the distribution of income, it is entirely relevant to use a Clarkian marginal productivity approach. The contribution of a factor of production must somehow be disentangled from the contributions of other factors, and the theory of marginal productivity may, with greater or lesser success, be called upon for this purpose. But if it is the second (creation) view that is to be used, then marginal productivity is entirely irrelevant except in a sense to be discussed below. On this second view, the necessarily indivisible entrepreneur is responsible for the entire product. The contributions of the factor inputs, being without any entrepreneurial component, are irrelevant for the ethical position being taken.

Of course, it is true that also on this second view, the entrepreneur producer must, in order to create the product, acquire the services of the necessary productive factors. (And, in fact, competition may force him to compensate them to the full extent of their respective marginal products.) However, it should be plain that this view does not claim rights in the product for the entrepreneur on the grounds that, since he has fairly purchased these factor services, production has now been carried on with *his* factor services. In this view, the entrepreneur's rights rest strictly on the vision and initiative with which, at the time when he owned *no* productive resources, he undertook to marshal them for his purposes.

It is not my purpose to choose between these two interpretations of the ethical implications of producing. Rather, I want to draw attention to the existence of the second view and to emphasize that it is diametrically opposed to the first view. In choosing which of these views to endorse (if, indeed, one wishes to endorse either of them at all) or which of them to ascribe to particular writers, it is necessary to consider carefully whether it is the active human *creativity* of the producer that is to be underlined and recognized or the ownership of the physical or other *ingredients of production*.

FINDERS, KEEPERS, AND SPECULATIVE PROFITS

The points made in the preceding section may perhaps throw light on certain matters raised in discussions concerning the ethics of property and income distribution. Oliver[34] has noted that sometimes writers presenting ethical positions based on "what a man has produced," introduce the notion of finders-keepers. "The man . . . that first discovers and claims title to natural resources thereby gains ownership." Oliver points out that Locke's position bases ownership in natural resources (with which one has mixed one's labor) partly on discovery. For Oliver, finders-keepers is a rule that bears no relation at all to the ethical deservingness associated with having produced something. Our insight into the entrepreneurial view of production may perhaps be of some help in this respect.

Briefly, it seems that Locke's labor theory of property rights is best understood as involving a combination, possibly a confusion, of *both* the factorial and the entrepreneurial views of production. We recall our earlier reference to Myrdal's and Weisskopf's understanding of Locke in terms of the contrast between active, live labor, and passive, dead nature. This certainly supports the theory that Locke viewed labor not merely as a factor of production, but as also involving the uniquely human element we have identified with entrepreneurship. Again, the initially puzzling view Locke presents, in which title to natural resources is acquired by the mixing of labor, becomes understandable when the mixing of labor with the natural resource is perceived as the grasping of the entrepreneurial opportunity offered by the available but as yet unappropriated resources. The finders-keepers rule that Oliver discovers in Locke thus represents essentially the same ethical view as that underlying the entrepreneurial view of production. In this view, a producer is entitled to what he has produced not because he has contributed anything to its physical fabrication, but because *he perceived and grasped the opportunity* for its fabrication by utilizing the resources available in the market. This is clearly an example of finding and keeping.

These insights appear relevant to some comments by Samuelson on the normative aspects of speculative profits. Where a crop failure generates speculative profits, Samuelson points out that the successful speculator need only be a trifle quicker than his rivals in order to make his fortune. In his absence, the socially advantageous consequences of his speculation (i.e., the curtailment of relatively less urgently needed consumption at earlier dates, making possible some more urgently needed consumption at later dates) would occur seconds later through the activities of other speculators. Even if one accepts "a Clarkian naive-productivity theory of ethical deservingness," Samuelson remarks, one can hardly justify the capture of all the profits by the successful speculator who saved society from no more than a few seconds of unwise consumption. Without commenting on the substance of Samuelson's normative criticism of speculative profits,[35] it seems useful to remark that, as we have seen, a Clarkian ethical approach is wholly inappropriate anyway in dealing with entrepreneurial profits. What *might* be of greater relevance would be the entrepreneurial view that, as we have seen, consists essentially in precisely a finders-keepers ethic. According to such an ethic, an opportunity perceived and grasped confers ethical deservingness. Necessarily, this perceives the gain from grasping the opportunity as having been deserved, despite the possibility or even the likelihood that others might have perceived and grasped the same opportunity seconds later. No one is bound, of course, to subscribe to this entrepreneurial ethic; in fact one may reject it precisely on Samuelson's grounds, if one chooses. But it does seem appropriate to judge the deservingness of one particular example of entrepreneurial profit on the approach relevant to a defense of the deservingness of entrepreneurial profits in general.[36]

THE ENTREPRENEURIAL ELEMENT
IN FACTOR OWNERS' DECISIONS

Although I have emphasized the distinction between the factor-of-production view on the one hand and the creation-entrepreneurial view on the other, it seems wise to point out a circumstance that operates to blur, to some extent, the sharp line we have drawn between these views. This circumstance is the presence of an entrepreneurial element in *every* human action and decision, including, especially for our purposes, the decisions of factor owners.

The isolation of a purely entrepreneurial element in production is, of course, an analytical device. Human action in its totality is made up of an entrepreneurial element (to which is attributable the decision maker's awareness of the ends-means framework within which he is free to operate), *and* an economizing element (to which we attribute the efficiency, with respect to the perceived ends-means framework, of the decision taken).[37] Analytically, we conceive of factor owners as pure economizers operating within an already-perceived market framework. Entrepreneurs, on the other hand, we perceive as becoming aware (with no resources of their own at all) of changed patterns of resource availability, of technological possibilities, and of possibilities for new products that will be attractive to consumers. But flesh and blood resource owners are, of course, also to *some* extent, their own entrepreneurs, just as flesh and blood entrepreneurs are likely to be owners of some factor services themselves.

It follows that when a producer hires the services of productive agents, entrepreneurship has, in fact, been exercised not only by "the" entrepreneur, but also by the factor owners in deciding to sell. While productive services may be viewed as flowing passively from the productive agent, it is the factor owner's decision (from which all elements of entrepreneurship cannot be entirely absent) that permits the flow to proceed in the adopted channel, rather than in alternative processes of production. In the case of labor in particular, the factor owner's decision to permit the service flow is required at every minute of his service. So that when we say, in an apparently "factor-of-production" view of the matter, that a factor has produced a product, we are, *in real-world cases,* referring *both* to the factor as producer and to the factor owner as, at least to some extent, entrepreneur. Now, it seems of great importance to emphasize the two quite different senses of production so involved. It seems, at the same time, helpful to notice how easily the two views on production can become combined or confused. This will perhaps account not only for the view my interpretation has ascribed to Locke, but also for the circumstance that the literature has failed almost entirely to notice explicitly the possibility of an entrepreneurial, factorless view of the ethical implications of producing. The single but outstanding exception is the sentence in Knight cited earlier, in which it is the entrepreneurs who are seen in the strict sense as the producers, with the factor owners merely furnishing them with productive services.

NOTES

1. J. S. Mill, *Principles of Political Economy,* ed. William J. Ashley (London, 1923), p. 218.

2. See G. Myrdal, *The Political Element in the Development of Economic Theory* (Cambridge: Harvard University Press, 1954), pp. 71ff.; R. Schlatter, *Private Property: The History of an Idea* (New Brunswick: Rutgers University Press, 1951), ch. 7; C. B. Macpherson, "The social bearing of Locke's political theory," *Western Political Quarterly* 7 (1954): 1–22; A. Ryan, "Locke and the dictatorship of the bourgeoisie," *Political Studies* 13 (1965): 219–30.

3. Myrdal, *Political Element.* Strictly speaking, Locke did not actually assert that, by mixing his labor with a nature-given resource, he has thereby "produced" the result. However, he has certainly been understood as having implied as much. Thus, commenting on the notion "that, if a man 'makes' something, it is his," Oliver cites Locke as having given expression to this idea in his labor theory of property rights (H. M. Oliver, *A Critique of Socioeconomic Goals* [Bloomington: Indiana University Press, 1954], p. 27). This is further discussed later in this chapter.

4. M. Friedman, *Price Theory: A Provisional Text* (Chicago: Aldine, 1962), p. 196.

5. M. Friedman, *Capitalism and Freedom* (Chicago: University of Chicago Press, 1962), p. 167. On this, see also Oliver, *Critique of Socioeconomic Goals,* p. 37. In an extensive critique of Oliver's discussion, M. N. Rothbard, *Power and Market, Government and the Economy* (Menlo Park, Calif.: Institute for Humane Studies, 1970), p. 183, makes it clear that he supports the same underlying ethic.

6. Friedman, *Price Theory*, p. 196.

7. J. B. Clark, *The Distribution of Wealth* (New York and London: Macmillan, 1899), p. 3.

8. J. Locke, *An Essay concerning the True Original, Extent and End of Civil Government*, paragraph 27.

9. J. A. Schumpeter, *The Theory of Economic Development* (Cambridge: Harvard University Press, 1934), p. 76.

10. On this, see, for example, the discussion in F. Machlup, *The Economics of Sellers' Competition* (Baltimore: Johns Hopkins University Press, 1952), pp. 226–28. See also chapter 10 in this book [Israel M. Kirzner, "Alertness, luck, and entrepreneurial profit," in *Perception, Opportunity, and Profit* (Chicago: University of Chicago Press, 1979)].

11. Schumpeter, *Theory of Economic Development*, p. 143.

12. Ibid.

13. See ibid., p. 153; Machlup, *Economics of Sellers' Competition*, p. 226; Knight, *Risk, Uncertainty and Profit*, p. 271.

14. On all this, see my *Competition and Entrepreneurship* (Chicago: University of Chicago Press, 1973), ch. 2.

15. Knight, *Risk, Uncertainty and Profit*, p. 271; emphasis on the central clause supplied. Similar statements are to be found in F. Hawley, *Enterprise and the Productive Process* (New York: Putnam, 1907), pp. 85, 102, 112, 127.

16. J. P. Day, "Locke on property," *Philosophical Quarterly* 16 (1966): 207–20, reprinted in *Life, Liberty, and Property: Essays on Locke's Political Ideas*, ed. G. J. Schochet (Belmont, Calif.: Wadsworth, 1971), p. 109. All page references will be to this reprint.

17. See Day, "Locke on property," pp. 109–10; and see note 3 above.

18. Locke, *Essay*, paragraph 33.

19. Ibid., paragraph 28.

20. Day, "Locke on property," pp. 113ff.

21. On all this, see ibid.

22. Myrdal, *Political Element*, p. 74. It should be noted, however, that just as the later classical economists used expressions like "trouble," "sacrifice," and "pain" synonymously with "labor"—and are for this reason described by Myrdal as having viewed labor strictly as the "trouble caused by effort" (ibid.)—so too does Locke occasionally (see paragraphs 30, 34) seem to identify the justification for ownership of the product of one's labor as resting on one's having been he "who takes pains about it."

23. See the reference in E. Halévy, *The Growth of Philosophic Radicalism* (Boston: Beacon Press, 1955), p. 45, to Hume's view that "we are the proprietors of the fruits of our garden, and of the dung of our flock by virtue of the normal operation of the laws of association."

24. See Oliver, *A Critique of Socioeconomic Goals*, p. 33; see also the sources referred to above in notes 4 and 7.

25. See A. C. Cutler, "Some concepts of human rights and obligations in classical Protestantism," in *Natural Law and Natural Rights*, ed. A. L. Harding (Dallas: Southern Methodist University Press, 1955), p. 16.

26. I. Kant, *Philosophy of Law*, ed. Hastie (Edinburgh, 1887), p. 92.

27. Schlatter, *Private Property*, p. 256.

28. Ibid.

29. On the question of the influence of Locke's labor theory of property on the later classical labor theory of value, there has been controversy. Myrdal, *Political Element*, pp. 71ff.; Halévy, *Growth of Philosophic Radicalism*, p. 44; and W. A. Weisskopf, *The Psychology of Economics* (Chicago: University of Chicago Press, 1955), pp. 22ff., 145, all assert a direct influence. See, however, J. A. Schumpeter, *History of Economic Analysis* (London: Oxford University Press, 1954), pp. 120, 310–11; see also I. M. Kirzner, *The Economic Point of View* (Princeton: Van Nostrand, 1960), pp. 25, 190, nn. 8, 9.

30. Myrdal, *Political Element*, p. 72; see especially Myrdal's reference to Rodbertus.

31. Weisskopf, *Psychology of Economics*, pp. 25, 145.

32. For further discussion of the entrepreneurial element in the decisions of factor owners, see below, pp. 184–85.

33. Oliver, *Critique of Socioeconomic Goals*, p. 37.

34. Ibid., p. 42.

35. Samuelson's discussion is in his "Intertemporal price equilibrium: a prologue to the theory of speculation," *Weltwirtschaftliches Archiv* 79 (December 1957): 209. For further comment, see Kirzner, *Competition and Entrepreneurship*, ch. 6.

36. See Schlatter, *Private Property*, p. 191, n. 2, for references to use made of Locke's labor theory to condemn the ethical status of entrepreneurial profit.

37. See further, Kirzner, *Competition and Entrepreneurship*, ch. 2.

ENTREPRENEURSHIP, ENTITLEMENT, AND ECONOMIC JUSTICE

Nozick's entitlement theory of justice plays a crucial role in his carefully and brilliantly crafted case for the minimal state. Accepting the theory, it appears, sweeps away with one stroke all those demands for state interference with the market that rest on the claims of distributive justice. The persuasive elegance with which Nozick develops his position can leave few thoughtful, moralist critics of uncurbed capitalism unimpressed, at least, by the strong claims that Nozick advances, precisely on the grounds of economic justice, for the free market. It is the thesis of this chapter, however, that Nozick's theory of entitlement, important though it undoubtedly is for any defense of the morality of laissez-faire, does not—at least without significant reformulation— solve all the difficulties that exist in respect to the justice of the market. Pursuing this theme, I will offer a suggestion for supplementing, or perhaps reformulating, Nozick's theory that may not only equip it to handle the difficulties to which I will draw attention, but may, in fact, render its defense of the morality of the market even more straightforward and subject to fewer qualifications than Nozick apparently believes justified.

Nozick's theory depends largely, in its application to the market, on the view that with few definite exceptions, the market adheres to the principles of justice both in the *original acquisition of holdings* from the natural state and in subsequent *transfers of holdings* in market transactions. The difficulties to which I draw attention here pertain to the claim that the market is fully consistent with the principles of justice in transfer. This claim carries conviction only if we are prepared to incorporate into our entitlement theory certain somewhat novel views concerning the morality of the entrepreneurial role.

Presented at a meeting of the Austrian Economic Seminar, New York, May 1978.

Reprinted from *Perception, Opportunity, and Profit: Studies in the Theory of Entrepreneurship* (Chicago and London: University of Chicago Press, 1979), 200–224 and 261–66, with permission of Palgrave Macmillan; original source is *Eastern Economic Journal* 4 (1978): 9–25.

Recognizing this aspect of the entrepreneuial role makes it no longer useful to distinguish as sharply as Nozick does between justice in original acquisition, on the one hand, and justice in transfer. So that, while the entitlement theory may indeed be deployed to defend the morality of the market—and with fewer reservations, perhaps, than in Nozick's own statement—this will have been achieved only through a fairly substantial reformulation of that theory.

JUSTICE IN TRANSFER, VOLUNTARINESS, AND ERROR

For now, I accept Nozick's entitlement theory of justice without reservation. If an object was originally acquired justly from nature, and if all subsequent transfers of the object have been justly accomplished, then, we will say, the present holder of that object holds it justly, and no aesthetic or moral considerations concerning desirable distribution patterns can, without injustice, permit the state to tamper with the rights of the present holder. The issue that concerns us is whether this theory, when applied to the results of the free market, can certify these results as being in accord with just principles. Let us, for the time being, accept Nozick's own conclusion[1] that the free operation of the market system is consistent with past acquisition of initial holdings. Our concern will be with the justice of market transfers.

Now Nozick has not, he explains,[2] attempted in his book the task of specifying the details of the principles of justice in transfer. The general outlines of his position on the justice of market transfers are, however, clearly implied: What has been acquired through market transaction has been justly acquired for the simple reason that such transactions are *voluntary*. The money a professional athlete receives from spectators eager to watch his performance is justly his because those who paid have done so willingly. They preferred to watch the athlete at the given money price rather than to retain the money without witnessing the performance.[3] Because a property system excludes taking anyone's goods or money without his consent, whether by theft or fraud, because such a system permits transfer only by gift or voluntary market exchange, it follows that such a system has room only for transfers that are just.

The view assigning so critical a role to voluntariness in just transfers is surely highly appealing, and we will accept it fully as the basis for our discussion. Involuntary transfers, I have said, are ruled out in the market by definition; only voluntary exchanges qualify as market transactions.

The question I wish to raise has to do with the extent to which *error*, in the decisions of market participants to engage in exchange, erodes the voluntariness—and hence the justice—of the transfers effected by such exchange. Now it might appear that consistent application of our definition of market transactions as being voluntary avoids any difficulty for the justice of market transfer arising out of error. If, say, a seller sells an item in error, then either the error was so serious as to definitely impair the voluntariness of the sale, or it was not. That is, either the error on the part of the seller was so fundamental that we are compelled to say he did not *really* wish to sell at all (i.e., that his consent to sell was utterly erroneous and was thus no consent at all) or else it was not serious enough to impair the voluntariness of the sale. If the error *was* serious enough to render the sale involuntary, then we should simply pronounce the exchange a total mistake and thus not a permissible market transaction at all. Unjust though we must consider the purchase to have been, it was, we should say, not a market transaction but simply an involuntary transfer. If, on the other hand, the voluntariness of the sale was *not* undermined by the error, then the transfer remains a just one. Either way, it seems, the possibility of error presents no problems for the justice of market transfers. Defenders of the market have, after all, always made it clear that fraudulent transactions are a form of theft and are—with or without state action—to be expunged from the market system.[4] But surely a fairly persuasive case can be made for a less comfortable view of the matter. Such a case may perhaps gain plausibility from a consideration, first, of the degree to which the market process *depends*, in fact, on the profitability of entrepreneurial trading with market participants who have, at least to some extent, erred.

EQUILIBRIUM, DISEQUILIBRIUM, AND ERROR

For the economist's model of market equilibrium it is not only possible, but indeed necessary, to imagine a world without error. As Hayek explained forty years ago, equilibrium is defined as the state of correct foresight.[5] Were, then, a market economy to be continuously in equilibrium, it would be indeed easy to defend the voluntariness—and hence the justice—of all market transfers, since every one of them would reflect decisions made with complete awareness of market conditions. In no way could it be claimed that any exchanges were entered into out of ignorance.

But it is now well understood that the function of equilibrium models is hardly to portray the real world. Rather, such a model serves to illuminate the nature of the equilibrating market forces that are at work during the states of disequilibrium that, in fact, prevail at all times.[6] And it is the essence of states of disequilibrium that the decisions being made are quite different from those that would have been made in an errorless world. It is, further, the case that insight into the equilibrating forces of the market generated by the conditions of disequilibrium reveals them to operate through entrepreneurial discovery and exploitation of the errors characteristic of disequilibrium. A simple example illustrates the matter effectively.

It is one of the features of models of competitive equilibrium that, in the market for a given good, no more than one price can prevail during the same period. Before equilibrium has been attained, however, many prices for the same goods may be simultaneously paid and accepted by different buyers and sellers. The disequilibrium situation in which many prices prevail in this way generates a spontaneous equilibrating tendency toward the elimination of such gratuitous price differentials. The existence of a price differential constitutes an attractive opportunity for entrepreneurial profit. Eager seekers of profit will tend to grasp these opportunities until their competitive activity has squeezed out all such opportunities, that is, until prices have become uniform throughout the market.

Consideration of this simple example immediately shows how heavily the equilibrating process rests on the profitability of acting to take advantage of the errors of others. We notice at the very outset that the multiprice situation characteristic of disequilibrium reflects widespread ignorance on the part of buyers and sellers. Those who paid the higher prices were clearly unaware of the sellers who were prepared to accept, and in fact did accept, lower prices; and those sellers who accepted the lower prices were obviously unaware of the buyers who offered and paid the higher prices. The entrepreneur who discovers and moves to exploit the profit opportunities presented by the multiprice situation is buying at low prices from those who are unaware of the possibility of selling at higher prices. He, on the other hand, is buying at the low prices in order to sell at higher prices to those who are, in turn, unaware of the possibility of buying at lower prices. The equilibrative aspects of the market process depend, in an essential way, upon the lure of the profits made possible by the errors of those with whom the entrepreneur deals. In fact, the insights gained from the simple illustrative example we have used apply not only to this simple case but to the most complicated of markets, involving production in any number of stages, inputs in any number and any variety, and outputs of any degree of multiplicity and heterogeneity. The coordination and allocative properties of competitive markets depend entirely on the attractiveness of pure entrepreneurial profit opportunities; such opportunities arise only out of the less-than-perfect omniscience of those from whom entrepreneurs buy, and of those to whom they sell.

The questions I wish to raise concerning the justice of market transfers thus emerge fairly clearly. If the market depends heavily on the exploitation of profit opportunities made possible only by the errors of others, and if goods purchased from sellers who sold only as a result of error and money received from buyers who bought only as a result of error are considered unjustly acquired, then surely the justice of the market has been fatally compromised. It will not do to declare that transactions entered into in error—being "involuntary"—are excluded by definition from the class of market transactions, since a market process without "erroneous" transactions is unthinkable. The only logical possibility for defending the general morality of market transactions must be to maintain that the errors that characterize disequilibrium markets do *not* affect the voluntariness of the transactions completed. The profits won by entrepreneurs taking advantage of the errors of others are, one would have to maintain, not unjust, as measured by Nozick's "voluntarism" yardstick of justice in transfer. Can such a position, we must ask, in fact be maintained?

THE MORALITY OF ENTREPRENEURIAL PROFIT: A BRIEF DIGRESSION

It will be seen that the question I have raised about the justice of market transfers generally has led us to question, in particular, the justice of pure entrepreneurial profit.[7] The form in which this last question is posed makes it rather different from other challenges to the morality of profits. It may be useful to digress very briefly in order to explain this difference. The roots of the matter lie, in the first place, in the theory of profit one chooses to embrace, and, in the second place, in the theory of justice one wishes to apply.

Most criticisms of capitalism made on moral grounds have denounced profit as unjust. Usually such criticism has rested on one or another of the theories of economic justice that Nozick has, persuasively, rejected in favor of the entitlement theory. Entrepreneurial profits are likely to violate many of the patterns of distributive justice one might wish to promote. In addition, the critics saw profits as generated by, say, the exploitation of labor or the unfair exercise of economic power; or else what they were criticizing as profit was not pure entrepreneurial profit at all, but the interest on capital.[8]

The question that I, on the other hand, have raised about entrepreneurial profit and, indeed, about all market transfers rests on what has been described as an *arbitrage theory of pure profit;*[9] and it has been raised against the specific background of Nozick's entitlement theory. The arbitrage theory sees profit as generated by the existence of different prices in different parts of the market for what are, economically if not physically, identical goods. Such differentials can arise only as the result of imperfection in knowledge. It is this theory of profit that, in the context of Nozick's "voluntariness" criterion of justice in transfer, is responsible for the question raised here.

OPTIMUM IGNORANCE, DELIBERATE MISTAKES, AND GENUINE ERROR

We return to consider the possible challenge to the justice of market transfers, arising out of the errors on the basis of which market transactions are completed. Here I discuss and reject one possible way of dismissing this challenge altogether. In subsequent sections the question itself is examined.

One way that one might reject the challenge of injustice based on error is to deny altogether the possibility of genuine error. One might, that is, maintain that while market transactions are indeed frequently entered into as a result of incorrect knowledge or expectations, this *never* involves genuine error. After all, one who knows his vacation may be ruined by bad weather and nonetheless travels to the resort and occupies his hotel room cannot, when bad weather indeed arrives, be said to have really erred in the sense of having consented to do something which he did not "really" wish to do. After all, he deliberately erred; he deliberately risked his money; he gladly took his chances; every transaction he entered was a wholly voluntary one. To the extent that *every* decision made in error is made either through deliberately accepting an uncertainty (such as bad weather) concerning which accurate knowledge is simply unavailable, or through deliberately choosing not to spend the resources necessary to remove the possibility of error,[10] every decision has been deliberately and hence voluntarily made. A deliberate decision not to acquire costly knowledge is, after all, made voluntarily. If we rule out deception, where, for example, an entrepreneur misleads a seller into thinking no one else is prepared to pay a higher price,[11] the fact that someone sells to an entrepreneur at a low price (knowing full well that diligent search *might* yield the possibility of selling at a higher price) can surely not raise doubt concerning the voluntariness of the sale (even though it is true that, had the seller known that higher prices were being paid, he would not have sold at the lower price).

This line of argument denies that *genuine* error (in the sense of a decision's being made in unwitting ignorance of pertinent information) can be made at all. *All* mistakes are seen as the result of deliberately assumed risk. No mistakes can raise questions concerning the voluntariness of decisions made.

I have elsewhere argued at length that genuine error can and does indeed occur.[12] Without repeating that discussion here, I will simply point out that decisions are often made in ignorance of the very need or possibility of acquiring information that might be freely available. It is one thing to know that one is ignorant and to deliberately maintain one's ignorance because of the high cost of gaining knowledge. It is quite another to be ignorant simply because one has no inkling that one is ignorant, because one has no idea that information exists, or indeed that any such thing is imaginable, in the relevant context, as information. Surely the latter kind of ignorance is abundantly present; genuine error is alive and well. We cannot rule out the possibility that market decisions have been made not out of deliberately accepted ignorance, but out of genuine error. The "voluntariness" of such decisions still calls for examination.[13]

MISTAKES: LAW AND MORALITY

The question of erroneously made decisions has, of course, been treated thoroughly by jurists in regard to the law of contracts. And the kinds of error occurring during disequilibrium that have given us concern—where, say, sellers would not have sold at the price they accepted had they known the true eagerness of buyers elsewhere in the market—are, in the legal literature, *not* seen as affecting the validity of transactions completed. Providing the entrepreneur-buyer did not explicitly deceive the seller concerning the facts—extrinsic to the goods sold—about which he has been misinformed (and providing no fiduciary type of relationship between them exists that might render the buyer's silence concerning the truth a form of implied deception), the law finds no grounds to invalidate market transactions into which one of the parties has entered under mistaken assumptions concerning present or future market conditions. "Tacit acquiescence in the self-delusion of another, if nothing is said or done to mislead, or silence which does not make that which is stated false, draws with it no legal liability,"[14] we are told. And the kinds of self-delusion referred to include that of the landowner who sells his land for the price of grazing land when in fact it contains valuable minerals, or who is ignorant of the fact known to the buyer that a railroad is intended to pass through it. "If the parties are at arms' length, neither of them is under any obligation to call the attention of the opposite party to facts or circumstances which lie properly within his knowledge, although he may see that they are not actually within his knowledge."[15] The law thus takes a hard-boiled view of commercial transactions—an attitude often loosely and imprecisely identified as caveat emptor—that does not see a mistake (except where it is *induced* by one's trading partner) as legitimate cause for the invalidation of a completed transaction or commitment. Apparently the law does occupy a position close to that (rejected in the preceding section) which sees a mistake merely as a deliberately assumed gamble that failed, rather than as representing lack of true will to participate in the transaction as it turned out.[16]

But the *legal* validity of entrepreneurial transactions in disequilibrium markets is not at all what is of concern to us and was never in question. Of course the legal system within which the capitalist economy operates recognizes the validity of the market transactions that make up the system. We have been concerned with possible challenges to the morality of that very legal system that sustains capitalism. What answer, we have been asking, can one give those who might contend that market transfers violate Nozick's canons of justice in that error (which invariably characterizes market transactions) introduces an ineradicable moral stain of *involuntariness* into the very fabric of these transactions? It is noteworthy that the jurists expounding the hard-boiled attitude of the law toward mistake go out of their way *not* to defend the morality of those who benefit by the law's tough-mindedness. "No doubt" we are in fact told, "such dealings would be repugnant to a man of high honor and delicacy."[17] The view of fraud taken by the law is carefully distinguished from the view of moralists.[18] It will not do simply to denounce moralists who fail to include, in their assessment of the morality of market transactions, the enormous social benefits these transactions generate. To be sure, these benefits ought not to be overlooked by the moralist.[19] But Nozick's demonstration of the justice of the free market cannot, surely, be pronounced complete if the *voluntariness* of market transfers, upon which Nozick's case depends, can possibly remain under a cloud. What does one say to the critic who argues that the law permits the gullible to be *cheated*? ("Fraud is difficult to prove" is a repeated refrain;[20] and, anyway, what is not *technically* fraud may, to men of honor, be seen as cheating all the same.) And, in the broadest of senses, can it not be said that the market process *depends* on at least a mild form of "cheating"?

ON CHEATING AND THE JUST PRICE

No examination of the possibility of injustice in market transfers can avoid some reference to recent discussions of the medieval doctrines of just price. Earlier scholars understood the medieval writers to have seen *cost of production* as the criterion for justice in pricing. An unjust price for a good was one that diverged from its true value as defined by production costs, with the latter "determined by a fixed standard of living on the part of the producers and . . . not to include any element of *interest*."[21] An unjust price was thus seen as unjust not primarily because it involved deceit by the one party (or at least an error on the part of the second), but simply because justice requires that each party to an exchange receive the true value of what he has given up. If divergence from the true value is described as involving "cheating," this must then mean either merely that without deceit it would presumably be impossible to secure more than the true value of what one gives up, or that to cheat is to be *defined* purely in terms of divergence from true value. (Compare the phrase Nozick used in describing the old question about the possibility of profits: "How can there be profits if everything gets its full value, if no *cheating* goes on?"[22]) For decades after 1870, economists found it necessary to explain how inadequate such a conception of justice in transfer, ignoring all demand considerations, must be considered. And in Nozick's entitlement theory little room seems to be assigned for divergence from production costs as a criterion for injustice in transfer. (In referring to the possibility of "gouging," Nozick seems quite content to leave to buyers the responsibility of looking out for themselves.[23])

More recently, however, historians of medieval economic thought have emphasized references in the scholastic writings to market price as the criterion for justice.[24] And such references are occasionally couched in language suggesting that to take advantage of imperfect knowledge of market conditions on the part of one's trading partner is to violate the canons of the just price.[25] But it appears to be incorrect to ascribe to the medieval writers the concern for the possible injustice of disequilibrium market transfers I have expressed here. Whether, with Schumpeter and De Roover, one is prepared to credit Aquinas and the medieval writers with a sophisticated understanding of the relationship between cost of production and long-run equilibrium price, or whether, with Hollander, one is not prepared to do so, it seems fairly clear that for Aquinas actual market price is understood as being always the equilibrium price. It was because the market price was therefore seen as expressing the true value of a good, reflecting "the entire set of objective and subjective elements which forms the community estimate,"[26] that it was considered unjust to take advantage of a buyer's ignorance of the market price. It is true that pure profits were, as Hollander has explained, generally frowned upon by Aquinas, but this was clearly on grounds other than the taking advantage of the ignorance of one's trading partners. In other contexts it was clearly not considered unjust to take advantage of another's ignorance. A number of writers have drawn attention to Aquinas's view that a seller may charge a high price for grain in a place where it is dear, even though he knows that others are following with more supplies—a fact that, if known to the buyers, would have led them to refuse to pay the present higher price.[27] Clearly a price paid only out of ignorance of the true facts does not, in this view, by itself mark it as unjust.

Aquinas's justification for this permissive position clearly implies that the market price at a given instant is the true equilibrium price relevant to questions of justice. The present high value of the grain is its true present value. The anticipated arrival of additional supplies of grain can be expected to lower the market price *in the future,* so that a seller who sells at today's price does not act unjustly in failing to disclose what will happen in the future.[28] One can understand that if the market price is considered the just price because it reflects the current "community estimate" of value, then information concerning the future possessed by a single market participant may not be seen as altering the present community estimate; and his exploitation of his superior information need not, therefore, be seen as unjust according to the criterion adopted. But if one questions the justice of market exchange precisely because it occurs under conditions one of the parties is ignorant about (so that his consent to the deal might be said to hinge on a wholly erroneous perception of the relevant circumstances) then the scholastic insight into the justice of market price has not helped us answer our question. Our awareness that market prices are never equilibrium prices does not encourage us to accept the market prices as just because they are somehow expressive of *all* relevant circumstances. These prices, we must recognize, necessarily reflect the very errors that have occasioned our concern.

THE BASE FOR THE JUSTICE OF THE MARKET:
THE ETHICAL AND ECONOMIC BUILDING BLOCKS

I will argue that the difficulties raised concerning the justice of disequilibrium market transactions can be resolved definitively by (1) accepting a particular *ethical judgment,* and consistently applying it in conjunction with (2) the acceptance of a particular economic insight into the nature of disequilibrium market transactions. The ethical judgment referred to has been called the "finders-keepers" ethic.[29] The economic insight is that which permits us to perceive the discovery of a hitherto unknown market use for an already-owned resource or commodity as the discovery of (and consequently the spontaneous establishment of ownership in) a hitherto *unowned* element associated with that resource or commodity. I will argue that acceptance of the morality and justice of a market system does imply the acceptance of these ethical and economic ways of seeing things. Many who consider a market system just may not perhaps have explicitly articulated their own position to themselves in precisely these terms, but upon reflection they will probably recognize my exposition as faithful to their own view. It should be noted that it is not my purpose to insist on the *acceptance* of these views. My purpose is only to show that there exist plausible (and, at least implicitly, apparently widely accepted) moral and economic insights upon which a consistent defense of the justice of the market can be constructed. These insights, we will discover, remove the difficulties we have encountered so far. Moreover, they can easily be grafted onto a suitably reformulated entitlement-theoretic interpretation of market justice. Let us consider separately and more carefully

each of these ethical and economic insights, building blocks for constructing the case for the justice of the free market.

FINDERS, CREATORS, AND KEEPERS

The finders-keepers ethic has been discussed only slightly in the literature on the ethics of private property.[30] In fact, it seems fair to conclude that
most writers on the justice of private acquisition from nature of hitherto
unheld resources, do *not* accept it. The mere fact that an individual has
stumbled on a rich deposit of a valuable natural resource does not (without at least some effort on his part, say, some mixing of his labor with the
resource) entitle the discoverer, according to this view, to claim title to it
merely on the grounds that he found the resource. Mere discovery has
not placed the discoverer in any kind of privileged position with respect
to the hitherto unheld resources. If the rest of mankind were seen, up
to the present, as enjoying rights of access to and common use of these
hitherto unheld resources, then these rights are seen as in no way dis-
lodged by the mere event of the discovery.

To introduce plausibility into the notion of finders-keepers,[31] it
appears necessary to adopt the view that, until a resource has been discovered, *it has not*, in the sense relevant to the rights of access and common use, *existed at all.* By this view it seems plausible to consider the
discoverer of the hitherto "nonexistent" resource as, in the relevant sense,
the *creator* of what he has found.[32] It becomes, then, fairly easy to understand how the finder can be held justly entitled to keep that which he
has "created."

It should be noted that ownership-by-creation is quite different from
ownership-by-just-acquisition-from-nature, as the latter is spelled out in,
say, Nozick's entitlement theory. Ownership by acquisition occurs against
the prior background of *given* unheld resources even if no one is aware
of their existence. Acquisition is, in fact, a kind of "transfer" from nature
to the first holder. Ownership by creation, on the other hand, involves
no notion of transfer at all. The finder-creator has spontaneously generated hitherto nonexistent resources and is seen, therefore, as their natural owner.

The adoption of a finders-keepers ethic does not, of course, rule out
scope for acquisition from nature in the usual (Nozick's) sense.[33] The
first man to land on Mars can hardly claim title to it as its "creator." To
establish just ownership in an unheld resource whose existence everyone

is fully aware of, it is certainly necessary to follow the criteria considered appropriate to just acquisition from nature.

Moreover (and this will be of some importance later), it does not seem necessary to choose between adopting the finders-keepers ethic absolutely and not accepting it at all. It seems possible to view some kinds of creation-by-discovery as conferring just natural ownership, while in other circumstances (perhaps those in which discovery was *wholly* accidental, or those in which discovery by one person came on the heels of years of exhausting search by another), one may not be so prepared to recognize the actual discoverer as the sole just keeper of his find. Certainly the cases in which we might invoke the ethics of finders' remaining keepers call for systematic analysis and classification. My purpose has merely been to emphasize the possible role a finder-creator view of discovery can play in a theory of justice.

ENTREPRENEURIAL DISCOVERY AND CREATIVITY

We turn to the second of the building blocks referred to earlier: the economic insight that the discovery of a hitherto unknown market use for an already-owned resource or commodity constitutes the discovery of a hitherto *unowned* element associated with that resource or commodity. In the conventional view (apparently shared by Nozick), once a unit of resource has been acquired, ownership has been established in it with respect to *all* its properties and powers, whether or not these have been known or imagined. In the view now being considered, on the other hand, those aspects of a thing that are unknown remain, so to speak, nonexistent. Their discovery constitutes the discovery of a hitherto unknown, nonexistent, and hence unowned dimension of the thing. An owner owns only those aspects of his property of which he is aware. Acceptance of this way of viewing the matter has far-reaching implications for the perception of the entrepreneurial role in the market.

The entrepreneur perceives and exploits opportunities in the market that others have not noticed. He discovers, for example, that a quantity of oranges is being sold, for eating, throughout the market at $5, while consumers would gladly pay a total of $12 for these same oranges converted to orange juice and marmalade, at a total manufacturing cost, above that of the oranges, of $4. Entrepreneurial discovery of the $3 profit opportunity—of buying oranges for $5 and selling them for $8 (i.e., the $12 obtainable from the sale of juice and marmalade less the other costs of $4)—represents, in the view being discussed, the discovery of $3 value in the oranges that did not previously exist. Up to the moment when the entrepreneur's vision "saw" the juice and marmalade the oranges represent, oranges had value only for eating, a value the market set at $5. The entrepreneur has discovered $3 additional value in the oranges. He may, then, be held to have created this additional value in these oranges.[34] It is as if the entrepreneur found orange juice and marmalade in nature, where no one had perceived their existence; he has created the orange resource that can provide juice and marmalade.

Pursuing the matter further, it may be held that *any* price differential discovered and exploited by the entrepreneur constitutes the discovery of hitherto unknown and nonexistent value (even where no new, physically different, use is entailed). If orange juice can be bought at $3 (in one market) and sold at $4 (with no additional costs involved) in a second market, this means that those who were buying and selling at $3 did not know of the presence of those sufficiently eager for juice to be willing to pay $4 for it. Entrepreneurial discovery of this may, then, be seen as the discovery in the first market of a hitherto unsuspected intensity of potential value in orange juice. The entrepreneur may be held to have created this additional value by introducing these oranges to the second market.

It should be observed that this view of entrepreneurial discovery and creativity arises out of an understanding of the entrepreneurial role in a strictly arbitrage sense.[35] According to this view, the entrepreneur adds nothing to the production process other than his alertness to the production possibilities already existing. He provides no services, managerial or other; he simply notices that inputs can be obtained at a total outlay less than the sales revenue obtainable from output. We see the entrepreneur as creator not in the sense of the physical producer, but strictly in the sense of his being the discoverer of an available opportunity.

ENTREPRENEURSHIP AND THE EXPLOITATION OF ERROR

Acceptance of the finders-keepers ethic and of the economic insight into entrepreneurial discovery discussed in the preceding sections clears away the difficulties surrounding the justice of disequilibrium market transactions to which attention has been drawn. The central feature that distinguishes the market in disequilibrium from the model of market equilibrium can, after all, be stated in terms of the scope open for entrepreneurship. In the equilibrium model, all profitable opportunities have already been discovered and exploited. Nothing remains for entrepreneurs to discover and to create. In the disequilibrium market, it is precisely the changes introduced by entrepreneurial discovery of existing errors (and the consequent opportunities for profit), that constitute the market process and that are, in fact, the *meaning* of the label describing the market as in disequilibrium.[36]

It follows that entrepreneurial profits captured during the disequilibrium market process can be defended as new value that entrepreneurs have discovered and thus created. The equilibrating market process is thus perceived not simply as economic theory has traditionally shown, as a process tending to correct the misallocation of resources, but as a process of the continued net *creation of values,* as it were ex nihilo, as goods tend to move from lower-valued to higher-valued uses.

But what of the difficulty that such entrepreneurial activity in disequilibrium has involved transactions with trading partners who would never have bought or sold (at prices they accepted) had they known the true state of the market? What of the possibility that these transactions, having been made in error, lack the critical element of true voluntariness, that the consent given to these sales and purchases was in reality no consent at all? Reflection shows that, given the basis of the views discussed, these difficulties no longer obtrude.

If a man sells oranges, knowing full well their usefulness for marmalade and juice, because of some serious misunderstanding on his part, we may wish to say that the sale really lacked consent and is thus invalid. The oranges, including their potential in producing juice and marmalade, were his; without genuine consent they cannot justly become owned by another. But consider the man who sells oranges for $5 because he is unaware that, as potential raw material in producing juice and marmalade, they are worth $8 to the entrepreneur to whom he sells. The shadow clouding his consent arises from the existence of the $3 of additional value about which he is ignorant. But we have seen that this additional $3 value may well be held *never to have been possessed by the seller at all.* This $3 value was discovered (indeed *created*) by the entrepreneur's purchase and subsequent sale. So the error on the part of the seller (on the basis of which we sought to invalidate the sale) can, by the present view of things, hardly be held to affect the conclusiveness of the consent of the seller to the sale of what was his to sell in the first place.

It thus turns out, not at all accidentally, that the reasoning that justifies pure entrepreneurial profit on the grounds that the entrepreneur has "created" previously nonexistent value is at the same time able to protect one who purchases or sells any good at a disequilibrium price from the charge that it was sold to him or purchased by him only on the basis of error and hence of flawed consent. Market transfers are, according to this view, just because no one consents voluntarily to a transaction except insofar as it gives him a satisfactory exchange for what he sees himself as giving up. And until someone discovers that what is given up is more than the owner sees, no more than that exists, in the sense relevant to this view of economic justice.

It should be observed that this justification of entrepreneurial alertness to the errors made by others does *not* extend to the justification of fraud, properly defined. Nor does it necessarily rule out the possible view that at least some cases of nonfraudulent exploitation of error be considered morally questionable. Fraud is not covered by the reasoning that justifies market transfers because fraud involves the deceitful *inducement* of error, either positively or—where a fiduciary type of relationship exists—tacitly, on the basis of which consent is fraudulently obtained. And even some cases of nonfraudulent exploitation of error may be condemned, despite an otherwise general acceptance of the justification of disequilibrium market transfer we have discussed. It seems entirely possible to restrict one's adoption of the "finders-creators-keepers" ethic to only some kinds of entrepreneurial finds and creations. Perhaps it may seem that to take advantage of prior knowledge of information that will be commonly known in five years' time is justified, but that exploiting the knowledge that everyone will surely know in five minutes is going too far.[37] The point has not been to show that all possible forms of entrepreneurial exploitation of error sanctioned by the law are rendered immediately morally acceptable by application of the finders-keepers ethic. The purpose has been to show that this ethic can plausibly be deployed to rebut possible blanket condemnation of market processes on grounds of error and consequent lack of genuine consent.[38]

MODIFICATIONS IN THE ENTITLEMENT THEORY

We are now in a position to spell out how Nozick's entitlement theory needs modification if it is to effectively demonstrate the possible justice of the market system. The entitlement theory maintains the following definitions: (1) a distribution of holdings is just if all those are entitled to the holdings they possess under the distribution; (2) one is entitled to a holding only if he has acquired it from the unheld state in accordance with the principle of justice in acquisition, or if he has acquired it in accordance with the principle of justice in transfer from someone else entitled to the holding.[39] Our discussion calls for modification of Nozick's view that these latter definitions under (2) "exhaustively cover the subject of justice in holdings."[40]

For Nozick, the justice of holdings depends "historically" on the justice of the original acquisition from the unheld state, and on the justice of each of the subsequent transfers of the holding. Our discussion of the finders-keepers ethic, and its application in the justice of entrepreneurial creation, indicates first that Nozick's definitions have not definitively covered all cases of holdings that may be considered just, and, again, that the lines Nozick draws between original acquisition and acquisition by transfer are not as sharp as his discussion suggests.

The framework of Nozick's definitions sees things as being held either as the result of original acquisition from an unheld state or else as the result of acquisition by transfer from a previous holder. Our discussion has pointed out a third possibility: a thing may be held as the result of the holder having, in the relevant sense, created it ex nihilo, by finding it.[41] To be sure, the possibility that a thing has been, at one level of discourse, created from the state of nonexistence, does not preclude its having been acquired (either originally or by transfer) from what, at a different level of discussion, is treated as an earlier state of existence. Oil discovered in an unsuspected location may, at one level, be treated as not having existed before; at another level, it did already exist. Nozick's schema is certainly an exhaustive one at this latter level; but our discussion has shown that discourse may be fruitful when the third possibility we have mentioned enters as an important additional class of holdings.[42]

Recognition of this possibility, the holding of a thing as a result not of its acquisition from the unheld state, or from a previous holder, but of its having been created, introduces a certain fuzziness in the line Nozick draws between holdings resulting from original acquisition and those resulting from acquisition by transfer. In his schema, transfer involves only the acquisition of a previously held thing. For us, transfer may well involve, besides the acquisition of what was already held, the creation of an entirely new dimension of the holding, something not only not previously held, but something that did not, in the relevant sense, exist previously at all.[43] Recognizing this complexity in transfers, especially in market transfer, has enabled us to perceive the possible justice of the entrepreneurial discoveries that may be expressed in disequilibrium market purchases and sales.

Another implication in the entitlement theory relates to the justice of original acquisition. As we will see in the following section, it appears that some of Nozick's views that flow from his treatment of the justice of original acquisition arise from his decided lack of enthusiasm for the possibility that many cases of original acquisitions may qualify, at least in part, for justification under the finder-creator-keepers ethic. To the implications of this possibility we now turn.

NOZICK AND THE LOCKEAN PROVISO

Nozick has not attempted to spell out in detail the proper principles of justice in original acquisition or in acquisition by transfer. Nonetheless, he has devoted a good deal of attention to what he has termed the "Lockean Proviso." And, while Locke himself enumerated the proviso in relation to the original acquisition from nature, Nozick has pursued its implications insofar as it introduces complications into the justice of acquisition by transfer.

Locke's theory of justice in original acquisition, requiring only that the would-be expropriator of an unowned object mix his labor with it, was qualified by the proviso that there be "enough and as good left in common for others."[44] Nozick explains that, by this qualification, Locke meant "to ensure that the situation of others is not worsened."[45] While Nozick sharply limits the scope of the Lockean proviso as it enters into his own entitlement theory of justice,[46] he does, without hesitation, strongly accept the principle that justice in original acquisition requires that such acquisitions shall leave no one else in a worse situation than he would have been in without it. In fact, Nozick seems almost relieved to be able to invoke this principle in cases involving appropriation of the entire stock of a limited, life-giving resource, to which critics of the private property system have traditionally pointed as exemplifying the injustice of the system. The case of "someone who comes upon the only water in the desert several miles ahead of others who also will come to it and appropriates it all"[47] is a violation of the proviso circumventing original acquisition. And even, Nozick argues, where one appropriates only one of many water holes in the desert, but it subsequently happens that all the other holes dry up, the Lockean proviso stringently limits what he can do with "his" hole.[48]

My emphasis on the role of discovery and creation in justifying title to a holding enables us to question the rather sweeping scope that Nozick, at least in principle, assigns to the Lockean proviso. (Nozick believes that, in practice, "the free operation of a market system will not actually run afoul of the Lockean proviso.")[49] Clearly, once we admit that the discovery of an unknown thing justifies its finder's holding it on the grounds that, in the relevant sense, he created it, as it were, ex nihilo, the entire basis of the Lockean proviso becomes vulnerable to challenge. Is it really true that, where a discoverer appropriates all of a limited deposit of resource, he is worsening the situation of others for whom this deposit was completely unknown and nonexistent? This question seems so obviously to call for a negative answer that, indeed, Nozick finds himself forced by it to accept, in effect, a limited finders-keepers ethic. Nozick circumscribes the Lockean proviso by observing that where a researcher synthesizes a new substance out of easily available raw materials he may justly refuse to sell except on his terms since by so doing he does not harm others, who are free to do what he had done. Moreover, Nozick adds, one who appropriates the total supply of a new substance by finding it "in an out-of-the-way place" has not worsened the situation of others: "If he did not stumble upon the substance no one else would have." But Nozick immediately qualifies this by pointing out that in the latter case, "as time passes, the likelihood increases that others would have come across the substance," justifying, Nozick suggests, possible limitation on bequest by the first discoverer.[50]

Nozick's limited recognition of the exemption of discovery from the Lockean proviso does not appear to go nearly far enough. For Nozick, even appropriation of an object after its discovery may be considered to worsen the situation of those (possibly in later generations) who would have found the object for themselves. But our insight into the creative aspect of discovery suggests a different view of the matter on two separate grounds. First, we must maintain that one who *might* at a given date have created an object ex nihilo has hardly been hurt because a second individual in fact did create the object first. It was the latter individual who was the creator, not the former. A finders-creators-keepers ethic cannot, it must be maintained, confer any claim on those who *might have,* but did not in fact, create. Nozick's concern for the harm done to those who would have themselves discovered the new substance is based on the view that, whether discovered or not, the new substance *has* always existed, for both present and future generations. So that the basis of Locke's proviso—that others have some claim on unowned objects, requiring that they therefore not be harmed by appropriation—applies also to undiscovered substances. But if we recognize that an undiscovered substance does not, in the relevant sense, exist for those who are not aware of it, then Nozick's concern loses its justification.

But perhaps even more important is a second reason we cannot share Nozick's view that the discoverer of a new substance is justified to hold it only to the extent that it would not have been discovered by others. For Nozick, Lockean acquisition of an unowned object from nature seems to be justified only in the negative sense that such appropriation (where, of course, it does not violate the proviso) has not harmed others. That is, one who has mixed his labor with the unowned resource, of which ample supply is left for others, has not acquired just title on the basis of any powerful positive moral claim. He has acquired title because mixing one's labor with the resource *is* the act of appropriation, and compliance with the Lockean proviso ensures that no *in*justice is involved in this acquisition. But acceptance of a finders-creators-keepers ethic confers just title on the discoverer-creator not in the negative sense that such title involves no injustice to others, but in the positive sense that justice requires that the creator be recognized as the owner of what he has created: to deny the creator title would be to inflict injustice on him. From this view of the ethics of creation, it is by no means clear that Locke's proviso has necessary relevance to discovery at all. If justice requires that the creator of an object be recognized as its owner, then this *may* remain true even if it might be shown that others who might, say, have otherwise discovered the object for themselves can be considered as having been rendered worse off by the creation.

The consideration advanced tends to exempt from the Lockean proviso a substantial proportion of the cases—all those involving discovery—that Nozick includes under the heading of "original acquisition from the unheld state." On this basis, the troublesome water hole in the desert cases must, where they have involved discovery, be viewed as indeed involving no violation of strict justice, despite whatever other moral stricture one may invoke to criticize selfish behavior by a just owner, especially in situations involving threat to life. Moreover, it should be pointed out that consistent application of the reasoning developed earlier suggests that the Lockean proviso cannot claim necessary relevance even for cases in which discovery does not seem obviously to be involved. I have argued that genuine entrepreneurial discovery and creation may occur even with respect to objects whose existence is known to all.

Consider the case (referred to only by implication in Nozick's discussion) of the unheld sole water hole in the desert which *everyone* in a group of travelers knows about, which one of the travelers, by racing ahead of the others, succeeds in appropriating. For Nozick this case, involving as it does no discovery at all, clearly and unjustly violates the Lockean proviso: the other travelers who, in the absence of appropriation by their fellow, would all have enjoyed some water without cost, are now forced to pay a price (even a monopoly price) for that same water. For us, however, this view is by no means the only one possible. We notice that the energetic traveler who appropriated all the water was not doing anything that (always ignoring of course, prohibitions resting on the Lockean proviso itself) the other travelers were not equally free to do. The other travelers, too, could have raced ahead. Assuming, for simplicity, that all the travelers were of equal strength and speed, there would have ensued a gold rush in which each would have, let us say, captured *some* water. As it happened, the other travelers did not bother to race for the water. May it not be that they were less alert, entrepreneurially, to the possibility that someone else might indeed appropriate all the water than the energetic traveler? Should we not, then, say that the latter was the first to discover the true market value of the unheld water? For the others, the water was indeed known, but the worthwhileness of its application was not known. Perhaps they mistakenly thought there was more water available than could possibly be drunk; perhaps they mistakenly thought that no one would or could race across the desert faster than they were traveling, or perhaps they gave the water no thought at all. It does not seem obvious that these other travelers can claim that they were *hurt* by an action they could themselves have easily taken had they been as alert as the successful appropriator. What, one must ask, even under conditions involving the appropriation of known substances, is so obviously acceptable about the Lockean proviso, as interpreted by Nozick?

THE JUSTICE OF THE MARKET

It turns out, then, that the insight into entrepreneurial discovery, coupled with the possibility of a finders-keepers ethic, has not only solved the difficulties raised earlier, but has enabled us to perceive possible justification for the free operation of a market system with fewer qualifications than those that Nozick, on the basis of the Lockean proviso, was impelled to introduce.

A finders-keepers ethic, we have observed, may *not* be found compelling. Even if the basic idea is accepted, there remains ample room for moral reservations concerning particular cases of application of the ethic. Nonetheless there does seem to be a certain plausibility in the notion of ownership through creativity. This plausibility may help explain how so many observers of the market appear to find it consistent with economic justice in the face of the denunciations of the moralist critics of capitalism. We have explored the sources of this apparent plausibility and have scrutinized its ability to serve as possible support for the morality of the market. For this purpose, Nozick's entitlement theory has served as a crucial framework. That our discussion has suggested certain modifications in the framework itself has, I hope, been a positive contribution.

NOTES

1. R. Nozick, *Anarchy, State, and Utopia* (New York: Basic Books, 1974), pp. 178–82.

2. Ibid., p. 153.

3. Ibid., pp. 160–64. See also Nozick's extensive discussion of the voluntariness of market transactions, pp. 262–65.

4. See the discussion of this point in J. S. Mill, *Principles of Political Economy*, Ashley ed. (London: Longmans, Green, 1909), pp. 796ff.; M. N. Rothbard, *Power and Market* (Menlo Park: Institute for Humane Studies, 1970), p. 34; H. B. Acton, *The Morals of Markets* (London: Longmans, 1971), p. 4; Nozick, ibid., p. 152. See also the discussion in G. Tullock, *The Social Dilemma* (Blacksburg: University Publications, 1974), p. 11.

5. F. A. Hayek, "Economics and knowledge," *Economica* 4 (1937), in *Individualism and Economic Order* (London; Routledge and Kegan Paul, 1949), p. 42.

6. L. Mises, *Human Action* (New Haven: Yale University Press, 1949), p. 249. See also F. H. Hahn, *On the Notion of Equilibrium in Economics* (Cambridge: Cambridge University Press, 1973), pp. 7ff.

7. It ought perhaps to be emphasized that it is not only a relatively small class of business entrepreneurs the justice of whose acquisitions are being questioned. As Mises pointed out (*Human Action*, p. 253), every acting individual displays entrepreneurial characteristics. Since almost all market transactions involve less than perfect

omniscience, the errors they reflect might seem to cast a shadow over the justice of *all* market transfers. Pure entrepreneurial profit may be present, to some extent, in any sale and in any purchase.

8. For some discussion of the morality of profits, and of the arguments of its critics, see Acton, *The Morals of Markets*, ch. 2.

9. See Mises, "Profit and loss," in *Planning for Freedom* (South Holland, Ill.: Libertarian Press, 1952), pp. 108ff.; see also I. M. Kirzner, *Competition and Entrepreneurship* (Chicago: University of Chicago Press, 1973), pp. 85ff.

10. To do this is again to deliberately accept an uncertainty—namely, the possibility that, *without expenditure of the resources needed to remove the possibility of error*, error may occur—concerning which accurate knowledge is simply unavailable. There is no way, without expenditure of those resources, to know whether error will or will not occur.

11. We prefer, for present purposes, not to press this position in even more uncompromising form, which might maintain that one who has been deceived has, again, merely refrained deliberately from spending the resources necessary to ensure against deception.

12. See chapter 8 [Israel M. Kirzner, "Economics and error," in *Perception, Opportunity, and Profit* (Chicago: University of Chicago Press, 1979)]. The view denying scope for error within economic analysis has been stated by G. J. Stigler, "The Xistence of X-efficiency," *American Economic Review* 66 (March 1976): 216.

13. Despite our insistence on the prevalence of genuine error, we must of course readily grant that many cases in which an entrepreneur appears to be exploiting the ignorance of others *do* result merely from the deliberate judgment of others, in the face possibly of the very same information available to entrepreneurs, concerning a future that, they are well aware, is highly uncertain.

14. G. S. Bower and A. K. Turner, *The Law of Actionable Misrepresentation* (London: Butterworths, 1974), p. 104.

15. S. E. Williams, *Kerr on Fraud and Mistake*, 6th ed. (London: Sweet and Maxwell, 1929), p. 76.

16. For a fascinating pioneer discussion of both the morality and the law surrounding exchanges made on the basis of incomplete or faulty information, see Gulian G. Verplanck, *An Essay on the Doctrine of Contracts: Being an Inquiry How Contracts Are Affected in Law and Morals by Concealment, Error, or Inadequate Price* (New York, 1825). Verplanck showed remarkable awareness of the element of pure (entrepreneurial) profit in all exchanges and of how this implies the impracticality of a legal system that insists on "full disclosure" in all exchanges.

17. Bower and Turner, *Law of Actionable Misrepresentation*, p. 106.

18. Williams, *Kerr on Fraud and Mistake*, p. 76. An oft-cited opinion of Cardozo does, however, appear to argue that the law simply reflects the "morals of the market place"; so that where, as in the case of partners, morality calls for loyalty to one another, or where, as in the case of trustees, morality calls for not "honesty alone, but

the punctilio of an honor the most sensitive," this should and will find expression in the law. See the quote in H. Manne, *Insider Trading and the Stock Market* (New York: Free Press, 1966), pp. 20–21.

19. See Mises, *Human Action*, p. 147. For a recent plea not to reach conclusions concerning the morality of particular economic practices (specifically, insider trading) before thoroughly exploring the welfare consequences of these practices, see Manne, *Insider Trading*, p. 15.

20. See, e.g., Manne, *Insider Trading*, p. 18.

21. W. J. Ashley on the "Just price," in *Dictionary of Political Economy*, ed. R. H. I. Palgrave (London: Macmillan, 1896), 2:500.

22. Nozick, *Anarchy, State, and Utopia*, p. 262 (italics in original).

23. Ibid., p. 161.

24. B. W. Dempsey, "Just price in a functional economy," *American Economic Review* 25 (September 1935): 471–86, reprinted in *Economic Thought: A Historical Anthology*, ed. J. A. Gherity (New York: Random House, 1965); R. de Roover, "The concept of the just price: theory and economic policy," *Journal of Economic History* 18 (December 1958): 418–34, reprinted in ibid.; J. A. Schumpeter, *History of Economic Analysis* (New York: Oxford University Press, 1954), part 2, ch. 2; J. T. Noonan, *The Scholastic Analysis of Usury* (Cambridge: Harvard University Press, 1957); S. Hollander, "On the interpretation of the just price," *Kyklos* 18 (1965): 4; M. N. Rothbard, "New light on the prehistory of the Austrian School," in *The Foundations of Modern Austrian Economics*, ed. E. Dolan (Kansas City: Sheed and Ward, 1976).

25. See, e.g., the view of Cajetan, cited in de Roover, "Concept of the just price," p. 29.

26. Hollander, "On the interpretation of the just price," p. 625.

27. See de Roover, "Concept of the just price," p. 28; Hollander, "On the interpretation of the just price," p. 624.

28. See Hollander, "On the interpretation of the just price," p. 624.

29. H. M. Oliver, *A Critique of Socioeconomic Goals* (Bloomington: Indiana University Press, 1954), p. 42.

30. See above chapter 11 ["Producer, Entrepreneur, and the Right to Property," pp. 173–87 in the present volume], and the discussion there of the views of Oliver.

31. It seems particularly important to distinguish the finders-keepers ethic from the ethic of "first come, first served" that Vickrey, for one, has described as of dubious quality. W. Vickrey, "An exchange of questions between economics and philosophy" (1953), reprinted in *Economic Justice*, ed. E. S. Phelps (Penguin Books, 1973), p. 58.

32. The notion of the discoverer as creator should, of course, be linked with the view of F. H. Knight, that it is not the factors of production that produce the output, but the entrepreneur who decides to enlist the services of these factors (F. H. Knight, *Risk, Uncertainty and Profit* [New York: Houghton Mifflin, 1921], p. 271). See also F. B. Hawley, *Enterprise and the Productive Process* (New York: Putnam, 1907), pp. 85, 102, 112, 127.

33. See p. 206 for a discussion of the (very limited) recognition of the ethical significance of *discovery* in Nozick's system.

34. It was Schumpeter (*Theory of Economic Development* [Cambridge: Harvard University Press, 1934], translated from the German work published in 1911) who emphasized the *creative* role of the entrepreneur. It should perhaps be noted that the writer has elsewhere demurred from Schumpeter's view of the entrepreneur as *disrupting* earlier states of repose (I. M. Kirzner, *Competition and Entrepreneurship* [Chicago: University of Chicago Press, 1973], pp. 72ff.). See also above, chapter 7 [Israel M. Kirzner, "Entrepreneurship, and the market approach to development," in *Perception, Opportunity, and Profit* (Chicago: University of Chicago Press, 1979)]. The position taken here in the text is not, I believe, inconsistent with my earlier insistence on the *equilibrating* role of the entrepreneur, seen as responding to the existence of as yet unexpected opportunities. For individuals in a society, of whom none has as yet perceived the existence of a profitable opportunity, this opportunity may properly be said not yet to exist: its first discoverer may be properly seen as its creator. Nonetheless, the theorist analyzing the social role of entrepreneurial discovery is surely entitled to point out that, before the discovery of a productive opportunity, its existence did mean that society has failed in some sense to achieve its greatest possible level of output. It is not improper, at *this* level of discourse, to insist on the entrepreneur as *responding* to the opportunities "out there," of which he becomes aware.

35. See note 9.

36. See Kirzner, *Competition and Entrepreneurship*, chs. 1 and 2.

37. P. A. Samuelson has derided the social utility of the vast speculators' profits won by entrepreneurs several seconds more nimble than their fellows in assessing new information (*Weltwirtschaftliches Archiv* 79 [December 1957]: 209). One may question the validity of Samuelson's argument at the utilitarian level (see, e.g., Kirzner, *Competition and Entrepreneurship*, p. 224; also above pp. 183–84), while recognizing the possibility that one may *not* choose to extend one's finders-keepers ethic (if, indeed, one subscribes to it at all) to defend the morality of the case discussed by Samuelson.

38. To put the point somewhat differently, the discussion in the text *has* sought to show that *all* market transactions can be seen as in no way involving imperfect consent. This was done on the basis of the insight that all entrepreneurial gain reflects not exploitation of error, but creation (i.e., finding) of new value. At the same time this may *not*, of itself, be seen as *justifying* all cases of such gain, since one may not wish to recognize the justice of *every* finder, under *all* conceivable circumstances, becoming a keeper.

39. Nozick, *Anarchy, State, and Utopia*, pp. 150–55.

40. Ibid., p. 151.

41. See in the following section for a discussion of the limited degree to which Nozick appears ready to recognize an ethical role for pure discovery.

42. For the biblical version of an entitlement theory based on *divine* Creation, see Psalms 24:1, 2; 115:16.

43. It may be objected, both to the argument of the text itself and to its application of the finders-keepers ethic, that if I discover new, hitherto unnoticed value in my neighbor's property, that the additional value ought, according to the finders-keepers ethic, be mine *without* any transfer of the property at all. To the extent that the new value can be consumed without violating the rights of the neighbor, this seems not unreasonable. (One thinks of the legal questions raised when it was discovered, through the invention of flying, that air rights over land were more valuable than hitherto realized.) In general, where the newly discovered value cannot be consumed without violating existing rights, it will be in the interest of the discoverer to buy up *those* rights, in order to enjoy the new values *he* has discovered.

44. John Locke, *An Essay Concerning the True Original, Extent and End of Civil Government*, ch. 5, sec. 27.

45. Nozick, *Anarchy, State, and Utopia*, p. 175.

46. Ibid., p. 178.

47. Ibid., pp. 179–80 and the footnote on p. 179.

48. Nozick's position on this point has potentially far-reaching implications for the justice of monopoly positions in production obtained through sole acquisition of needed resources. For a discussion *not* involving the issue of the justice of such monopoly cases, but from the perspective of their alleged harm to society, see Kirzner, *Competition and Entrepreneurship*, pp. 236–42, where a variety of considerations are weighed against one another. The discussion in the subsequent paragraphs in the text, questioning Nozick's views, points not to any vindication of monopoly producers from possible charges that their activity in some sense harms society, but to a defense of the moral legitimacy of monopoly resource ownership even were it to be shown that the rest of society would, in some sense, be better off were such monopoly not present.

49. Nozick, *Anarchy, State, and Utopia*, p. 182.

50. Ibid., p. 181.

DISCOVERY, PRIVATE PROPERTY AND THE THEORY OF JUSTICE IN CAPITALIST SOCIETY

Critics of the capitalist system have accused it of many faults. Some of these perceived problems have been the subject of debate among economists. Economists have argued over the economic merits of a system without conscious direction under an overall plan. The *justice* of a capitalist system, too, has often been the subject of criticism and debate. But the problem of economic justice under capitalism has, in the main, in recent years been debated by philosophers rather than by economists. This is perhaps because this debate has, in principle, assumed the economics of capitalism to be well understood and agreed upon, so that judgments concerning the justice or absence of justice in the system could be made purely on philosophical and ethical grounds. In this chapter[1] I shall argue that the common understanding of the economics of capitalism which has served as the basis for the philosophical debate has in fact suffered from certain serious weaknesses. When these weaknesses are corrected, I shall maintain, hitherto overlooked key features of capitalism come into view which can be seen to have important philosophical and ethical implications—implications totally overlooked in the standard philosophical debates. In particular, I shall argue, an adequate understanding of the economics of the capitalist system reveals the crucial role played in this system by *discovery*. Once the economic role of discovery is properly understood, I shall maintain, most of the features of capitalism which have provoked the charges of injustice become visible—even without any new ethical argumentation—in a totally different light. In other words the discovery theory of justice in capitalist society offers a defense of capitalist justice not by articulating novel philosophical or ethical positions but by offering a fresh economic understanding of how the capitalist economic system actually works.

From *The Meaning of Market Process: Essays in the Development of Modern Austrian Economics* (New York and London: Routledge, 1992), 209–26 and 232. Reprinted with permission of Walter de Gruyter; original source is *Journal des Économistes et des Études Humaines* I (October 1990): 209–24.

THE CHARGE OF CAPITALIST INJUSTICE

Claims that capitalism perpetrates economic injustice have traditionally taken a variety of forms. At one level, the basic institution of capitalism, private property, has been attacked philosophically at its very roots. In the view of these critics, there is an inherent injustice committed whenever a nature-given resource is privately appropriated. Such appropriation is seen as the private grabbing of something belonging naturally to all mankind. (In some variants of this attack, even the notion of self-ownership by the individual is fundamentally denied on these grounds.) A system in which all transactions are built on such an unjust foundation is a system in which the consequences of injustice are being continually extended.

A different level of attack is that directed at the inevitable inequality of incomes under capitalism. Quite apart from accusations that private property is an inherently unjust institution, quite apart from charges that markets permit direct forms of unjust exploitation (such as the exploitation of labor), this attack focuses on the inherent immorality held to be represented by economic inequality. Even if no individual in the system sought to act unjustly, the inevitable inequality of incomes in a market society is, in these attacks, denounced as an ethical monstrosity *per se* (see, for example, Nielsen 1985).

But the main thrust of the widespread skepticism concerning the justice of capitalism seems to be pointed at the phenomenon of pure profit and its consequences. Even those prepared to recognize the ethical acceptability of private property, even those who recognize no overwhelming ethical imperative prescribing equality of incomes, are frequently deeply disturbed by the apparent consequences of entrepreneurial profits. This ethical concern is fueled by an intuition that such profits have not been "deserved" ("earned") by the entrepreneur, and must in some way, therefore, have been unjustly won at the expense of the other market participants (in particular, at the expense of laborers).[2] The pattern of income distribution under capitalism is seen as unjust because capitalism permits— is in fact built upon—the pursuit of entrepreneurial profits. The circumstance of income inequality is seen as ethically offensive primarily because this is the inevitable and unfortunate consequence of the capture of profits. The institution of private property comes to be condemned to the extent that it is identified as the vehicle for the entrepreneurial pursuit of profits.

In preparation for our own exposition of the discovery theory of economic justice, we shall here briefly review two classic defenses of capitalist economic justice, those associated with the names of John Bates Clark and Robert Nozick. Each of these defenses, directly or indirectly, depends on particular assumptions concerning private property rights and the role of pure profits. We shall also draw attention to certain weaknesses (relating particularly to these assumptions concerning private property and pure profit) in each of these defenses, with regard to the criticisms they are confronting. We shall then be in a position to identify certain perspectives on the economics of capitalism (and highly relevant to the issue of its economic justice) shared by both the critics of capitalist justice and its classic defenders. It is by demonstrating the unfortunate narrowness of this economic understanding of capitalism that we hope, in subsequent sections of the chapter, to offer a more adequate defense of the justice of the capitalist system.

PRIVATE PROPERTY, PURE PROFIT, AND THE
CLASSIC DEFENSES OF CAPITALIST JUSTICE

It was the economist John Bates Clark who, at the turn of the century, offered the most explicit defense of capitalist distribution of incomes. He wrote a substantial book to demonstrate that, in static equilibrium, each participant in the productive process of the market system receives the full value of his marginal productive contribution (Clark 1899). In the words of Milton Friedman, the Clarkian ethic supporting the justice of capitalism can be expressed as: "To each according to what he and the instruments he owns produces" (1962:161f.).

Clark's defense consisted of showing how, in equilibrium, the price per unit of each productive service is the measure of the market value of its productive contribution at the margin. (This demonstration was, in fact, an important step in the development of the neoclassical theory of resource price.) For Clark it was axiomatic that justice can require no more than that each resource owner receive the market value of what he and his resources have produced. It was also apparent to Clark that, in a world in which production is always the outcome of jointly used resource services, the concept "what a resource has produced" is to be measured by the marginal product of the resource (i.e., the incremental output forthcoming through adding one unit of this resource to an unchanged mix of the remaining resource inputs). Finally, Clark was quite uncurious regarding the validity of a resource owner's title to the resources he holds. He simply accepted that a laborer is unquestionably entitled to the fruit of his labor, that a landowner has arrived at his title justly, that the owner of capital is in fact its legitimate owner.

It will be seen that Clark's defense of capitalist justice simply ignored possible challenges to the very idea of private ownership. Moreover he simply ignored challenges to capitalist justice based on an axiomatic egalitarian ethic. Clearly he believed that by demonstrating the justice of the marginal productivity mode of distribution he had implicitly justified any entailed departures from an equal distribution of income. Clark's defense of capitalist justice consisted, in essence, in showing that each resource used by the capitalistic entrepreneur commands a fair price (measuring fairness by value of productive contribution). If each resource owner receives a just income, fully reflecting his productive contribution, no charge of injustice can be fairly leveled at the capitalistic entrepreneur. If part of the product is received as income by others than the laborers who have sweated to produce it, this must reflect some productive contribution made by these others and not any surplus unjustly exploited from the laborers.

The problems raised by this Clarkian defense stem from his virtually complete silence on two crucial ethical aspects of the capitalist economy: (a) the source of just title in resources and (b) the legitimacy of pure economic profit. As noticed above, Clark displays no curiosity concerning the source of resource ownership. He simply assumes that laborers own their bodies, landowners their land, and capitalists their capital. There is nothing in the Clarkian defense of capitalism which justifies the incomes received, in return for resource services rendered, by those who, lacking legitimate title to these services, may somehow have appropriated them from their rightful owners (possibly society as a whole). One might fully accept Clark's defense, as far as it goes, but then assert its irrelevance on the grounds of the fundamental injustice of private title to nature-given resources (if one believed in the injustice of such title). This gap in Clark's defense has often been noted.

Clark's silence in regard to the legitimacy of pure economic profit is a little more complicated to interpret, but equally troubling for the defense of capitalist justice. Clark did not have to deal with pure profit, because he confined his demonstration to the static world of equilibrium, in which pure profit is completely absent. For Clark, profit is an ephemeral, transient phenomenon associated with dynamics, which can be safely ignored in attempting to come to grips with the permanent features of the capitalist system. What Clark accounted for was the justice of the major component of what earlier economists had called profit, namely the segment which neoclassical and subsequent economists have called, not profit, but *interest*.[3] But a critic of capitalist justice could reasonably point out that *pure* profit (as entrepreneurial profit is often called) is an obvious and prevalent feature of the capitalist economy. It cannot be dismissed as a kind of trivial, frictional phenomenon. Its presence means, presumably, that resource incomes must, to a greater or lesser extent, fall short of the full value of the relevant marginal products.

Pure profit must, precisely from the Clarkian perspective, raise serious economic and ethical questions. Such profit seems, on the face of it, unjustified both economically and ethically. There seems, on the face of it, no economic explanation for the ability of the entrepreneur to capture any difference between input prices and output prices. Competition should surely be expected to ensure the absence of such differences. Any differences which somehow exist cannot be justified as the marginal product value of any resource service. (Remember that pure profit is what is left after subtracting, from the market value of output, the market values of *all* resource services that contributed to the production of that output.) It appears totally unjustified within the Clarkian criterion for economic justice.

Robert Nozick's defense of capitalist income distribution is embodied in his entitlement theory of justice, published exactly three-quarters of a century after Clark (1974:chs. 7, 8). Nozick's point of view is that, so long as no individual in a system has violated the rights of any others, the results of that system cannot be pronounced unjust, no matter how unequal the resulting distribution of income may be. For a capitalist system to consist solely of transactions free of unjust violation of rights, we must require that all titles to property be consistent with principles of just original acquisition from nature and just transfer of title. In this way we would be able to state that all present holdings are justly held, since each of them rests on an unblemished chain of just transactions, leading back all the way in time to just original acquisition from nature. Nozick's defense of capitalist justice boils down to carefully articulated claims that the institutional foundations of the capitalist economy may indeed be consistent with the principles of just title.

For Nozick, if two just holders of title voluntarily agree to an exchange transaction, no matter what the circumstances may be which induce such agreement, the subsequent reallocation of ownership can in no way be declared unjust. If a star professional basketball player becomes a millionaire as a result of many poor but eager spectators buying tickets, out of their hard-earned meager wages, to watch professional basketball games, there is, for Nozick, nothing unjust in the resulting inequality of income. The athlete is the beneficiary of voluntary exchange; the money he receives was freely given up in exchange for the opportunity to witness his prowess. Nor is the situation rendered more unjust, in the entitlement view, if the individual becoming a millionaire is not a professional athlete but a landlord renting out apartments (justly owned by him) to desperately poor tenants. No one has violated any rights of others; the tenants voluntarily pay the rent in order to secure dwelling space. The entitlement theory is uninterested in the motives which may have "compelled" a tenant (or a ticket-holder) to pay for dwelling space (or tickets to basketball games). The urgency of need for a purchased item need not taint the voluntariness of the transaction, for purposes of evaluating the justice of the transfers effected. "Whether a person's actions are voluntary depends on what it is that limits his alternatives. If facts of nature do so, the actions are voluntary. . . . Other people's actions place limits on one's available opportunities. Whether this makes one's resulting action non-voluntary depends upon whether these others had the right to act as they did" (Nozick 1974:262). With capitalism defined to exclude the violation of the rights of others, it follows that there is nothing to flaw the voluntariness of market transactions. The resulting pattern of income distribution can therefore never be an unjust one, as long as the rules of the capitalist game are scrupulously respected.

Within the confines of its own scope, the entitlement theory is unquestionably a powerful addition to the defense arsenal on behalf of the justice of capitalism. However, we must carefully note the limitations circumscribing the scope of the theory. First, the theory presumes the possibility of just original acquisition of items from nature. No matter how impeccably all subsequent capitalist market transactions meet the criterion of voluntariness, the justice of private property title rests ultimately upon the initial private appropriation of that which is subsequently transferred in markets. There is nothing within the entitlement theory itself which provides us with a rationale for justice in original appropriation from nature.

Nozick appeals to the classic ideas of John Locke on this point, but is ultimately forced by consideration of the "Lockean proviso" to modify the original Lockean formulation (Nozick 1974:177). Nor is Locke's principle of initial ownership (based on "mixing one's labor" with unowned natural resources) obviously or universally convincing.[4] The entitlement theory seems to require some independent support for its initial premises. But there are additional reasons for concern with the adequacy of the entitlement theory as a defense of capitalist justice. This has to do with the sense in which market transactions can indeed be described as voluntary.

The entitlement defense of capitalism is doubtless correct in asserting that, by definition, market transactions necessarily fulfill the legal requirements for voluntariness. But it is yet possible to question the ethical significance of the voluntariness of many, if not all, market transactions. This is because the market transactions which result in the winning of pure economic profit must in retrospect be judged to have been made, in part, as a result of "sheer error" on the part of one or other of the relevant participants. Pure profit arises when an entrepreneur is successful in selling an item at a price higher than the sum of the prices of everything necessary to deliver the item to its buyer. Such profit could hardly arise unless those from whom the entrepreneur buys have been unaware of the price to be paid by those to whom the entrepreneur sells, and unless those to whom he sells have been unaware of the sum of the prices accepted by those from whom the entrepreneur bought. Pure profit must mean that those selling at the low price are unaware of the true higher market value of that which they sell; those buying at the high price are unaware of the possibility of buying the same item elsewhere in the market at a lower cost. It follows that those trading with the profit-making entrepreneur must, in the light of subsequently revealed profits, "regret" their trades. Those who sold for the low price would never have done so had they then known what they subsequently know; nor would those who bought at the high price have done so had *they* known then what they subsequently find out to have been the case. Whenever it turns out that an action was taken under mistaken assumptions, it may be possible to question the true voluntariness of the action. It may be argued that the agent did not "really" wish to do that which he did do—even though at the time he did it he did it gladly. To be sure the law (and perhaps also a certain hard-boiled moral perspective) may not recognize the mistake as substantial enough (or excusable enough) to invalidate the transaction, yet the observer may be less than certain that justice in transfer, requiring as it does voluntariness in transfer, is fully satisfied in such situations. After all, it may be held, willing consent based on mistaken assumptions (even without intent by anyone to defraud) may perhaps fall short of that informed consent which permits us to describe a transaction as fully voluntary, for purposes relevant to the requirements of justice.

But, it must be pointed out, the possibility of the winning of pure profit is central to the operation of the capitalist market system. From this perspective the entitlement theory, confined as it is to a capitalism in which all transactions are, by definition, *wholly* voluntary, appears not to have grappled with the phenomenon of pure profit.

It is with respect to these limitations in regard to the classic defenses of J. B. Clark and R. Nozick that we believe it useful to draw attention to what we shall call the *discovery* elements in the market system. It will be helpful, in preparation for the exposition of the discovery perspective, to identify, by way of contrast, a perspective shared both by these classic defenders of capitalist justice and by those who have sharply questioned the justice of capitalist distribution. We shall argue that this perspective overlooks a highly significant and characteristic feature of the economics of the capitalist system.

THE "GIVEN-PIE" PERSPECTIVE

This perspective on the economics of capitalism which we wish to criticize, a perspective shared, it seems, by *all* the participants, so far, in the debates on capitalist justice, can be labeled the "given-pie" perspective. The question that seems to be pondered, in the debates thus far, is how, in order to achieve distributive justice, a given pie is to be shared out among the claimants to it. This pie is given, in the sense that *its origin is not relevant to the justice* of its distribution.

Now, certainly it would be palpably false to assert that participants in the debate have failed to recognize possible ways in which justice may require that we recognize the productive contributions of claimants to shares in output. It has of course been recognized that those who have baked a pie may justly claim a share of it. Nonetheless it remains true that, at least *with respect to the ingredients that went into the production of the pie,* with respect to the original productive resources of a society, it has been simply assumed that the original productive resources were already "there." Criteria for justice did not, it appears, depend on how these resources came to be "there" in the first place. More specifically, no room, in these debates on distributive justice, is left for the possibility that the pattern of just distribution of output may depend on *who originated* the inputs that made its production possible. The question asked about original inputs is rather how an individual can establish just title to them now (*after* they have somehow come to be "here"), or whether, being "here," they somehow belong to society as a whole.

The question of who originated original inputs is, apparently, not asked because it appears to be a nonsense question. Original inputs, i.e., inputs that have not themselves been produced but exist in nature, could not have been originated by any person, because such origination would be inconsistent with their not having been produced. That which is produced, is produced out of inputs. These inputs may themselves have been produced out of other inputs. An original input, one that is itself not produced, could not have been originated—it was simply "there."

Thus the given-pie perspective seems, at first glance, a sound one. Sooner or later, in the analysis of justice in the ownership of produced output, we are pushed back, in principle, to consider the just ownership of original inputs. Criteria of justice may, possibly, be agreed upon with regard to the output forthcoming from original inputs—once it can be settled what justice has to say about ownership of such original resources. But in order to say something about just ownership of original resources, we must, in the given-pie perspective, remember that these original resources are—given pies. And, since pronouncements concerning the justice of produced output depend on what we say concerning just title to the original inputs, it turns out that ultimately our theories of distributive justice boil down to principles asserted about the just distribution of given pies. Whether a Rawls considering, from behind a veil of ignorance, just title to differentially superior personal qualities and talents, or a Nozick considering the validity of Lockean principles concerning initial private acquisition of nature-given land resources, our philosophers of justice agree on treating all non-produced resources as belonging to a category to which the notion of human origination is irrelevant. In what follows, we shall point out that this stance excludes the possibility of hitherto undiscovered resources entering into the economic world except as a result of luck. We shall, by contrast, argue that a most important human element in the economic process is made up of the *discovery* by individuals of hitherto unperceived resources or of other opportunities for gain (including pure profit opportunities). Let us turn to examine this notion of discovery.

THE MEANING OF DISCOVERY

One who enjoys a desirable situation is, in economic discussion, usually viewed as having reached his present happy state as a result of either of two possible kinds of circumstances. Either such a situation is seen as the deliberately achieved outcome ascribable to an earlier plan, or it is the fortunate result of a stroke of good luck. Economists discuss the first of these possibilities under the theory of *production*. The outcome produced is attributed to the deliberate deployment of inputs. In terms of the Clarkean ethic discussed earlier, just title to output arises out of the ownership of and marginal contribution made by the respective productive inputs. On the other hand, a situation the fortunate occurrence of which is ascribed to pure luck is viewed as in no way ascribable to human will and motivation. Beneficiaries of luck, from this perspective, are often seen as possessing no inherent claim, in justice, to that which good fortune has swept into their laps. We wish here to draw attention to a neglected, but extremely important, third alternative. A desired situation may be enjoyed not as the result of a deliberate plan of production, not as the result of sheer good fortune, but *as a result of perceptive discovery made by a human being*. It will be instructive to contrast an act of discovery with an act of deliberate production.

   1. An act of production is the outcome of a plan; an act of discovery
      is spontaneous. (Deliberate search, during which known inputs
      are systematically deployed to comb available data for some
      searched-for item, is a special kind of production. The deliberate
      production of information, e.g., looking up the meaning of a word
      in a dictionary or looking up a telephone number in a telephone
      directory, is not discovery, in the presently discussed sense of the
      word.)

2. An act of production can be seen as conforming to the criteria for economic efficiency: the producer employs inputs in an optimal mix; he maximizes the output of any given mix of inputs; he minimizes the cost of production of any aimed-at output result. An act of discovery contains no such expression of constrained maximization; it involves no plan, no allocation—merely the grasping of a perceived, available, objective.

3. Credit for a pure act of production (one containing no element of discovery) accrues to the owners of the combined inputs. *All* the output is seen, along Clarkian lines, as ascribable to the productive contribution of owned inputs. Credit for a discovery accrues to the discoverer whose alertness brought the discovered item to his notice. But this alertness is not itself in the nature of a possessed input deployed to achieve a planned result. Alertness is not *deployed*. The discoverer simply notices that which has hitherto escaped attention (including his own). Thus one does not, in the discovery context, treat "alertness" as an ingredient to be mixed with others in order to achieve a planned result, and therefore as the bottled-up form presently taken by its future marginal contribution (as productive resources are viewed in marginal productivity theory).

4. The aimed-at result of an act of production can be seen as having *already existed,* in embryonic form, in the input bundle responsible for the outcome. The decision to produce is simply the decision to pull the switch that effortlessly converts inputs into output. The future, in a world of only production decisions, is fully inherent in the present. History is merely the inexorable, inevitable unfolding of that which is already here, in bottled-up form. But discovery is quite different. Each discovery is a genuine novelty; it does not consist of the conversion or unfolding of earlier inputs. There is nothing at all inevitable about an act of discovery; we cannot, *ex-post*, describe the outcome as having been *caused* by anything that existed in the past. Prior to the discovery, the state of the world—even taking into account the alertness of the (persons who subsequently turn out to be the) discoverers—was not such as *to ensure* the subsequent course of events, in so far as these express discoveries subsequently made. The discoverer is in fact injecting something totally new into history. History consists, in part, in a series of total surprises, wholly unpredictable.[5]

DISCOVERY AND LUCK

But if an act of discovery is not able to fit into the box labeled "production," it is also not able to fit into that other box labeled "luck." It really does require a box of its own. An individual whose alertness inspires a discovery is not to be treated as merely the fortunate beneficiary of good luck. Theorists of justice tend to dismiss the justice of claims made by those who have benefited from good luck; they dismiss these claims because these fortunate claimants did nothing to bring about their present fortunate circumstances; they have therefore not "deserved" their good fortune. It is our concern here that such dismissal not lead also to summary dismissal of claims *of an entirely different* character—those made by discoverers. An act of discovery, even though it is not an act of deliberate production, is the expression of human motivation and human alertness. That which has been discovered might *never* have been discovered but for this motivation and alertness; it is quite wrong to see the discovery as merely the product of blind chance.

To see how a discoverer may be held to "deserve" that which he has discovered, even though he has not deliberately produced it, consider the following. If the discovery is to be dismissed as due entirely to pure luck, it follows that the earlier *failure* to have discovered (what is discovered later) must be excused as having been the result of bad luck. No one who has made a belated discovery should be able to berate himself for having done anything wrong in the past, for having made any error, since all earlier failures are to be ascribed, not to any earlier human shortcoming on his part, but simply to atrociously bad fortune. But in fact we know from our everyday experiences that truly deplorable errors—as judged subsequently by their perpetrators—do occur. That is, we know that desirable situations were entirely within our grasp, but were let go merely as a result of oversight. We blame ourselves for these past lapses, we do not simply shrug our shoulders, regretting our atrocious past luck. But if earlier failures to see what is staring us in the face are indeed seen as a series of deplorably "stupid" errors on our part, it follows that our alert discovery of what is now staring us in the face must be ascribed to us, not to blind luck.

We must, that is, distinguish sharply between one who has produced nothing, discovered nothing—who was in fact unalertly slumbering—who wakes up to find a windfall in his lap,[6] and one who has alertly grasped an attractive opportunity that came within reach. A pure windfall may correctly be described as being wholly "undeserved" (i.e., as not being attributable in any sense to the fortunate beneficiary), but an alertly grasped opportunity may quite plausibly, we suggest, be considered to fall into an entirely different ethical box.

It must of course be conceded that even though we emphasize the alert and motivated perception of the opportunity which constitutes the core of the act of discovery, we must also recognize that luck alone may indeed be responsible for the *very existence* of the opportunity waiting to be discovered. Certainly the discoverer of an attractive opportunity may count himself fortunate in having been at the right place at the right time. But, we wish to emphasize, to the extent that being at the right place at the right time does not in itself ensure that one will realize one's good fortune, luck cannot be pronounced as responsible for the discovery of the opportunity inherent in the situation. In fact, we suggest, it is plausible to treat the discoverer of a hitherto unperceived opportunity as its *creator*, its originator. That which is grasped by the discoverer did not, in a relevant sense, exist at all prior to its discovery.

DISCOVERY AS CREATION

To see this creative character of the discovery act, it is sufficient to notice that an unperceived opportunity, an unperceived resource, is, in an important sense, an opportunity or a resource without relevance for human history. As far as understanding the historical flow of events is concerned, nothing depends on the existence of resources of which everyone has been ignorant.

Let us recall that in an act of discovery (unlike the act of production) the outcome is not attributable to the contributions made by inputs. No inputs can guarantee a discovery. A discovered outcome is not a result already embedded, in embryonic form, in any bundle of resources. The outcome of an act of discovery is thus originated *entirely* by that act. A newly discovered island rich in natural resources has been created, for purposes of social science, in the act of its discovery. Its earlier physical existence may be significant for chains of purely physical causation; of course the island "really did exist" even though no one knew of its existence. Its presence may well have influenced the weather, or the flow of ocean currents, whether or not any human being was aware of its existence. But as far as directly concerns human decision making and economic values—and human ethical judgments—the island entered into existence at the moment of its discovery. Its discoverer was its creator, for all purposes of direct human concern.

While the discoverer of the island may indeed consider himself lucky to have been in the position to notice the island, he may plausibly claim that even after having been placed in that lucky position the island's discovery was by no means assured. The island, not yet existing in the relevant social sense, could well have remained forever undiscovered but for the discoverer's motivated alertness. It was that alertness which brought the island, with all its resources, within the purview of human concern, human valuations, and human planning for the future.

The inspired hunch which leads the discoverer to notice islands where others see only clouds, to notice opportunities for innovative products or innovative applications of technology which others fail to see, is as creative, in its own context, as the inspired vision of the sculptor who sees, in marble and chisel, not merely marble and chisel but a sublime form waiting to be brought forth. Recognition of this creative aspect of the act of discovery seems to underlie a widely shared ethical conviction, that embodied in the notion of "finders, keepers."

THE FINDERS, KEEPERS ETHIC AND PRIVATE PROPERTY

It seems plausible to interpret the fairly widespread view that the first finder of an unowned object is its just owner as the moral conviction that this finder is the discoverer and thus, in the significant sense, the creator of that object. We wish to suggest that this finders, keepers ethic undergirds the widespread acceptance of the legitimacy of private property and, ultimately, of the possibility of justice under capitalism. In this section we explore the relevance of the finders, keepers ethic for the institution of private property.

Traditionally, defenses of the institution of private property have relied on the observations of John Locke concerning the legitimacy of private acquisition of unowned, naturally available useful things, through the mixing of one's labor with those useful things. We have already noted (in our references to Nozick's entitlement approach) that critics have questioned the validity of the Lockean approach, and have, moreover, pointed out that a proviso circumscribing this approach enunciated by Locke himself may in practice render that approach quite irrelevant for a justification of private property in the real world. The validity of Locke's approach rests on (a) the (arbitrary?) assumption of the justice of self-ownership by individual human beings (without this assumption one could hardly talk of an individual mixing "his labor" with nature-given objects, since the labor he mixes may be held to belong justly to society as a whole); and (b) the belief that mixing one's labor with an object does indeed confer private title to it upon the laborer; critics have challenged this belief as quite arbitrary.

The problems arising out of the Lockean proviso follow from Locke's qualification of his doctrine to make it applicable only to those situations where, even after the individual has mixed his labor with the nature-given objects, there remain plenty of these same objects for others to enjoy as well (Locke 1937). Commentators have pointed out that in the real world of economic scarcity this proviso seems to make Locke's justification of private acquisition almost entirely irrelevant. We wish to suggest that a finders, keepers approach, based on the ethical implication of seeing discovery as creative, may offer a more convincing basis for original acquisition of property from the state of nature.

The finders, keepers approach would assign just title to the one who, discovering an unowned (because undiscovered) resource, grasps it first. The justice of his title is then seen as stemming from the creative character of the pure act of discovery (rather than being derivative from the self-owned resource which the appropriator has mixed with the resources).[7] For this view on the justice of original acquisition, no Lockean proviso need be held to apply. The rationale behind the proviso has been interpreted (Nozick 1974:177) to be that such private acquisition cannot be just if it harms others (and, unless there is plenty left over for others, private acquisition must limit the common pool available to others). But, from the perspective of a finders, keepers ethic based on the creativity of discovery, this rationale may reasonably be held not to be relevant to acts of pure discovery. An act of discovery (even if it results in private appropriation of a hitherto undiscovered *scarce* resource) does not necessarily harm others, since this resource never did exist for these others. My discovery now of a resource has not stopped you from enjoying this object now (or even in the future), since as far as you are concerned *now* (i.e., at the second prior to my discovery) this resource has not existed (and its future existence has not been anticipated). The possibility that, were I not now to have discovered this resource, you would, very likely, have discovered it a little later yourself (so that my grasping of my discovery has limited your potential future enjoyment) seems to be not really a relevant circumstance at all. The circumstance that you might, at some time in the future, have created the object which I am now in fact creating hardly means that I am harming you (by "preventing" *you* from creating *this* object). Once I have created the object through its discovery, there is simply no way for you to create it independently; it already does exist, for human purposes. No one can, before hypothesized future discovery, in fact predict that discovery. It would, when it were to occur, have to be an act of pure origination so that, at the moment of my present discovery, the hypothetical future discovery by you is simply conjecture. To say now that you were somehow "going" to make the discovery in the future is to rewrite history in the light of future events—events which are in no way implicit in the course of prior history. Within the finders, keepers ethic there is simply no room for any Lockean proviso.

FINDERS, KEEPERS AND THE JUSTICE OF CAPITALISM

Once we have satisfactorily grounded the notion of just original acquisition—and thus the institution of private property—in the discovery act, the road is open for a more comprehensive defense of the justice of the capitalist market system. Such a defense may be built along Nozickian entitlement lines, but with an added dimension capable of dealing with the gap we noticed in that entitlement theory. That gap was its possible weakness in regard to the justice of pure profit. Pure profit, we pointed out, may not be wholly defensible within the entitlement approach, since the pure error (involved in the transactions which make pure profit possible) may be held to invalidate the prima facie voluntariness of the relevant transactions. Our discovery perspective permits us now to perceive a new dimension in profit, a dimension obscured in the "given-pie" perspectives which we have cricitized.

It turns out, from this discovery perspective, that the very features of pure profit which seem to raise problems within the entitlement approach are sufficient to prove profit to be *a wholly discovered* gain. The problem with pure profit, it will be recalled, was that there seemed no way of "justifying" it in terms of productive contribution rendered (since by definition it is what remains after deducting *all* necessary costs of production, including transportation and transaction costs necessary to deliver output to its ultimate buyer). Moreover, it will be recalled, the very circumstance that pure profit is in the nature of a surplus, not strictly necessary to be paid to the primary sellers in order to persuade them to sell (that which is later resold at a profit), appears to raise serious questions concerning the informed voluntariness with which the ultimate buyers pay the higher, profitable price. (Or, alternatively, the willingness of the ultimate buyers to pay the higher price raises questions concerning the informed voluntariness with which the first sellers agreed to sell for the low price.) Our present perspective enables us to perceive that, precisely because the primary sellers have no inkling of the immediate availability of obtaining higher prices, and precisely because the ultimate buyers have no inkling of the immediate availability of what they buy at lower prices than they are paying, the gap between the low and the high prices constitutes for them an undiscovered opportunity. The entrepreneur who buys at the low price and sells at the high price is grasping a discovered opportunity. From the finders, keepers perspective he is justly entitled to this grasped gain because, in the relevant sense, he has *created* it.

Indeed, our understanding of the primary role of entrepreneurship in the market system permits us to see the entire capitalist system *as consisting essentially of acts of discovery*. From the *ex ante* perspective there is no market transaction which does not involve, to some degree, an attempt to peer ahead through the fog of uncertainty, in order to grasp opportunities which might easily escape recognition. In the ceaseless flow of dynamic competition, sellers modify their judgments on what prices they can command, buyers modify their judgments on what prices it is necessary for them to offer to pay. These bids and offers constitute attempted acts of discovery. The justice of market outcomes cannot be assessed without incorporating the extent to which gains derived from these discovery acts fit the guidelines of the finders, keepers rule.

Standard theories of capitalist justice, it emerges, appear to have treated the market as if it were, at all times, in full general equilibrium. Such a model of the market contains no scope for entrepreneurship, no scope for pure error, no scope for overlooked costlessly available opportunities—in short, no scope for discovery and for its ethical implications. Once we exorcise the "given-pie" incubus—an incubus very much implicit in a strictly equilibrium view of the market—from discussions of market justice, the door is open for careful introduction of the possible relevance of a finders, keepers rule. The finders, keepers ethic provides a plausible basis for defending the justice of the capitalist system. Such an ethic offers a fresh basis—unencumbered by any Lockean proviso—for original private acquisition from nature. Such an ethic offers, in addition, a solid theory supporting the possible justice of pure profit. To the extent that capitalist resource incomes involve a discovery element, they, too, may be held justified, at least in part, by the finders, keepers ethic. Together these insights significantly supplement the standard defenses of capitalist justice. They certainly do not declare capitalism to be free of all moral blemishes (since, in any event, strict justice is not the sole criterion for morality between human beings). They certainly do not pronounce all actions taken under historical capitalism to have been moral, or even just. They do, however, suggest that the capitalist system need not be rejected out of hand as being inherently unfair. Moral improvement may be sought within the framework of private property and free exchange, without the conviction that to participate in capitalism is to participate in an inevitably flawed human institution.

NOTES

1. This paper draws heavily from my recent book, *Discovery, Capitalism, and Distributive Justice* (1989), to which the reader is referred for many additional observations concerning the matters and arguments put forward somewhat dogmatically in the present paper. See especially chapter 7 in that book for certain qualifications to the discovery approach which, for space reasons, could not be considered in this chapter.

2. The Marxist doctrine of capitalist exploitation of labor can be seen as one particular form which this category of attack has taken.

3. For some critical comments on Clark's references to pure profit, see Kirzner (1989:50–5).

4. For some critical discussion of this point, see Nozick (1974:174f.) and Epstein (1979:1227f.).

5. For such a view of history, see especially the work of Shackle (1972:351f.). See also Shackle (1970).

6. For present purposes we ignore the (possibly significant) element of discovery required in fact to recognize the windfall that has already been deposited in one's lap.

7. The self ownership of the individual may be seen as a special case of the general discovery approach.

REFERENCES

Clark, J. B. (1899) *The Distribution of Wealth*. New York and London: Macmillan.
Epstein, R. A. (1979) "Possession as the root of title." *Georgia Law Review* 13:1221.
Friedman, M. (1962) *Capitalism and Freedom*. Chicago: University of Chicago Press.
Kirzner, I. M. (1989) *Discovery, Capitalism, and Distributive Justice*. Oxford: Basil Blackwell.

Locke, J. (1937) *An Essay concerning the True Original Extent and End of Civil Government*. New York: Appleton Century Crofts, section 27.

Nielsen, K. (1985) *Equality and Liberty, a Defense of Radical Egalitarianism*. Totowa, N.J.: Rowman and Allanheld.

Nozick, R. (1974) *Anarchy, State and Utopia*. New York: Basic Books.

Shackle, G. L. S. (1970) *Decision, Order and Time in Human Affairs*, 2nd ed. Cambridge: Cambridge University Press (originally published 1969).

Shackle, G. L. S. (1972) *Epistemics and Economics: A Critique of Economic Doctrines*. Cambridge: Cambridge University Press.

A CRITIQUE OF KIRZNER'S FINDERS-KEEPERS
DEFENSE OF PROFIT

THEODORE BURCZAK

Israel Kirzner has for many years developed and championed a theory of the market as a discovery process. He argues that an understanding of the market process derived from the work of Hayek and Mises offers a more realistic and descriptive portrayal of a capitalist market economy than does the theory dominating mainstream economics depicting the market economy as a perfectly competitive, general equilibrium system. Kirzner also insists that if the Austrian theory were more widely accepted, the popular idea that it is possible and desirable to challenge the justice of the outcomes of a market process guided by the rule of law would be discredited. As he puts it, understanding the market as a discovery process makes end-state notions of distributive justice "highly problematic" (Kirzner 1995:46). In a similar vein, Hayek (1976) maintains that in a market economy, conceptions of social justice are a "mirage." For Kirzner, a proper conception of the functioning of the market process, combined with the widely held acceptance of a finders-keepers ethic, should also produce an acceptance of the justice of free market outcomes, especially entrepreneurial profit.

While Kirzner's theory of the market as a discovery process has considerable descriptive merit, it has some shortcomings, and this paper exploits these deficiencies to challenge his normative conclusions. After presenting Kirzner's theory of the market discovery process and his belief that supplementing this theory with a finders-keepers ethic undermines notions of distributive justice, this paper criticizes two claims supporting his normative defense of market outcomes.

David Prychitko and an anonymous referee provided very helpful comments on an earlier version of this paper. Support for this research was provided by the Bartlett Junior Leave Program at Denison University.

From *The Review of Austrian Economics*, vol. 15, no. 1 (2002): 75–90. © 2002 Kluwer Academic Publishers. Reproduced with permission of Springer New York via Copyright Clearance Center. A few, minor corrections have been made.

First, Kirzner's defense of the justice of entrepreneurial profit is based upon treating the wage-for-labor-time exchange as legitimate. Yet there are good reasons—some of which we will see are consistent with Kirzner's own defense of entrepreneurial profit—for doubting the justice of the wage-for-labor-time exchange and hence the justice of the profits generated in capitalist firms created by such exchanges. The paper argues that the profits earned by a capitalist firm employing wage-labor can only be considered as just if we deny that human beings are responsible agents while employed by an entrepreneur. If, however, we consider hired human beings always to be responsible agents, as is true in David Ellerman's (1992) rendition of the labor theory of property, Kirzner's defense of entrepreneurial profit generated in a capitalist enterprise is weakened.

Second, the paper criticizes Kirzner's thesis that in a market economy everyone has, in principle, an equal opportunity to be an entrepreneur directing a productive enterprise or to be an entrepreneur engaging in speculation. According to Kirzner, in a market economy that places no statutory limits on the economic activities in which an individual may participate as long as those activities do not infringe upon the property rights of others, every person in principle has the same opportunity of acting upon an entrepreneurial insight as any other. Specifically, ownership of wealth provides no entrepreneurial advantage: a poor person who notices an opportunity for entrepreneurial gain is in principle no less able to seize this opportunity than is a wealthy person. Kirzner reaches this conclusion because he believes that credit markets in a free economy do not systematically discriminate amongst types of borrowers. Thus, a poor entrepreneur who notices a speculative or productive opportunity has the same access to credit, after transactions costs are taken into consideration, as a wealthy entrepreneur. This conclusion has been called into question by credit rationing models demonstrating that asset-poor individuals who are not able to provide collateral to lenders will be unable to obtain credit, *no matter the interest rate they are willing to pay*. The credit rationing literature erodes the underpinnings of Kirzner's application of the finders-keepers ethic to the evaluation of entrepreneurial profit because it implies that all individuals do not in principle have an equal opportunity to be an entrepreneur. To extend an old adage, "It takes money to make money entrepreneurially," and this possibility further challenges Kirzner's belief that a finders-keepers ethic can undergird the normative conclusion that entrepreneurs should necessarily be able to keep the profits that they find.

Given these two criticisms, this paper maintains that it is possible to accept Kirzner's *arbitrage* theory of profit and the finders-keepers ethic in situations where everyone in principle can be a finder, but still reject his defense of profits generated through productive creativity and speculation. To be clear, the paper does not challenge the justice of the finders-keepers ethic per se, but rather its use to evaluate the justice of profits received through speculation and by the entrepreneur organizing a capitalist firm. Thus, the finders-keepers ethic has only limited applicability in a normative defense of incomes generated in an unregulated capitalist market economy.

I. THE ARBITRAGE THEORY OF PROFIT AND FINDERS-KEEPERS

The Austrian theory of the market process starts from a perspective about the nature of human knowledge that is compactly summarized as "subjectivism." According to the Austrians, knowledge of economic opportunity, technology, potential market demand, and resource availability is subjective in the sense that each individual has his own perception of cost conditions, market demand, and resource availability. These perceptions may be unique to each individual, and thus they may turn out to be wrong. One entrepreneur, for instance, may be out-competed by another, because his perception of feasible technology proves to be too costly. The main point here is that conventional economics generally treats all this knowledge as *given* to economic actors. Knowledge of profit opportunities, technology, and resource endowments is objective knowledge, and the economic problem is how to utilize this knowledge in a way to achieve the optimal level of economic output. In contrast, for the Austrians, economic knowledge is partial, dispersed, ever-shifting, and potentially wrong. The economic problem is then how to coordinate individual actions sparked by subjective perceptions and imaginings.

The central actor in the Austrian conception of the market process is the entrepreneur. Entrepreneurs are alert to the possibility of economic gains, or profits, that arise from disequilibrium price discrepancies. For instance, an entrepreneur may profit from arbitrage: buying a commodity from a low-priced producer and immediately reselling it at a higher price to a consumer who, the entrepreneur alertly notices, values the commodity more highly. Prior to the intervention of the entrepreneur, the producer and consumer are ignorant of each others' existence. The consumer was unaware that the producer offered the commodity for sale, and the producer did not notice the potential customer willing to pay more than he was asking. Entrepreneurship can also be speculative: the entrepreneur speculates that a commodity currently selling for a low price will sell for a higher price in the future, after taking into consideration the interest expense of carrying the commodity. Finally, entrepreneurship can take the form of what Kirzner calls "productive creativity": buying low priced inputs and combining them to produce a commodity with a higher price. For instance, an entrepreneur might buy oranges and rent capital and labor-time to manufacture orange juice that consumers value more highly then the inputs individually. The lure of profit is to find and act upon these price discrepancies in order to try to get something for nothing (Kirzner 1979a:11). In Kirzner's (1979a:150) words, "What the market process does is to systematically translate unnoticed opportunities for mutually profitable exchange among individuals into forms that tend to excite the interest and alertness of those most likely to notice what can be spontaneously learned."[1]

Central to the Austrian understanding of entrepreneurship is that it is an activity entailing no opportunity cost. To see this most clearly, we can contrast entrepreneurship with deliberate search behavior. Searching involves looking for opportunities that are known to exist, and it can be understood to involve the comparison of costs and benefits. For instance, when we search for a library book, we have good reason to believe it exists, and it is sensible to ask whether the benefit we expect to receive upon locating the volume is worth the additional time we expect that it will take to find it. Entrepreneurial behavior is different than search. We act entrepreneurially when we notice a potentially valuable resource that, prior to its discovery, we had no idea existed. For instance, if when searching for a library book, we happen to perceive a different—previously unknown to us—book that stimulates a startling insight, this alert noticing is entrepreneurial in nature. The flash of inspiration that caused us to perceive this book did not involve the deliberate forfeit of any other opportunity. We did not weigh the expected additional costs with the expected additional benefits.

Given that there are no opportunity costs associated with entrepreneurship, Kirzner also advances the potentially questionable claim that entrepreneurial activity does not require the prior ownership of any resources. Take the case of arbitrage in which we notice a resource that we can purchase, with a check drawn upon an account with a zero balance, and immediately resell at a higher price, enabling us to deposit the proceeds in our checking account before the initial check clears. In the case of speculation or productive creativity, we may have to borrow the funds to finance our purchase of the low-priced resources, since the higher-priced output will not be available for sale until the future. But again, as long as we are able to obtain the credit needed to initiate the speculative or productive endeavor, we do not need to possess any assets to be an entrepreneur.

From Kirzner's (1992a:224) subjectivist perspective, the profit that the entrepreneur earns by acting upon perceived price discrepancies is a discovered gain, a gain that did not exist for human purposes until its discovery. Thus, he believes that "it is plausible to treat the discoverer of a hitherto unperceived opportunity as its *creator*, its originator. That which is grasped by the discoverer did not, in a relevant sense, exist at all prior to its discovery" (Kirzner 1992a:221). Entrepreneurial discovery creates an opportunity of whose existence others were previously ignorant. Understanding market exchange as motivated by the discovery of previously unnoticed and unthought of gain allows us, in Kirzner's view, to apply the widely held ethical belief in finders-keepers to evaluate the justice of entrepreneurial profit. Kirzner observes that many of us accept the rule of finders-keepers, or first come–first served, when we need to decide how to reward property rights to a scarce resource with no previously existing property title that is, in principle, available to any particular person to appropriate. If this observation is correct, and if we understand profit to be the reward for alertly grasping previously unnoticed economic gain, then we should, from Kirzner's perspective, accept the justice of entrepreneurial profit. This is the essence of what Kirzner characterizes as an arbitrage theory of profit and his use of it to advocate a finders-keepers ethic to evaluate the justice of market incomes.

This analysis allows Kirzner to draw broader conclusions about the justice of wage and property incomes earned in a market economy. He argues that all exchanges exhibit an element of entrepreneurship. Sellers of factor services must always decide whether a particular offer should be accepted or whether they should hold out for a higher price. In an economy out of equilibrium that is permeated by true ignorance of possible opportunities, every decision to sell or to buy is contingent upon an entrepreneurial judgment. As such, Kirzner believes that all incomes contain an element of entrepreneurial profit, and the legitimacy of these incomes can therefore also be evaluated with a finders-keepers ethic. In effect, he asserts that finders-keepers supports the justice of all income receipts resulting from uncoerced exchanges in a market economy. Thus, it is unnecessary (and perhaps even inappropriate) to apply other criteria to evaluate the justice of the market determination of income.

Insofar as entrepreneurship takes the form of pure arbitrage this paper has no qualms with an application of the finders-keepers ethic to justify profit incomes. Arbitrage does not involve renting laborers. Nor does it require prior asset ownership. However, unless it is undertaken by an independent contractor, productive creativity calls for the employ-ment of wage-labor. There is reason to doubt whether finders-keepers is sufficient to justify entrepreneurial profit in this context. In addition, this paper will argue that in contrast to Kirzner's belief, both productive cre-ativity and speculation do require the possession of resources, so that the receipt of entrepreneurial profit in these cases is not in principle available to everyone, as the finders-keepers ethic requires.

2. PROFIT, PRODUCTIVE CREATIVITY, AND THE LABOR THEORY OF PROPERTY[2]

Unless the entrepreneur is an independent contractor, productive cre-ativity involves buying or renting inputs, including labor time, at a low price and selling the output produced by these combined inputs at a higher price. A critical question in determining the justice of entrepre-neurial profit earned through this method is to examine the justice of the wage-for-labor-time exchange. To accomplish this task, we will begin by evaluating Kirzner's essay, "Producer, Entrepreneur, and the Right to Property" (1979b), in the light of David Ellerman's (1992) version of the labor theory of property. This comparison raises the issue whether it is legitimate to treat labor as an input, or in other words, for workers to assume the legal status of things.

Kirzner begins his attempt to justify entrepreneurial profit received through establishing a firm by seeking to pinpoint who bears responsibil-ity for production. He argues that we should consider an individual who makes the entrepreneurial decision to initiate a joint production process to be the responsible agent of production. After all, if the entrepreneur did not hire the factors of production that constitute the firm, there is no guarantee that anyone else would have assumed this role. Thus, if the entrepreneur had not taken the initiative, the product of the firm may have never appeared. As the responsible agent, entrepreneurs should appropriate the product and receive the profits (and losses) from the enterprise.

Kirzner draws this conclusion by first differentiating between the concepts of productivity and responsibility. For Kirzner, responsibility refers to the necessarily human and willful initiative to undertake production. To be productive, on the other hand, does not require the exercise of human will. A resource can be productive simply if its presence contributes to the realization of an entrepreneur's decision to produce a commodity.

To clarify this conceptual distinction we might consider the contribution of a gun in an armed robbery. The gun helps to realize the robber's vision of a successful burglary, and as such is productive. But since it is an inanimate object without a will, the gun cannot share responsibility for the crime with the robber. Given this distinction between productivity and responsibility, Kirzner (1979b:189) maintains that it is pure entrepreneurship that "is responsible—in the sense relevant to the ethical connotation of 'what a man has produced'—to the *entire* product." "[T]he necessarily indivisible entrepreneur is responsible for the entire product. The contributions of the factor inputs, being without an entrepreneurial component, are irrelevant for the ethical position being taken" (1979b:195). He quotes Frank Knight to reinforce this view:

> Under the enterprise system, a special social class, the businessman, direct economic activity: *they are in the strict sense the producers, while the great mass of the population merely furnishes them with productive services, placing their persons and their property at the disposal of this class* (quoted in Kirzner 1979b:189).

We can accept the separate links that Kirzner establishes between entrepreneurship and responsibility and between responsibility and the creation of the entire product. The controversial issue to notice at this juncture is the rather curious position rented workers assume in this analysis. It would seem that in order for the entrepreneur to be regarded as the solely responsible agent of a joint productive venture, workers must play a similar role in the firm as do guns in a robbery: they are the instruments of the entrepreneur's will.

Ellerman's version of the labor theory of property challenges Kirzner's conclusion that the entrepreneur should be the sole appropriator and receiver of profit in the capitalist firm by pursuing a line of argument that is similar to Kirzner's. For Ellerman, like Kirzner, the relevant question is to determine who is responsible for production in the capitalist firm. Once the responsible agent of production is identified, Ellerman proposes that we can call upon the "juridical principle of imputation" in order to establish the just appropriator of the entire product. This widely-accepted principle maintains that people should be held legally accountable, or responsible, for the consequences of the actions for which they are factually responsible. Kirzner also appeals to the juridical principle of imputation in his defense of entrepreneurial profit.[3] Despite this similar appeal, the two differ in their judgments of who bears the factual responsibility for production in a capitalist firm. In Ellerman's view, the agent responsible for production is not Kirzner's indivisible entrepreneur alone, but all the workers—mental, manual, and entrepreneurial—who labor in the firm together.

Understanding Ellerman's definition of the concept "appropriation" is crucial to grasp the meaning of his labor theory of property. There are two dimensions to his notion of appropriation. First, appropriation refers to being the first owner of a newly created asset. For instance, a car that emerges at the end of an assembly line is not yet owned by anyone. It is not born with a property right automatically already attached to it. Someone must become the first claimant, creating a property right to the vehicle. Second, Ellerman uses the term appropriation to mean being the last owner of a productive input. For instance, in the same automobile factory, some agency must be the last title holder to the inputs, e.g., the electricity and labor time, extinguished or used up in the process of production. He thus speaks of the appropriation of the entire product, by which he means being the first owner of produced output as well as being the last owner of the used up productive inputs. As we will see, Ellerman views legal responsibility for the results of economic activity to entail appropriation of the entire product.

While Ellerman's theory begins from the Lockean position that people have a natural right to the product of their labor, he understands the nature of this right differently than Locke. Ellerman defends the position that the right to the entire product of one's labor is an inalienable right that should not be transferred, even with consent. The typical employment contract in a capitalist enterprise is consequently illegitimate. This contrasts with Locke who believes that it is just for a person to sell his labor time to, say, an entrepreneur, giving the entrepreneur the legal right to appropriate the entire product resulting from the laborer's efforts. Ellerman points out that when worker B sells his labor time to entrepreneur A thereby granting A control rights over B's labor time and allowing A to appropriate the entire product of B's labor, the worker is no longer legally responsible for the results of his productive activities. The entrepreneur becomes the last owner, and hence appropriator, of his employee's labor time. As such, the worker assumes the legal status of an inanimate object while employed by the entrepreneur.

It is worth quoting Ellerman at length to see how he conceives the legal "thingification" human beings undergo when they become rented laborers in a conventional firm.

> A person has the legal role of a thing from the viewpoint of decision-making if the person is not a legal party to the decisions about the services performed in that role. The owner of an entity rented out is . . . not a legal party to the decisions about the entity's use. Therefore when the entity hired out is a person, the person has the legal role of a thing. The person in the role of the owner of the entity hired out, that is, in the labor-seller's role, is not a legal party to the decisions made within the scope of the employment contract. Decision-making power is not delegated from the employees to the employer; the employer decides in his own name. The legal decision-making authority is alienated and transferred to the employer (Ellerman 1988:1118).

Since they do not participate in the appropriation of the entire product of the firm, hired laborers are not legally responsible for all of their actions while on the job. Nevertheless, they remain factually responsible for the results of their intentional actions. Central to Ellerman's theory of property is that it is impossible to alienate factual responsibility. Current law only pretends that it can be alienated when it fails to apply the juridical principle of imputation to the capitalist firm.

One purpose of law courts is to determine factual responsibility for criminal behavior in order to assign legal responsibility. When jurists do this, they are applying the juridical principle of imputation. When legal responsibility does not line up with factual responsibility, most people believe that an injustice exists that needs to be rectified. In the realm of production and resource allocation, Ellerman considers one of the roles of economists to be the identification of the factually responsible agents of production, in order to determine how the juridical principle of imputation should be instituted in an economic context. It is impossible to alienate responsibility for one's actions, whether one is a bank robber or an employee, and if the juridical principle of imputation is to apply in production, all workers should participate in the appropriation of the entire product of the firm. In particular, workers should be the last owner of their labor time. Ellerman concludes that because it is factually impossible to alienate responsibility for one's actions, it is unjust for a worker to be transformed by a legally recognized labor rental contract into the means (a thing without legal responsibility) to an entrepreneur's ends.

The comparison between a bank robber and an employee may illustrate why Ellerman believes that workers' consent to give up legal responsibility for the entire product of their labor efforts in exchange for a wage is unjust. If a rich murderer uses a considerable cash payment to entice a willing poor person to bear the legal responsibility for the murder, a court would not recognize this contract by jailing the pauper for the crime, even if he agreed to the exchange. Such a contract violates the juridical principle of imputation. Likewise, an entrepreneur's appropriation of the entire product and his receipt of profit from a productive firm employing wage-labor are based on what Ellerman regards as a fraudulent wage-for-labor-time exchange. For an economist who accepts all the implications of the juridical principle of imputation, the only way in which joint production can be justly organized is if it occurs in a labor-owned, self-managed firm in which all manual, mental, and entrepreneurial workers participate jointly in the appropriation of the entire product.[4]

In his attempt to identify the entrepreneur as the just appropriator of the entire product, we have seen that Kirzner also makes an implicit appeal to the juridical principle of imputation. This principle animates his linkage between the entrepreneur's responsibility for creating (finding) the firm's output and the entrepreneur's just receipt (keeping) of pure profit. But if we investigate Kirzner's reasoning more carefully, it is apparent that his finders-keepers theory of entrepreneurial profit harbors a potential contradiction and that he errs in his specification of the agent(s) factually responsible for production. Kirzner insists that there is "an entrepreneurial element in *every* human action and decision" (1979b:197), including the choice to supply labor services at every moment of production (1979b:198). He notes that picturing a capitalist enterprise to be the result of an entrepreneur's decision to combine non-entrepreneurial, purely productive inputs is merely an analytical convenience in order to highlight the entrepreneurial role in facilitating the market process. In a real world clouded with uncertainty, workers also act entrepreneurially when they decide to accept a particular job rather than another, conceivably more rewarding one (Kirzner 1992b:94–100). It is thus apparent that from Kirzner's perspective it is impossible to sustain Knight's description of real world, flesh and blood workers as passive, nonresponsible beings that are no different than inanimate capital goods subject only to the directing entrepreneur's will. Yet the crucial question remains: if workers are in possession of their decision making powers, or their entrepreneurial wills, at every minute of their services, how can we justify the legal treatment of workers in a capitalist enterprise as things that share no legal responsibility for production? How can we defend the singular entrepreneurial agent as the sole appropriator of the entire product of a joint productive enterprise, as Kirzner does?

One possibility is to think of employees as independent contractors, so that we interpret what workers sell to the entrepreneur to be the *product* of their efforts, and not control over their labor activities. To take this approach would mean that what Kirzner calls "productive creativity" collapses into arbitrage. This is the gambit that Prychitko (1998) attempts in his defense of Kirzner's application of the finders-keepers ethic to the positive ethical appraisal of the entrepreneur's appropriation of the entire product. Prychitko argues that we could conceive of individual workers as self-managed firms of one, who sell the products that their labor efforts are responsible for creating to the highest bidder that they can discover. Since Ellerman's labor theory of property requires that firms be self-managed if they are to adhere to the juridical principle of imputation, and since workers might be thought of as self-managed firms of one, Prychitko (1998:84) reasons that there is no contradiction between the labor theory of property and a finders-keepers defense of profit.

While this interpretation may have analytical purchase for some readers, a typical employee in a capitalist enterprise working on, say, an assembly line would surely not be astonished if he were fired for stepping off the line to talk to his stock broker on a cell phone. He would not be surprised because he knows that he has not sold the product of his efforts to the directing entrepreneur. He has rented his time to that entrepreneur, who thus enjoys the right, within limits, to command the employee as she pleases during the contracted period. The actual servitude resulting from a labor-rental contract and the appropriation of an employee's labor time by the hiring entrepreneur do not disappear by analytically construing an employee to be a self-managed firm of one.[5] If one accepts the juridical principle of imputation, as Kirzner does, it appears that Ellerman's normative conclusions cannot be so easily dodged.

3. ENTREPRENEURIAL PROFIT AND CREDIT RATIONING

In his book, *Discovery, Capitalism, and Distributive Justice* (1989), Kirzner fleshes out his portrayal of the actors on both sides of the labor market as entrepreneurial. He does this to reinforce the applicability of finders-keepers to an ethical evaluation of all income receipts in a capitalist economy, including wage incomes, and not just pure profits. Because real world labor markets are never in equilibrium, self-owners of labor time must act, in part, as entrepreneurs since wage incomes are never guaranteed prior to their receipt. Kirzner (1989:116) describes the entrepreneurial nature of the labor supply decision as follows:

> Inevitably the laborer must determine for himself—in an open-ended world fraught with inescapable uncertainty, pervaded by the sheerest of utter ignorance—which job to apply for, which job to accept, and what wages and working conditions to hold out for. This means that the more successfully "entrepreneurial" laborer will in fact enjoy a job offering wages, working conditions, prestige and prospects for advancement, which may substantially exceed those won by a fellow laborer with equal talents *qua* laborer, but with less potential as an entrepreneur.

The decision of a worker to sell his labor time is entrepreneurial because the worker has to judge which producer, in what industry, offers the greatest chance for his labor to be most productive and hence to be rewarded with the highest possible wage.

Yet one wonders whether this kind of analysis undermines Kirzner's intentions. After all, if workers are entrepreneurs when they evaluate different employers in search of the most "profit" (or the highest wage), what prevents workers from using these same entrepreneurial insights to initiate their own productive enterprise? Is there, in his view, any difference between an entrepreneurial employee and an entrepreneurial employer?

Kirzner seems to suggest that workers who do not employ their entrepreneurial facilities to direct a productive enterprise prefer to take fewer risks than those who do. He asks us to imagine two men, Jones and Smith, who each own no resources but who both believe that cab driving is a rewarding economic activity. Kirzner contrasts the case of Jones, who borrows money to rent a taxicab and becomes an independent cab driver, with the case of Smith, who rents his labor time to an owner of a fleet of taxicabs. Both the independent contractor Jones and the wage-laborer Smith act entrepreneurially when deciding to work in the taxi-driving industry. For Jones, there is no guarantee that the cab driving business will generate enough revenue to cover all of his opportunity costs. Smith, also, "never was *assured* of anything at all. . . . In selling his driving services to Brown, the fleet owner, Smith is not simply transforming these services into their fully known cash value, he is taking a step into the dark, uncertain entrepreneurial future, guided by his entrepreneurial hunches" (Kirzner 1989:118). The only difference between Jones and Smith appears to be that Jones is willing to take the risk of running his own firm to exploit the perceived opportunity in the taxi business, while Jones is not willing to incur this risk.

There are two problems with Kirzner's analysis and conclusion. First, in this example, the amount of risk incurred by Smith and Jones is not very different, contrary to Kirzner's claim. Since Jones borrowed the money to finance the purchase of his cab, if the cab business is not profitable, all he runs the risk of losing is the labor time he devoted to the enterprise. The lending bank or capitalist bears all the risk if Jones does not generate enough revenue to pay back his loan. But this is the same exact loss to which Smith is exposed. If the fleet owner Brown goes out of business and is unable to pay Smith his wage, Smith will have lost perhaps the same amount of labor time as Jones. On the other hand, if the cab business proves to be extremely successful, Jones will gain entrepreneurial profit, while Smith will receive no more than his contracted wage. What then prohibits Smith from starting his own cab driving business? For that matter, if Kirzner is right that factor owners are all making the same kinds of entrepreneurial judgments, why would anyone ever choose to work for someone else if credit were easily accessible to all?

Kirzner's discussion of the cab drivers Smith and Jones reveals that he sees the entrepreneurial profit that accrues to the independent contractor Jones as readily available to Smith. Nothing stands in Smith's way of himself receiving this profit except either (i) his choice not to pursue it, or (ii) his inability to notice that being an independent contractor has more potential rewards, without incurring any more risk, than does being an employee in a firm offering taxi services. It is apparent that Kirzner thinks that perceptible opportunities for gain are "*in principle* available to others," not just to the entrepreneurs who happen to notice and grasp them (1995:40, emphasis added). For Kirzner, lack of fungible assets poses no barrier to acting upon entrepreneurial insights. Thus, he can write: "Entrepreneurial profits . . . are not captured by owners, in their capacity as owners, at all. They are captured, instead, by men who exercise pure entrepreneurship, for which ownership is *never* a condition" (1979a:94). He draws this conclusion because he believes the asset-poor cannot be systematically denied credit in an unregulated market economy.

If Kirzner is right that anyone can borrow to finance a speculative or productive investment project, whether or not they can demonstrate any collateral, then he is correct that any perceptible opportunity for gain is in principle available to others. However, contemporary theories of credit rationing suggest that Kirzner's presumption that credit is available to anyone willing to pay market rates of interest is not an accurate description of reality.[6] If everyone does not, in principle, have equal access to credit, then in the context of both production in a capitalist firm and speculation, everyone does not, in principle, have the opportunity to be an entrepreneur.

Bowles and Gintis (1986:68–71) call Kirzner's belief that the possession and distribution of wealth do not affect the outcomes of economic processes the "asset neutrality proposition." They contend that the widespread acceptance of this proposition is due to the fact that the economics discipline is preoccupied with general equilibrium, perfect competition models, which practitioners use to show that the distribution of income would be the same irrespective of whether capital hired labor or labor hired capital (Samuelson 1957). The asset neutrality proposition supports the classical liberal belief that wealth-holders have the same power in the determination of economic outcomes as do households with few assets. Although the perfect competition, equilibrium foundations for this conclusion are not compatible with Kirzner's own thinking, the conclusion of the asset neutrality proposition parallels his contention that the possession of wealth does not determine whether or not an entrepreneurial opportunity will be realized. Bowles and Gintis, however, maintain that the asset neutrality proposition is false because credit markets are inherently plagued by imperfections that may prevent the asset-poor from obtaining any credit no matter how high an interest rate they are willing to pay, while those possessing assets suitable as collateral to lending capitalists will be able to obtain loans at market rates of interest.

Bowles and Gintis follow the model of Stiglitz and Weiss (1981) to make their case. Stiglitz and Weiss's work shows that asymmetric information may prevent the interest rate from being an equilibrating variable in the loan market. While demanders of credit may react in traditional fashion to interest rate movements, credit suppliers, like banks, are not necessarily eager to increase their lending when the demand price of loans rises. Banks care about the expected returns on loans, not simply the interest borrowers are willing to pay. The two classic problems of markets with asymmetric information—moral hazard and adverse selection—prevent there from being an isomorphic relationship between interest rates and expected returns. Since the willingness to lend is determined by the expected return on loans, the interest rate consistent with the optimal expected return for lenders may not be the interest rate that demanders are willing to pay.

The problem here is that lenders can surmise the types of risk borrowers might take, but they cannot know the decisions that borrowers will actually make after the loan contract is signed. Because lenders cannot know the risks borrowers will incur once a loan has been initiated, they attempt to infer this information from the interest rate borrowers are willing to pay when calculating their expected returns. In particular, lenders understand that as interest rates rise, borrowers have greater incentive to increase the risks they take and are thus more likely to default. The increased likelihood of moral hazard at higher interest rates means that high interest rates may not be correlated with increased returns for the lender. In addition, banks know that as interest rates rise, the pool of willing borrowers is more likely to include risk-loving borrowers who will take actions incompatible with the interests of the bank. Since banks have difficulty identifying these borrowers, if they do not attempt to infer who are risk-loving individuals from the interest rates potential borrowers are willing to pay, the probability of bad lending decisions increases with a rising interest rate, thereby lowering bankers' returns. In sum, the problem of adverse selection and the possibility of moral hazard mean that raising the interest rate in response to an excess demand for credit may influence the pool and behavior of borrowers in such a way that the expected returns of lenders decline. Because "the interest rate directly affects the quality of the loan in a manner which matters to the bank," credit markets may consequently experience *persistent* excess demand (Stiglitz and Weiss 1981:409).[7]

Although Stiglitz and Weiss do not draw any critical conclusions from the possible existence of credit rationing in an unregulated banking industry, Bowles and Gintis insist that credit rationing vitiates the asset neutrality proposition. One strategy banks employ in response to ignorance of the risks borrowers will take is to demand that loans be partly collateralized. As a result, the potential borrowers who are ultimately approved for loans are more likely to be those who possess assets that can be easily liquidated.[8] This means that wealth-holders possess a decided advantage when they seek loans to finance entrepreneurial endeavors, and it helps to explain the correspondence Kirzner (1979a:97) notices, and dismisses as insignificant for his theory, between individuals who undertake entrepreneurial activity and individuals who fill the capitalist role. That is, contrary to Kirzner's belief, entrepreneurs usually are capitalists because the asset-poor are unable to obtain credit, no matter the interest rate they are willing to pay, while owners of significant assets face no such restriction.

Kirzner recognizes that arguments for the existence of credit market imperfections damage his position that entrepreneurial opportunities are in principle available to everyone. He maintains, however, that most theories of financial market imperfection ignore the existence of transactions costs. He argues that if a potential entrepreneur is willing to pay the market rate of interest but is unable to obtain financing, this is not an indication that credit is being rationed but a sign that there are transactions costs requiring the entrepreneur to offer higher interest rates to make the loan worthwhile to the bank. For instance, Kirzner remarks that the reputation of a potential entrepreneur may be unknown to a bank, and thus he will be asked to pay above market interest rates. Although such a requirement could render the entrepreneurial endeavor unprofitable, we must face the fact that there are social costs of "securing recognition of one's competence and trustworthiness" that may result in some entrepreneurs facing higher borrowing costs than others (Kirzner 1979a:101). Kirzner thus echoes George Stigler's (1967) conclusion that it is inappropriate to label credit markets as imperfect simply because different would-be entrepreneurs with varying and unknown reputations are asked to pay higher rates than "the" market interest rate.[9]

While we can accept Stigler's (1967:289) dismissal of the existence of credit market imperfection when this charge "rests ultimately upon the inability of borrowers to get cheap funds," the charge of credit market imperfection levied by Stiglitz and Weiss and by Bowles and Gintis is linked to the apparent *inability* of some borrowers, particularly asset-poor individuals, to obtain funds at *any* price. "[I]t is a mistake," Bowles and Gintis (1990b:306) assert, "to treat the [the existence of credit rationing] simply as a reflection of the existence of *frictions* in exchange relations. . . . Friction will produce out of equilibrium alternations between excess demand and excess supply but not consistent . . . quantity constraints" that prevent access to credit to some potential entrepreneurs. A critical interpretation of the credit rationing literature calls into question Kirzner's employment of the Chicago School notion of transactions costs to buttress his claim that entrepreneurial opportunities are in principle available to all.

Kirzner also pursues another line of defense against the claim that credit markets are imperfect. "If a new idea holds forth promise, even after all trading costs have been taken into account, of a yield to capitalists higher than they can obtain elsewhere," he (1979a:102) argues, "their failure to exploit it constitutes an entrepreneurial error on their part." Thus he might explain the purported existence of credit rationing as another example of the pervasiveness of entrepreneurial error in an economy out of equilibrium. One wonders, however, if the inability to obtain credit from a lending capitalist by an asset-poor, would-be entrepreneur constitutes an entrepreneurial error on the part of the capitalist, where exactly does this error lie? Is the capitalist making an entrepreneurial error when declining *to lend* to the asset-poor entrepreneur? Or is the capitalist making the entrepreneurial error by failing *to notice* the opportunity that the asset-poor and frustrated entrepreneur sees? If the theory of credit rationing is correct in its conclusion that it is sometimes impossible for lenders to acquire the necessary information about the credit risks a borrower will take, it is difficult to see how we might interpret that *impossibility* and the credit rationing to which it leads as an entrepreneurial *error*, an error that a competitive market could potentially correct. If the second reading captures Kirzner's meaning (that the lending capitalist himself does not notice the actual opportunity seen by our frustrated entrepreneur), it would not challenge the conclusion that capitalists do have an advantage in acting upon entrepreneurial possibilities.

Both interpretations of the existence of credit rationing as an instance of entrepreneurial error undermine Kirzner's belief that entrepreneurial opportunities in the cases of speculation and productive creativity are in principle available to everyone.[10]

Kirzner (1995:38–39) asserts that "[w]hat the entrepreneur sees is a prospective increment of value which others, although in no way handicapped as compared with our entrepreneur, have somehow failed to see." If the asset-poor are systematically denied access to credit, we can be confident that all potential entrepreneurs face no handicap in seizing upon profit opportunities only in the case of pure arbitrage. The possibility of credit rationing means that when an opportunity involves production or speculation, an alert, asset-poor, would-be entrepreneur will face possibly insurmountable obstacles when attempting to grasp that profit when compared to a wealthy entrepreneur. Thus, what Kirzner calls entrepreneurial profit would seem to be partly enabled by the prior ownership of assets and thus not solely a reward for entrepreneurial alertness. If a "profit" opportunity requires the prior ownership of capital, perhaps it can and should be justified by what Kirzner calls "the fruit of the tree" ethic. That is, it is widely believed, according to Kirzner, that an individual may legitimately appropriate output that emerges from a justly-held asset. In cases where we might use the fruit of the tree ethic to justify an income receipt, there would be no need to apply a finders-keepers ethic. This ethic would be applicable only in the evaluation of pure arbitrage opportunities.[11]

Denying the applicability of the finders-keepers ethic in cases involving production and speculation appears, however, to put Kirzner's positive theory of entrepreneurship in grave jeopardy. Real world instances of a pure arbitrage that require no interest expense because they do not involve the passage of time are likely to be rare, if not existent. Most, if not all, profit opportunities have a speculative or productive element. In order to say that the fruit of the tree ethic alone justifies income receipts from speculative and productive activities, one would have to accept that all the relevant factors of production were paid according to the value of their marginal products. Yet this could be so only in a world where all gains from speculative trade and production were exhausted. In such a world, there would be little, if any, room for entrepreneurship. This line of reasoning undermines, in ways that this author rejects, the insights of Austrian economics concerning time, ignorance, and knowledge (Burczak 1994).

As an alternative, we might argue that pure profit opportunities are abundant in productive and speculative ventures, but that they are not in principle available to everyone because of the existence of credit rationing. Insofar as the finders-keepers ethic requires that any person may be a potential finder, this ethic cannot justify the receipt of pure profit. We might thus search for another ethic that is consistent with a world of ceaseless change and widespread ignorance and with a defense of free market outcomes. Our alternative interpretation indicates, however, that there are constraints on individual choice and impediments to entrepreneurial action. We might therefore legitimately conclude that these constraints and impediments call for a theory of *distributive* justice in order to understand the nature and possible ethical shortcomings of an unregulated capitalist market process. Perhaps the applicability of a finders-keepers ethic could be re-established in an institutional environment where the possession of wealth did not confer any entrepreneurial advantage.

4. CONCLUSION

There are two major problems with Kirzner's attempt to apply the rule of finders-keepers to a positive ethical evaluation of profit and capitalist income. First, we have seen that the profits an entrepreneur receives through the establishment of a capitalist enterprise employing wage labor may be unjust if we believe that individuals should always be legally responsible for their intentional actions and the results of their intentional actions. Ellerman's labor theory of property demonstrates that in a capitalist enterprise, employed workers assume the legal status of things. Considering that Kirzner employs liberal discourse that places the highest value on individual responsibility, Ellerman's demonstration should make uncomfortable those initially persuaded by Kirzner's defense of the justice of entrepreneurial profit. This is especially true since he attempts to ground the justice of profit in the responsibility of the entrepreneur for the entire product. Yet Ellerman's analysis raises the possibility that we consider workers as co-responsible with the directing entrepreneur for the entire product of the firm. If so, workers should share profits with the directing entrepreneur if we accept Kirzner's own arguments that the just receipt of income and responsibility for production are somehow linked.

Second, Kirzner's defense of the justice of profit relies upon the possibility that all individuals, in principle, have an equal opportunity to pursue entrepreneurial opportunities. The credit rationing literature calls into question this possibility. If asset-poor individuals are systematically denied access to credit, they will not be able to act upon disequilibrium price discrepancies that cannot be instantaneously realized, and thus they may not be able to receive entrepreneurial profit. Kirzner notes that in a world out of equilibrium all income receipts are partly due to entrepreneurial alertness. Inasmuch as the possession of wealth gives some individuals an entrepreneurial advantage in many market transactions, there would seem to be good reasons to challenge the justice of many income receipts in an unregulated market economy. The market process may be biased, systematically working for the benefit of the wealthy in avenues not open to the asset-poor. Thus, contrary to Kirzner's arguments against the notion of distributive justice, a subjectivist might legitimately conclude that government has an important role to play, in the name of justice, to redistribute wealth in order to make entrepreneurial opportunities in principle available to all.

NOTES

1. See Kirzner (1985:116) where he makes the distinction among arbitrage, speculation, and productive creativity.

2. This section borrows from and expands upon Burczak (1996/97:6–8). Some of the ideas expressed here are debated in an exchange published in *Rethinking Marxism*: Cullenberg (1998), Prychitko (1998), Boettke (1998), and Burczak (1998).

3. This paper simply attempts to draw out the implications of this widely held principle for a theory of economic justice without investigating more deeply its philosophic foundations. Ellerman grounds the principle in inalienable natural rights. Hayek (1960:71–84) argues that we assign responsibility to individuals for their actions in order to promote good social consequences. Burczak (2001) connects the juridical principle of imputation to an Aristotelian concern to foster human flourishing.

4. To be absolutely clear, a labor-owned, self-managed firm need not hold title to any of the capital equipment used in production. In Ellerman's understanding, a labor-owned firm is consistent with a workers' cooperative that rents all of the nonhuman means of production. A system of labor-owned firms also does not require either state planning or state ownership of productive resources.

Perhaps the widespread existence of what Cornuelle (1992) calls the "employee mentality" is due to the legal thingification workers experience in the capitalist enterprise. Ellerman's advocacy of labor-owned firms might be seen in light of Cornuelle's (1992:9) call for "ways to liberate people from their proletarian status."

5. In his famous article on "The Nature of the Firm," Coase (1988:54) quotes F. R. Batt to make a similar point about the nature of employment in a capitalist enterprise:

"The master must have the right to control the servant's work, either personally or by another servant or agent. It is the right of control or interference, of being entitled to tell the servant when to work (within the hours of service) and when not to work, and what work to do and how to do it (within the terms of such service) which is the dominant characteristic in this relation and marks off the servant from an independent contractor, or from one employed merely to give to his employer the fruits or results of his labor."

6. While this paper does not explore the merits of this empirical proposition, see D. Evans and B. Jovanovic (1989) for some evidence supporting the hypothesis that lack of financial capital may lead to the inability to obtain credit.

7. The Austrian literature of which I am aware is generally critical of Stiglitz's work. See, for instance, Thomsen (1992:29–62). But Thomsen (1992:42–43) does observe that "individuals in a Hayekian world could attempt to infer information from prices if it were profitable for them to do so." This observation is one of the central building blocks of the credit rationing literature. Zappia's (1997) interesting paper develops the theme that the recent "post-Walrasian" microtheory literature along the lines of Bowles and Gintis, and Stiglitz and Weiss, is compatible with a Hayekian perspective.

8. Because voluntary self-enslavement is not permissible in Western society, individuals who lack financial assets but who possess considerable human capital are not able to use their human capital as collateral. As Bowles and Gintis remind us, not all forms of wealth may be pledged as collateral in financial transactions.

9. McCloskey (1990) puts forth the identical argument in a critique of Bowles and Gintis (1990a).

10. Ionnides (1993) develops a related perspective on Kirzner's theory of profit.

11. For ease of exposition, the following paragraph makes no distinction between the "reap where one sows" ethic, arguing that a person may legitimately appropriate the product created by the sweat of his brow, and the fruit of the tree ethic.

REFERENCES

Boettke, P. (1998) "Rethinking ourselves: the individual, the community, and the political economy of post communism." *Rethinking Marxism*, 10(2): 85–95.

Bowles, S., and H. Gintis. (1986) *Democracy and Capitalism*. New York: Basic Books.

Bowles, S., and H. Gintis. (1990a) "Contested exchange: new microfoundations for the political economy of capitalism." *Politics and Society*, 18(2): 165–222.

Bowles, S., and H. Gintis. (1990b) "Reply to our critics." *Politics and Society*, 18(2): 293–315.

Burczak, T. (1994) "The postmodern moments of F. A. Hayek's economics." *Economics and Philosophy*, 10(1): 31–548.

Burczak, T. (1996/97) "Socialism after Hayek." *Rethinking Marxism*, 9(31): 1–18.

Burczak, T. (1998) "Appropriation, responsibility, and agreement." *Rethinking Marxism*, 10(2): 96–105.

Burczak, T. (2001) "The labor theory of property and the injustice of capitalist exploitation." *Review of Social Economy*, 59(2): 161–83.

Coase, R. (1988) "The nature of the firm." Reprinted in R. Coase, ed., *The Firm, the Market, and the Law*. Chicago: University of Chicago Press.

Cornuelle, R. (1992) "The power and poverty of libertarian thought." *Critical Review*, 6(1): 1–10.

Cullenberg, S. (1998) "Exploitation, appropriation, and exclusion." *Rethinking Marxism*, 10(2): 66–75.

Ellerman, D. (1988) "The Kantian person/thing principle in political economy." *Journal of Economic Issues*, 22(4): 1109–1122.

Ellerman, D. (1992) *Property and Contract in Economics*. Oxford: Basil Blackwell.

Evans, D., and B. Jovanovic. (1989) "An estimated model of entrepreneurial choice under liquidity constraints." *Journal of Political Economy*, 97(4): 808–27.

Hayek, F. (1960) *The Constitution of Liberty*. Chicago: University of Chicago Press.

Hayek, F. (1976) *The Mirage of Social Justice*. Chicago: University of Chicago Press.

Ionnides, S. (1993) "Comment on I. Kirzner's notion of pure profit." *Journal des Économistes et des Études Humaines*, 4(2/3): 329–33.

Kirzner, I. (1979a) *Perception, Opportunity, and Profit*. Chicago: University of Chicago Press.

Kirzner, I. (1979b) "Producer, entrepreneur, and the right to property." In *Perception, Opportunity, and Profit*, pp. 185–99. Chicago: University of Chicago Press.

Kirzner, I. (1985) *Discovery and the Capitalist Process*. Chicago: University of Chicago Press.

Kirzner, I. (1989) *Discovery, Capitalism, and Distributive Justice*. Oxford: Basil Blackwell.

Kirzner, I. (1992a) *The Meaning of Market Process*. London and New York: Routledge.

Kirzner, I. (1992b) "Commentary: entrepreneurship, uncertainty, and Austrian economics." In B. Caldwell and S. Boehm, eds., *Austrian Economics: Tensions and New Directions*, pp. 85–102. Boston: Kluwer Academic Publishers.

Kirzner, I. (1995) "The nature of profits: some economic insights and their ethical implications." In R. Cowan and M. Rizzo, eds., *Profits and Morality*, pp. 22–47. Chicago: University of Chicago Press.

McCloskey, D. (1990) "Their blackboard, right or wrong: a comment on contested exchange." *Politics and Society*, 18(2): 223–32.

Prychitko, D. (1998) "Hayekian socialism: rethinking Burczak, Ellerman, and Kirzner." *Rethinking Marxism*, 10(2): 75–85.

Samuelson, P. (1957) "Wages and interest: Marxian economic models." *American Economic Review*, 47(6): 884–912.

Stigler, G. (1967) "Imperfections in the capital market." *Journal of Political Economy*, 75(3): 287–92.

Stiglitz, J., and A. Weiss. (1981) "Credit rationing in markets with imperfect information." *American Economic Review*, 71(3): 393–410.

Thomsen, I. (1992) *Prices and Knowledge. A Market-Process Perspective*. London and New York: Routledge.

Zappia, C. (1997) "Private information, contractual arrangements and Hayek's knowledge problem." In W. Keizer, B. Tieben, and R. van Zijp, eds., *Austrian Economics in Debate*, pp. 264–84. London and New York: Routledge.

COMMENT ON "A CRITIQUE OF KIRZNER'S FINDERS-KEEPERS DEFENSE OF PROFIT"

It is a pleasure to respond to Theodore Burczak's penetrating and lucid critique of my use of the pure discovery element in the market process (to suggest a finders-keepers defense of the justice of entrepreneurial profit). I believe that Burczak's criticisms do not necessarily undermine my defense of entrepreneurial profit; and I believe that Burczak's criticisms, together with my present response, can usefully advance understanding of the place of economic justice in markets. I am grateful for this opportunity to comment on Burczak's paper.

Burczak's critique consists of two separate and independent lines of argumentation. I will take up each of these in turn.

A. BURCZAK'S FIRST LINE OF CRITICISM

This line of criticism relates to the legitimacy of the exchange of labor-time for wages, permitting the employer to retain what the laborer's work produces that is in excess of the wages paid. My defense of the justice of entrepreneurial profit (for those who accept the finders-keepers ethic) did not question this legitimacy. But Burczak, relying on the work of David Ellerman, flatly denies such legitimacy. Ellerman maintains (in Burczak's words) "that the right to the entire product of one's labor is an inalienable right" that should not (and, absent fraud or other injustice, cannot) be transferred, even with consent. "The typical employment contract in a capitalist enterprise is consequently illegitimate." This illegitimacy stems from the idea that a laborer, being a human being, not a "thing," necessarily retains "juridicial responsibility" for his actions. Just as a convicted criminal cannot transfer his responsibility for his crime to another, in exchange for money, so too can a worker not transfer the human responsibility for his actions to an employer in exchange for money. If the responsibility for his actions remains the worker's, it is illegitimate

From *The Review of Austrian Economics*, vol. 15, no. 1 (2002): 91–94. © 2002 Kluwer Academic Publishers. Reproduced with permission of Springer New York via Copyright Clearance Center.

for the employer to appropriate the fruit of what the worker (*not* the employer) has created by those actions.

Now, at first glance this thesis of Ellerman might not seem to affect my own defense of the justice of entrepreneurial profit, at all. My argument was, after all, not intended as a personal credo. It was intended (and explicitly presented) as an argument that should convince those who, for their own philosophical or other reasons, happen to accept the finders-keepers ethic. Burczak's critique would seem merely to require that I make it clear, in addition, that my argument is intended only for those (surely the vast majority of the public reading my argument) who do indeed accept the legitimacy of the wage-for-labor-time exchange (i.e., for those who have not been convinced to the contrary by Ellerman's work). However, this easy way out is not quite sufficient.

This is so because Burczak maintains that there are elements in my own work which, if followed consistently, must *require* me to accept Ellerman's thesis. So that, by grounding a defense of capitalist justice on an (implicit) denial of Ellerman's thesis, I have, Burczak suggests, contradicted myself. I believe, however, that no such contradiction in fact exists here in my work.

Burczak correctly points out that, like Ellerman, I emphasize the entrepreneurial (i.e., the "ultimately responsible") element in the laborer's decision (following on Mises's insight that each and every human action is, in a real sense, entrepreneurial). He, therefore, believes that I am logically required to accept Ellerman's conclusion that the wage-for-labor-time exchange is illegitimate, since such exchange consists of the illegitimate "thingification" of the laborer. Quoting Ellerman, Burczak writes: "The owner of an entity rented out is . . . not a legal party to the decisions about the entity's use. Therefore, when an entity hired out is a person, the person has a legal role of a thing."

I believe, however, that there is a logical non sequitur in Burczak's application of this reasoning to claim a contradiction between (a) my position that the laborer, *in choosing which job to accept,* is acting as (an "ultimately responsible") entrepreneur, and (b) my (implicit) acceptance of the legitimacy of the wage-for-labor-time exchange. Let me use Burczak's own example of the role of a gun in a bank robbery. The gun is "an inanimate object without a will, [it] cannot share responsibility for the crime with the robber." But surely one who owns a gun and knowingly rents it out to a known would-be bank robber *does* bear juridical and moral responsibility for his action; his renting out the gun, permitting the would-be robber to choose which bank to rob with it, does not imply that *he* (the owner of the gun) has become a "thing." Similarly, my observation that, in choosing an employer to whom to rent out his labor time, a laborer is acting entrepreneurially, does not, in itself, contradict the "thingification" which Burczak (following Ellerman) finds in the circumstance that the laborer's time now, once he has taken the job, "belongs" to the employer.

Strictly speaking the above is sufficient, I believe, to rebut the logical content of Burczak's critique of my position (as being contradictory). However, I find it difficult to resist pointing out, in addition, that, if one accepts the reasoning of the preceding paragraph, one has in one's hand (if one chooses to use it) an insight which might defend the legitimacy of the wage-for-labor-time exchange, *in spite of* one's accepting (as in fact I do certainly accept) that a worker never does lose ultimate moral responsibility for any actions he takes as an employee. Consider an owner of a gun who is asked to rent it for a day to a person whom he does not know to be a would-be bank robber. The owner may tell the would-be renter: "I am prepared to rent the gun to you for a day. However, since I do not know you, and fear you may use the gun for criminal purposes (for which I am *not* prepared to rent it to you), I propose the following: Let *me* retain the gun on my person for the entire day, except that I will accompany you wherever you wish to go during this day, and will gladly turn over the gun to you (whenever you wish to use it, for purposes which you will select), provided that your proposed use does not violate my moral code." Let us suspend our disbelief concerning the plausibility of any such bizarre proposal. Clearly if such a proposal *were* made and accepted, we would have a case where the owner of the rented gun (a "thing" for sure) has *retained* moral and juridical responsibility for its use *throughout its period of rental.*

I see no reason not to understand the laborer's position in an employment contract to be exactly that of my gun-owner; and the laborer's rented *time,* to be exactly similar to the gun. There is nothing in such a contract which appears to be illegitimate, unjust, or fraudulent.

Let us turn to Burczak's second line of criticism.

B. BURCZAK'S SECOND LINE OF CRITICISM

This line of criticism is based on the thesis that, in capitalist systems, those who do not possess capital may be absolutely unable to borrow capital funds at *any* rate of interest. A would-be entrepreneur (who "sees" an opportunity to capture pure profit through a productive enterprise, if only he could secure the needed capital funds) is in fact unable to grasp such profit, because he lacks capital. So that while one may describe the profit made by those producer-entrepreneurs who themselves possess capital (or who *do* have access to capital markets) as profits which they have "found," or "created," this does not necessarily render the capture of such profit legitimate, since others are *not* able to grasp such profit (even where they happen to be the first to "see" the opportunity which the successful capitalist-entrepreneur eventually grasped).

Now, although there may well be grounds for challenging the "credit-rationing models" upon which Burczak rests this line of criticism, my response here will *not* depend upon any such challenge. For the sake of argument only, let us accept the relevance of these models. My response to this second line of criticism takes the form of asking the reader to choose out of the following two, mutually exclusive, options: *Either* (a) the assumed requirement (for the capture of entrepreneurial profit) of *prior* ownership of capital means that such capital is to be treated as an indispensable *ingredient* in the recipe for grasping pure profit (i.e., as a "factor of production" in the "production" of profit), *or* (b) such a requirement does *not* have this meaning. Let us take up option (b) first.

In this option (b), while it is believed that an entrepreneur cannot capture pure profit unless he already possesses assets, such assets do not constitute a tool or instrument with which the entrepreneur's alert propensity to see and grasp profit opportunities is exercised. An entrepreneur sees the possibility of using some extra lumber which he happens to possess, to make some furniture. He expects to be able to sell the furniture for a price exceeding the costs of all needed inputs (including the opportunity cost of the lumber itself). The lumber is certainly a factor of production in the production of the furniture. But it is not to be seen, on this option, as a factor participating in the gaining of pure profit. It is the vision, energy, and initiative of the entrepreneur which has won him the profit—despite the fact that we may assume that, had he not already possessed the lumber, he might not have been able to acquire any. A mountain-climber who notices and grasps an unusually beautiful flower while on a hike, may be said to have "found" the flower purely as a result of his alertness. The flower is *not* the product of his strong legs, which made it possible for him to undertake the hike.

On this option (b), the pure profit gained has been "found," "created," by the entrepreneur alone. The fact that others who do *not* own lumber, *cannot* grasp such profit, even if their entrepreneurial vision is no less insightful than that of the lumber-owner, does not in the slightest alter the "found," "created," character of the profit so gained. *If* one accepts a finders-keepers ethic, one can surely see the legitimacy of such gain. While such legitimacy might certainly seem to be *enhanced* in situations where the successful entrepreneur has no differential advantage (such as, prior ownership of lumber) over other potential entrepreneurs, the presence of such differential advantage does not eliminate the finders-keepers basis for the justice of profit gained. The hiker who found the beautiful flower while mountain-hiking is not, surely, to be denied just ownership of the flower because crippled or older folk were unable to go hiking. (My own frequent references to the circumstance that *anyone* could have found what the successful entrepreneur has found—references which Burczak cites most relevantly—were observations that, based on my own non-acceptance of the conclusions of the credit-rationing literature, *enhanced* the persuasiveness of the finders-keepers ethic applicability. But the essence of the finders-keepers ethic does *not*, surely, depend in any way critically upon the possibility of such enhanced persuasiveness.)

All the above rests on option (b), in which the owned assets (required, according to Burczak's critique, for the capture of pure profit) are *not* seen as *ingredients* in such capture. Let us, however, now consider the other option, option (a).

Option (a) saw owned assets as an input into the "productive" process of grasping perceived pure profit. So that the grasping of pure profit *can no longer be seen as an act of pure discovery or "creation."* Those who do not possess capital assets simply cannot "produce" profit; those whose capital permits them to win profits cannot be said to have "found" these profits (since by my own definition, pure discovery, pure creation, pure "finding" *does not itself require any inputs whatsoever*). Clearly, according to *this* option the finders-keepers ethic cannot be used to defend the justice of pure profit, since nothing was "found."

In response to this possible line of argument I would merely point out that, on this option, "profit" has simply become reclassified as a return on capital (as it was seen by the classical economists and by Marx). On this view, there does not exist any category of pure entrepreneurial profit that cannot be imputed to a capital source. But, I must point out, the theory of justice which I proposed as a defense of capitalist profit, and which Bur-czak is criticizing, was proposed exclusively as a possible solution for the ethical puzzle posed by the phenomenon of pure entrepreneurial profit (for which no inputs whatsoever are required). By embracing option (a), we are not refuting the discovery-theory of justice, we are declaring that theory to be unnecessary, since the problem it set out to solve never does exist and never can exist (except, Burczak accepts, in the case of pure arbitrage).

Of course, declaring so-called entrepreneurial profit to be a return on capital, does not establish its legitimacy. Of course broader questions concerning the justice of capitalist income distribution require more comprehensive answers than that provided by the discovery-theory of the justice of pure entrepreneurial profit. My point here is only that, if option (a) is chosen, then Burczak's critique does not relate at all to my defense of the justice of pure entrepreneurial profit. Broader questions concern-ing the justice of capitalism, then, go beyond the scope of Burczak's paper—and certainly beyond the permissible length of this comment.